14.95

Israel's Law
and the
Church's Faith

Paul and His Recent Interpreters

BY

STEPHEN WESTERHOLM

WILLIAM B. EERDMANS PUBLISHING COMPANY
GRAND RAPIDS, MICHIGAN

The substance of the following articles by the author has been reproduced herein by the kind permission of the publishers:

"Letter and Spirit: The Foundation of Pauline Ethics," *New Testament Studies* 30 (1984), 229-248, by permission of Cambridge University Press.

"On Fulfilling the Whole Law (Gal. 5:14)," *Svensk exegetisk årsbok* 51-52 (1986-1987), 229-237.

Review of Hans Hübner, *Das Gesetz bei Paulus, Svensk exegetisk årsbok* 44 (1979), 194-199.

"Torah, Nomos, and Law: A Question of 'Meaning,'" *Studies in Religion/ Sciences Religieuses* 15 (1986), 327-336.

Library of Congress Cataloging-in-Publication Data

Westerholm, Stephen, 1949–
Israel's law and the church's faith.

Bibliography: p. 222.
Includes indexes.
1. Faith—Biblical teaching.   2. Law (Theology)—Biblical teaching.
3. Bible. N.T. Epistles of Paul—Criticism, interpretation, etc.—History.
I. Title.
BS2655.F2W44   1988   241'.2   88-11253
ISBN 0-8028-0288-5

Contents

Preface

Interest in what the apostle Paul had to say has never been confined to academics. Indeed, gradually—for revolutions of this order take time—the realization is growing among professional scholars themselves that Paul was not one of them. The places he frequented and the company he kept were, quite by design, not theirs. Nor are his writings scholarly treatises, but personal letters drafted in odd and fleeting moments of respite from pressures far from academic, and sent to motley first-century assemblies whose only entrance requirement was a confession of Jesus as Lord. If an apology is needed for the lack of a scholarly consensus on Paul, then perhaps we should bear in mind, along with other difficulties, the handicap under which professional students labor in trying to enter sympathetically a world so remote from their own.

The difficulties are real. Still, to judge from the number of library shelves given to our subject, they have not proved a deterrent; and not to be overlooked are the linguistic, historical, and critical skills which the scholar brings to the study of ancient texts. The result of the continuing effort is today's staggering literature on Paul. Few can be said to have mastered it, and both the interested layperson and the dedicated student are confronted by the dilemma of scarcely knowing where to begin. It is hoped that the following overview of the debate on a crucial area of Pauline thought will prove helpful for them and that scholars too may profit from this summary of the work which has been done and from the perspectives offered here on a number of time-worn issues.

This survey is not meant to be exhaustive. If we were to mention every scholar who has contributed to the debate, our study would be reduced to little more than a catalogue of names, useful only for reference. Omissions, always unfortunate and sometimes significant, are unavoidable. Thus Part One treats in some detail a limited number of scholars whose works mark important stages leading up to and shaping the current debate. Part Two deals more systematically with basic issues related to Paul's view of the law, thus attempting to answer the strictly separate, though occasionally overlapping, questions of where the state of the debate, and where the truth, may lie.

The present study has grown out of a series of papers reviewing literature for the *Torah/Nomos* seminar of the Canadian Society of Biblical Studies. Thanks are due to Dr. Peter Richardson for suggesting that I take on what has proved to be a rewarding task. My colleagues at McMaster University, Dr. Ben F. Meyer and Dr. E. P. Sanders (now also of Oxford University), have encouraged the project, read the manuscript as it became available, and made a number of helpful comments—for all of which I am grateful.

This book is dedicated, with appreciation and love, to my wife Gunilla. I confess that I fully expect it to be added to the growing list of works she will read some distant day when Jessica Joy, Martin Samuel, Paul Anders, and Monica Louise take less of her time. Meanwhile, in those odd and fleeting moments, day or night, when the house becomes unaccountably quiet, and at other times when it is not, she will continue to read and understand the apostle Paul.

Israel's Law
and the
Church's Faith

Chapter One

The Background of the Modern Debate

i. The Problem

Perhaps a century after believers in a resurrected Jesus first gathered in Jerusalem, an apology for the Christian faith was addressed by an unknown writer to an equally unknown Diognetus. This document is one of the treasures of early Christian literature. Christianity and its adherents are portrayed in a most attractive way; one could only wish that Christian behavior over the years more nearly matched its description here. The author achieves a particularly fine balance between Christian distinctiveness from the pagan environment and the positive contribution which Christians nonetheless make to society. Their moral standards are different, their allegiance is given to another world, and they are never really at home here. Yet they live in the cities of Greeks and barbarians, do good and show love even to those who abuse them, and so sustain the world as the soul sustains the body.

Not content with a commendation of Christianity, the author includes in his apology a denunciation of the follies of two perceived rivals, paganism and Judaism. The refutation of paganism simply repeats what had long since become a standard satire directed by Jewish and Christian authors alike at the heathen: how stupid can they be to use one stone to walk upon, another as an image for worship, or to reverence bronze no different from that used in making common utensils? Are not all images dumb and blind, unable to feel or move, subject to rot and decay? How can anyone call them gods?

The denunciation of Judaism, in spite of partial parallels in earlier literature, remains an astonishing piece of nearsighted polemic.

Our author admits that Jews worship the one true God of the universe. Yet he claims that they show themselves as foolish as the pagans in the way they worship him. How stupid, he writes, to offer God sacrifices of blood and burnt fat; the God who made the universe does not need such sacrifices any more than dumb idols do! And think of all the Jewish superstitions about the sabbath and circumcision, eating some foods and refusing others! How can anyone accept part of God's creation as useful and reject other parts as useless? Christians are right to distance themselves from the folly, the fussiness, and the pride of Jews.

The Jewish answer to all of this is self-evident: Jews abstain from certain foods because the commandments which God gave to Moses on Mount Sinai require such abstinence. Similarly, sacrifices, the sabbath, and circumcision were all included in the law God gave to Israel. What makes our author's polemic nearsighted is that the earliest Christians themselves were all Jews who worshiped the God of the Jews and acknowledged that Israel's law was God's law. The question how those with Christian faith should relate to the divine law of Israel was a burning issue in the first Christian century and has remained a crucial subject for Christian theology and ethics ever since. Different answers have of course been given; but the writer to Diognetus seems unaware even of the problem. Judaism seems so remote, so foreign and superstitious to him that he never even considers the Jewish claim to have a revelation from God or the implications of the fact that Christian faith itself affirms that claim to be true.

No one wrestled with the relation between Christian faith and Israel's law more intensely than the apostle Paul. His personal struggle was no doubt due in part to his background: before he became a Christian, he outshone his Jewish compatriots (so he insists) in exhibiting zeal for Israel's law. Then, too, as proponents of the law began to turn Paul's churches away from him, the matter was brought forcibly to his attention. Should the law God gave to Israel be imposed on non-Jews who wanted to become Christians? How could Paul demonstrate his claim that obedience to God's law is an inadequate base for acceptance by God? Why was the law given in the first place? What functions did it serve? These are among the questions which Paul was compelled to confront, primarily in his letters to the churches of Rome and Galatia.

Nor were the issues merely theological. At stake were such practical questions as whether Christians of Jewish and non-Jewish descent could share a common meal; whether the Christian mission to Jews would be compromised by the rejection of Jewish law and custom, or, conversely, whether the mission to non-Jews would be saddled with Jewish particularities which struck others as misanthropic, superstitious, and silly; and whether Christians as adherents of Jewish law could enjoy the protection which the Roman government afforded Jews, or whether, in departing from Jewish ways, they would be subjected to the suspicions and harassment which inevitably dogged a novel religion. It is a mark of the man that Paul addressed these issues almost exclusively in theological terms. But whatever verdict was given had wide-reaching consequences for the morality and practice of Christians, their relations with non-Christian Jews, and their attitude toward, and acceptance by, the non-Christian world in general.

The significance of the subject has attracted innumerable studies. In the pages that follow we will be surveying selected aspects of the twentieth-century debate. Nearly nineteen hundred years of intervening discussion must here be passed over in silence—with one notable exception.

ii. Luther's Answer

LITERATURE: Luther's lectures on Galatians are available in English translation in Vols. 26 and 27 of *Luther's Works* (see Bibliography).

For students who want to understand Paul's view of the law, there are scholars to this day who heartily commend a reading of Martin Luther; others, with even greater passion, would insist that Luther's writings are the source of monumental confusion and distortion. By contrast, students who want to understand the *scholarly debate* on Paul and the law will meet with a begrudged unanimity. Even the reformer's detractors could be prodded to concede that, for this purpose, *some* limited knowledge of Luther is essential.

Theologians of Catholic and Protestant persuasion have debated for centuries whether or not Luther correctly conveyed the apostle's thought; that debate cannot be reviewed here, though we may say by way of summary that, until quite recently, Protestant scholars tended to affirm, and Catholic scholars, to deny, that he did a fair job of it. For the last century or so the question has been the subject of a substantial literature by German Protestant scholars examining their own roots; though that literature is not the focus of our study, some of the problems raised will need to be noted. More recently, E. P. Sanders inaugurated a new stage in the discussion with a massively documented attack on German Lutheran understandings of the Judaism in which Paul was fostered; moreover, distorted views of Judaism, Sanders believes, have been accompanied by distortions of Paul's thought. This latest turn in the debate figures largely in what follows: Sanders's work will require extensive treatment, as will that of Heikki Räisänen, whose studies were at least in part inspired by those of Sanders. In addition we will inevitably be looking at other scholars on whom Sanders and Räisänen build, or with whom they pointedly differ. But the recent debate, too, is a response to positions whose prominence is due to the influence of Luther.

Our first task, then, is to provide the basis for *some* limited knowledge of Luther. The roots and development of his thinking are fascinating subjects in themselves but need not detain us here. We will confine our attention to the positions of the mature Luther as reflected in his great lectures on Galatians published in 1535, concentrating on issues which will prove crucial in our later discussion.

The Centrality of "Justification by Faith"

The doctrine of "justification by faith" is, for Luther, "the principal doctrine of Christianity" (26:106), just as the opposite notion, that one can be approved by God on the basis of one's own righteousness, is the "fundamental principle" of the world, the devil, and the Pope (27:146-147). If the doctrine of justification is ever lost, all true Christian doctrine will be lost (26:9); on the other hand, since all Christian doctrines are included in justification, "if it is sound, all the others are sound as well" (26:283). In fact, the doctrine of justification provides a "touchstone by which we can judge most surely and freely about all doctrines, works, forms of worship, and ceremonies of all men" (27:9).

It is evident throughout the lectures that Luther read and understood the Scriptures themselves with the doctrine of justification as his guide. Adam and Eve fell because they tried to be like God "by means of their own wisdom and virtue"; Abel's offering was accepted because it was offered "by faith," whereas Cain displeased God by offering "his works without faith" (27:145). For Luther it is important that even the commandments of Christ recorded in the Gospels not be confused with *the gospel,* the essential Christian message of justification. They are expositions of the law and as such, in Luther's scheme, they do not directly pertain to the doctrine of justification by faith (26:150, 372).

Implicit in these latter claims is Luther's fundamental distinction between law and gospel. The law requires that we do something for God ("works"); the gospel insists that we receive something from God (by "faith") (26:208, 272). Luther stretches the definition of "law" to include "whatever is not grace" (26:122). Such law may be divine and its demands holy, righteous, and good; but it must be kept distinct from the gospel where righteousness is based on faith alone. Using such distinctions Luther is able to divide all scripture between the two categories of law and gospel, command and promise. And he claims that even those texts in scripture which demand deeds are not opposed to, because they do not pertain to, the doctrine of justification (26:295). Justification by faith is thus the key to Luther's understanding of Paul, of the Bible as a whole, and of the religious experience and endeavors of all humanity.

As Luther defines the doctrine, it inevitably includes both a negative and a positive aspect: "We are justified neither by the righteousness of the Law nor by our own righteousness but solely by faith in Christ" (26:222). We may deal with the negative aspect first.

Luther's conviction that neither "the righteousness of the Law" nor "our own righteousness" forms the basis for redemption and acceptance before God draws on Pauline statements that the "works of the law" do not justify. To be sure, Luther recognizes that the Pauline phrase "works of the law" is not simply to be equated with "works" in general. Yet he believes that, if the works demanded by God's law do not justify, the same must apply all the more to works which humans may devise (26:141, 333). Indeed, Luther frequently distinguishes between the Jews and Paul's opponents on the one hand and, on the other, the proponents of "works" of his own day, and he is prepared to show a measure of magnanimity toward the former. After all, they could quite properly point out that their law and system of worship had been given to them by God (26:208). It was "no wonder," then, that they showed zeal in their defense of divine institutions (26:80). "Much worse" are the "heretics" of Luther's day, for they teach traditions and works which they themselves invent without support in scripture (26:52, 140). In the final analysis, however, the words of Paul apply to both: "If the Law of God is weak and useless for justification, much more are the laws of the pope weak and useless for justification" (26:407). Ultimately, the "papist," the Jew, the Turk, and the sectarian are all alike. Their forms of worship may differ. But all think that God will be favorably disposed toward them if they perform some specified deed and angry if they do not. The true God, however, has clearly stated

that he is pleased with no human righteousness at all, but only with
that of his Son (26:396-397).

Not "through ourselves," then, but only "through the help of
Another, the only Son of God, Jesus Christ" are we "redeemed from
sin, death, and the devil and endowed with eternal life" (27:145). The
"righteousness of faith" is not an "active" righteousness of our own,
but "a merely passive righteousness" in which we do nothing ourselves, but merely embrace the mercy and forgiveness which God
offers as his gifts through Christ (26:4-6).

The Inadequacy of "Works"

Why can one not be justified by "works"? Luther is eager to respond
to the question.

1. The power, wisdom, and majesty of God exceed by far what
the human mind can understand and what human nature can endure.
Any attempt to approach or comprehend him on one's own leads inevitably to a fall, to despair and death. This is why God came to us in
the person of Jesus. In his design we are to fix our gaze on Christ rather
than lose ourselves in speculations about the divine majesty.

> Take hold of [Jesus Christ]; cling to Him with all your heart. . . . When
> you do this, you will see the love, the goodness, and the sweetness of
> God. You will see His wisdom, His power, and His majesty sweet-
> ened and mitigated to your ability to stand it. (26:29-30)

But since righteousness by faith in Christ is God's appointed path to
himself, to approach him with one's own righteousness is to deny
God's righteousness, to go clean contrary to his demands, to infringe
on his prerogative of telling us how we may come to him, and to vainly
imagine that our puny works are sufficient to bridge the enormous
chasm between God and humanity.

2. Only the doctrine of justification by faith gives glory where
glory is due. "The doctrine of the Gospel takes away all glory, wisdom,
righteousness, etc., from men and gives it solely to the Creator"
(26:66). Naturally such a message is resisted and disdained by the
world, which finds irritating and intolerable the gospel's condemnation of all its pretensions (26:58); but it is God whom we must strive
to please.

Faith alone yields worship to God. Any reliance on human works
is idolatry. If God is to be acknowledged as God, we must cling to him

as the source of every good, our help in every situation of need. This, the substance of the first commandment of the Decalogue, is fulfilled by faith alone, which places all its trust in God, relies exclusively on his grace, believes and rejoices in his promises in the gospel, and so gives glory to God (26:227-229, 253-254). Those who, on the contrary, refuse to accept God's grace and his gift of eternal life, wanting to earn it by their own deeds, are in effect robbing God of his rightful glory (26:127). In attempting to justify themselves, free themselves from sin and death, overcome Satan, and gain heaven by force, they are taking upon themselves roles which belong exclusively to God (26:257).

3. The law requires perfect obedience; yet such obedience is nowhere to be found (26:273-274, 398). In this context Luther frequently emphasizes that God demands perfection in one's innermost heart. From his own experience he knew how an outward "cover" of sanctity could conceal inner attitudes of mistrust, fear, even blasphemy (26:70). Nor is that all. Experience told Luther that those who try to please God by their own deeds can never be certain whether God's standards have been met. Thus they end up multiplying sins of doubt, despair, and blasphemy in their hearts.

> When I was a monk, I made a great effort to live according to the requirements of the monastic rule. . . . Nevertheless, my conscience could never achieve certainty but was always in doubt and said: "You have not done this correctly. You were not contrite enough. You omitted this in your confession." Therefore the longer I tried to heal my uncertain, weak, and troubled conscience with human traditions, the more uncertain, weak, and troubled I continually made it. (27:13; cf. 26:387-388, 404-406)

4. In fact, all such efforts are doomed at the outset, for it is not only our patent sins but even our so-called "good works" which are unacceptable to God apart from faith. Luther never tires of citing Matt. 7:17-18: since a good tree bears good fruit and an evil tree bears evil fruit, truly good deeds, that is, deeds which God can approve, simply cannot come from sinful people. Faith must first make the doer a "good tree," and then "good fruit" will follow (26:255). Indeed, "good works" are themselves sinful if they are not done in faith, that is, with a proper attitude toward God (so Luther interprets Rom. 14:23). To try to please God with one's "good works" thus amounts to adding sins to sins (26:126)! Luther makes a similar point by citing John's Gospel: "That which is born of the flesh is flesh" (John 3:6). "Flesh" includes not

simply gross sins, but the highest morality, wisdom, and religion of which the world is capable (26:139-140, 216); all this, apart from the faith which acknowledges God's righteousness and gives him his due, remains the work of the "flesh" and unacceptable to God.

5. Humankind must be redeemed from the "present evil age" (Gal. 1:4), from bondage to the devil (26:39-40). For all the works we may do, we remain in the present evil age. And the devil for his part does not "stoop down one handbreadth" for all the works and righteousness we may accomplish (26:40-41). Only God through Christ is able to deliver us from his grasp.

6. The fact that the Son of God died for us is proof in itself that our sins cannot be covered by our works; to claim that they can is to commit the idolatry of giving glory to ourselves which belongs to Christ (26:145), the blasphemy of making the death of Christ useless (26:176, 185). This reminder should keep us on the one hand from trivializing our sins and, on the other hand, from despairing because of them. Surely those who believe God's Son died for their sin cannot regard such sin as "something trivial, a mere nothing," of "so little weight and force that some little work or merit of ours will remove it" (26:33), nor should they succumb to the temptation to despair, for to Satan's mention of their many sins they can simply reply that Christ died, not for righteous people, but for sinners (26:35-37).

At this point the reader may suspect that Luther is opposed to the law and good works; Luther insists that this is not the case. Both law and works have their place, their divinely appointed and absolutely essential functions. The point is simply that they must not be allowed to intrude in the matter of justification.

> When we are involved in a discussion of justification, there is no room for speaking about the Law. . . . This Bridegroom, Christ, must be alone with His bride in His private chamber, and all the family and household must be shunted away. But later on, when the Bridegroom opens the door and comes out, then let the servants return to take care of them and serve them food and drink. Then let works and love begin. (26:137-138)

The Function of the Law

What, then, is the proper place of the law? In commenting on Gal. 3:19, Luther suggests that the law has a twofold task. Its first use is "civic." "God has ordained civic laws, indeed all laws, to restrain transgressions" (26:308). The threat of punishment acts as a restraint on sin, a bridle on the wicked. The fact that sin is limited in this way is not an indication of human righteousness but, on the contrary, of unrighteousness. This is a very necessary function of the law, but not its "proper and absolute use" (26:310).

The law's primary and indispensable function is to serve as a "mighty hammer" (26:336) with which God may crush human self-righteousness and thus prepare otherwise complacent sinners to receive divine grace.

> If someone is not a murderer, adulterer, or thief, and abstains from external sins . . . he develops the presumption of righteousness and relies on his good works. . . . The proclamation of free grace and the forgiveness of sins does not enter his heart and understanding. . . . Therefore this presumption of righteousness is a huge and horrible monster. To break and crush it, God needs a large and powerful hammer, that is, the Law. (26:310)

> Therefore the Law is a minister and a preparation for grace. For God is the God of the humble . . . , of those who have been brought down to nothing at all. . . . When the Law drives you this way, so that you despair of everything that is your own and seek help and solace from Christ, then it is being used correctly. (26:314-316)

The picture which Luther frequently paints in this context is of the Israelites leaving the tents which represented their "peace and self-confidence" (26:150), having washed and made themselves as righteous, pure, and chaste as they could, now summoned into the presence of God to hear his law on Mount Sinai. To them in their holiness the law brought such terror, such recognition of their unworthiness to stand in God's presence, that they cried out for a mediator. The law had done its proper work (26:149-150, 311-312)!

Clearly the fact that commands have been given in scripture does not for Luther imply that they can be fulfilled. Nor, for that matter, are we to conclude that God is mocking humans by giving commands which he and they both know cannot be kept. Rather, Luther sees the human dilemma as so desperate that we are not only unable to obey God's commands but are also blind to our impotence. Our eyes are only opened when we have been confronted with God's demands and find ourselves unable to meet them.

The Law and the Christian

The law of God thus has a negative role in the process of justification, though it cannot serve as its basis. On the contrary, through justification believers are redeemed from the curse of the law, which was borne for their sake by the Savior (26:447-448). As we have seen, the believer's conscience must therefore be completely delivered from the threats and terror of the law (26:354). In this sense the entire law—its moral and ceremonial demands alike—has been abrogated for the Christian (26:156).

Furthermore, the "political" and "civil" laws of Moses are not relevant for the Christian, though Luther insists that the gospel does not free Christians from their obligation to obey the (political) laws of the state in which they live (26:448). Similarly, the ceremonial laws of Moses are not binding for believers though, since ceremonies are an essential part of "life in the body," and since things must be done in a decent, orderly fashion in the Church, the gospel allows the introduction of other ordinances prescribing times and places for people to gather to hear God's word (26:448; cf. 411-412). These, however, may be changed and omitted without sin.

Somewhat surprisingly, however, for Luther the law retains something of its "proper use" even in the lives of believers. To understand his thinking here, we must introduce his famous notion that the Christian remains in this life at one and the same time both righteous and sinner, *simul iustus et peccator.* The Latin phrase is retained in the literature to this day as a summary statement of this notion; for the Luther aficionado, "Luther's *simul*" is sufficient.

In Luther's definition, Christians are not people without sin, but those to whom God does not impute sin because of their faith in Christ (26:133). In this life, believers remain children of Adam; something of their "old vice" still clings to them. The "head of the serpent"—their unbelief and ignorance of God—has been crushed, but the scaly body remains (26:189). To be sure, God does not "see" such sin as remains, for it is concealed by the protective "wings" of the Savior. For Christ's sake "God reckons imperfect righteousness as perfect righteousness and sin as not sin, even though it really is sin." The paradoxical result, then, is that a Christian is "righteous and a sinner at the same time, holy and profane, an enemy of God and a child of God" (26:231-232).

Since, then, the Christian is still beset by sins of the "flesh," the law retains its function. While the Christian conscience is free from the law, the flesh must be subjected to it, disciplined by it, and thus brought to an awareness of sin (26:158, 341). Luther even claims that, to the extent Christians are "flesh," they remain "under the law" (26:342).

> As long as we live in a flesh that is not free of sin, so long the Law keeps coming back and performing its function. . . . There is still need for a custodian to discipline and torment the flesh, that powerful jackass, so that by this discipline sins may be diminished and the way prepared for Christ. (26:350)

Predictably, Luther finds virtue in this necessity. The virtue, too, is surely predictable.

> It is extremely beneficial to the faithful to be aware of the uncleanness of their flesh; for it will keep them from being puffed up by a vain and wicked notion about the righteousness of works, as though they were acceptable to God on its account. . . . We are not in a position to trust in our own righteousness, for we are aware of the uncleanness of the flesh. (27:85-86)

Does the moral law perform the more positive function of revealing God's will to the believer? Here we should remember that Luther divides all of scripture into law and gospel, commands and promise, and finds law and commandments in the New Testament as well as the Old. As far as the Mosaic law is concerned, Luther will not allow that the Christian is bound by any of its commandments, for to be subject to Moses in one respect is to bring on oneself "his whole regime." On the other hand, the Mosaic law does provide "examples of outstanding laws and moral precepts" (27:15); and anyone who has read Luther's profound interpretations of the Decalogue will realize that he could derive the entire duty of a Christian from this text, read in the light of the Christian Gospel. As far as the exhortations in the New Testament are concerned, they are intended to encourage and direct the believer, who, as we have seen, is not perfect in this life. But to the extent that faith is exercised, even such exhortations prove unnecessary (27:96). A good tree will bear good fruit spontaneously.

Thus, whereas the law cannot be satisfactorily kept without faith, a believer can be said to accomplish the law: partly because all his failings are forgiven for Christ's sake, and partly because what is done in faith and in strength given by God's Spirit is pleasing to God (26:260). Luther does not quote Rom. 8:4 without adding a gloss since, as long

as Christians live in the flesh, sin remains with them. But he does allow
that, through the gift of God's Son, the law may "begin to be fulfilled"
in believers (27:65).

* * *

As noted above, much of what has been said in even the most recent
scholarly literature can be appropriately seen as a response to Luther;
this consideration has determined the structure of Part One of our book.
Thus in Chapter Two, two scholars are reviewed who contest the claim
that justification by faith is the center of Paul's thought. In Chapter
Three, literature is discussed which disputes the characterization of
Judaism in Paul's day as a religion of works and self-righteousness.
The scholars treated in our fourth chapter oppose Luther's interpretation of a critical passage in Paul (Rom. 7) and suggest that Luther's
sensitive introspective conscience led him to misinterpret Paul's understanding of the law's function. In Chapter Five Luther's claim that
the righteousness of the law apart from Christian faith is itself sin is
tested in the work of three prominent Pauline scholars. Finally, in
Chapter Six we summarize positions which argue that Paul's various
statements regarding the law cannot be reduced to a coherent scheme,
whether the scheme be Luther's or any other. Obviously a number of
the scholars we discuss regard the work of Luther as rather a hindrance
than a help in understanding Paul; yet without Luther the current debate is inconceivable.

PART ONE

Chapter Two

Paul's "Polemical Doctrine": Wrede and Schweitzer

The names of William Wrede and Albert Schweitzer figure largely in reviews of New Testament scholarship; not quite coincidentally, Schweitzer himself wrote the best-known reviews. Perhaps, too, the nature of the genre, with its somewhat artificial stress on distinctive periods of scholarship and the "turning-points" between them, is weighted in favor of writers at the turn of the century who determined the direction in which research would move. In any case, a modern "Quest of the Historical Jesus" could begin at no better place than where the old *Quest* left off, in a review of Wrede and Schweitzer. That the same two scholars should be allowed to monopolize the first chapter of a discussion of modern Pauline scholarship seems hardly fair. But there are other criteria than fairness to be considered.

Concise, provocative, and popular in its appeal, Wrede's *Paul* remains to this day an excellent introduction to the academic study of Paul. Moreover, as we shall see, the displacement of the doctrine of justification from the center of Pauline thought is only one of many ways in which Wrede anticipates recent emphases in the scholarly literature. As for Schweitzer, not only do his Pauline studies mark a foretaste of things to come; even in translation his prose is inimitable in its imagery, spirit, and force. It is hard to resist the temptation to quote him liberally, and as close to the beginning of a book as the subject matter allows. When competing for attention with claims like these, a plea for fairness is bound to go unheard. So we begin with Wrede and Schweitzer.

Since Paul's view of the law cannot be isolated from other areas of his thought, I have tried to avoid too narrow a focusing of the issue. The broader canvas should also serve to bring what is distinctive about the approaches of the scholars discussed into better perspective. And, finally, a caveat to protect the innocent: what follows immediately is intended to represent the views of Wrede and Schweitzer. Many of the questions raised will be discussed in due course; but—it is a rule too seldom observed—fair reporting must precede scholarly assessment.

i. William Wrede

LITERATURE: Wrede, *Paul* (see Bibliography).

Fundamental to Wrede's presentation of Paul is his insistence that Paul was a man of his day—not ours. Paul's thinking was determined by laws we know not to be valid. He believed in beings which only children and poets speak of today. Where we see abstract terms, Paul, like all the ancients, tended to see real and effective powers. If, in spite of all this, countless of our contemporaries still believe that they share the views of the apostle, this is only because they misinterpret him. They spiritualize and psychologize, they read as metaphor what Paul took to be real, they make fundamental what is secondary and miss what is basic altogether. To present the true Paul to such readers is no easy task: "it is harder to interpret Paul's doctrine to one who half understands him than to one who knows nothing about him" (85).

Redemption

The distance between Paul and his modern would-be interpreters is nowhere greater than on the subject of redemption. Three questions must be answered if we are to understand his views: "(1) Wherein lies the misery from which the redemption releases us? (2) How and by what means does Christ bring the redemption to pass? (3) In what does the benefit of this redemption consist?" (92)

1. The popular view of Paul sees the problem of men and women outside of Christ as sin, and understands sin as the moral failings of the individual will. The problem posed for redemption is, then, how I, who have committed sins, can be made acceptable to a holy God, and the answer is found to lie in the atoning death of Christ, paying the penalty for, and thus freeing me from, my sins. Attention is focused on

the subjective peace of heart, purity of conscience, and assurance of grace felt by the "redeemed" individual. But this is grossly inadequate as a representation of what Paul means by redemption; his statements are general, sweeping, and objective. In a nutshell, Pauline redemption consists of "release from the misery of this whole present world" (92, referring to Gal. 1:4). Not deliverance from the torment of a guilty soul, but "a change in the very nature and conditions of existence" is the essence of redemption (112).

Why do the conditions of humanity need changing? Again, it would be too narrow an answer to speak simply of our ingrained propensity for sin. For Paul, life in "the present evil age" is characterized by bondage to "dark and evil powers" such as the flesh, sin, the law, and death (92). To our way of thinking, these are abstract terms; but the ancients attributed personality to such abstractions—after all, for them Love was a goddess! Similarly, Paul thinks of the law, sin, and the like as real and effective forces. He can speak of how "*sin,* finding opportunity in the commandment, deceived me and by it killed me*" (Rom. 7:11); or of how "death" is one of many "enemies" that have to be destroyed (1 Cor. 15:26). As a result, redemption, in Paul's mind, must involve deliverance from the evil powers that enslave us.

Of these powers, the "flesh" represents the limitations—indeed, the enslavement—imposed on us by our "finite, sensuous existence" (93) in a physical body on this earth. "Sin" must not be reduced to the sum of human wrongdoings, nor is our bondage to "sin" simply a metaphorical way of referring to our habit of "sinning." "Sin" is an active, enslaving power which accompanies the "flesh." "Sin clings indissolubly to the flesh, 'dwells' in the flesh, originates indeed in the flesh and its impulses" (93; cf. Rom. 7:17-20). We are slaves of "sin" simply because we live "in the flesh," the sphere where "sin" holds sway. Hence redemption must bring, not simply forgiveness for sins, but a change in the very conditions of an existence marked by bondage to "sin" and the "flesh."

Human misery is made more bitter still by the law. Without law there may be wrongdoing, but there can be no transgression, no violation of concrete commands (Rom. 4:15); in this respect, the presence of law aggravates human guilt. Moreover, the very command which prohibits lawless desires is used by "sin" to stimulate those desires within us (7:7-13). Hence the law, too, is a hostile power keeping humanity in bondage (v. 4). And inevitably, where the flesh, sin, and the law are present, death reigns as well (5:12-21); it, too, must be vanquished if we are to be redeemed.

And even this is not the full, dismal picture. "Angels, in our time, belong to children and to poets; to Paul and his age they were a real and serious quantity." And "Paul believes that mankind without Christ is under the sway of mighty spirits, demons, and angelic powers" (95). His letters are sprinkled with references to these "powers," "dominions," "principalities," and "authorities" (1 Cor. 15:24; Col. 1:16; 2:10, 15). Men and women are "slaves to the elemental spirits of the universe" (Gal. 4:3; cf. v. 9; Col. 2:8, 20). Such forces govern this age, they are its "rulers" (1 Cor. 2:6, 8), and they separate humanity from God (cf. Rom. 8:38-39). And, of course, these angelic beings stand behind sin, the flesh, death, and (perhaps surprisingly) even the law (cf. Gal. 3:19).

Such are the conditions of human existence before the intervention of the Christ. A redemption which means merely the forgiveness of sins and acceptance by God is too narrowly conceived; what is needed is a release from the whole present world and the evil forces which control it.

2. A change is brought about by the death and resurrection of God's Son. Christ, a superhuman, celestial being, "empties" himself of his heavenly status and enters the state of misery just described. He comes under the power of the law, "wears the flesh of sin," and subjects himself to the dominion of the spirits, who ultimately crucify him (98; cf. Gal. 4:4; Rom. 8:3; 1 Cor. 2:8). But, by dying, Christ leaves the sphere of these powers. "He no longer wears flesh, and therefore has nothing more in common with sin, law, and death" (99). Christ "died to sin" (Rom. 6:10); "death no longer has dominion over him" (v. 9). "Through his resurrection he enters upon a new existence, which is not subject" to these evil powers (99). He is thus the means by which God "disarmed the principalities and powers . . . , triumphing over them" (Col. 2:15).

Only such a view of Christ's death provides an adequate basis for understanding redemption. The evil forces enslaving humankind had to be overcome; and it is such a victory which Paul understands Christ to have achieved in his death and resurrection. Again, if we are to grasp how Paul thought this benefited us, the vicarious understanding of Christ's death (he died *instead* of us, as a substitute for us) is too narrow. Christ represents the human race in such a real way that what happened to him happened—in Paul's view, literally and objectively—to all. It is not just that all have derived benefits from his death; "one has died for all; therefore *all have died*" (2 Cor. 5:14). And if all die with him, then they also triumph with him over the evil powers. "We know that our old self was *crucified with him* so that the sinful body might be destroyed, and we might no longer be enslaved to sin. For he who has died is freed from sin" (Rom. 6:6-7).

Thus, "from the moment of his death all men are redeemed, as fully as he himself, from the hostile powers" (100). Such is the "change in the very nature and conditions of existence" brought about by Christ (112).

3. In popular piety, the "doctrine of salvation" is concerned with "what happens in the individual man." Since faith is seen as the means, its nature is carefully defined, and a vast literature is devoted to the "signs by which true and false, normal and defective faith can be distinguished" (113). But such a subjective, introspective, and psychological approach, Wrede says, has little support in Paul. Paul's concern is not with the individual but with the race, with humanity as a whole. Salvation is indeed individually appropriated by faith and baptism. But faith here refers simply to the acceptance of the message of redemption; no attempt is made to define the psychological state of the believer. Similarly, baptism is effective objectively; the thoughts or feelings of the one baptized are of no interest to Paul. Nor is baptism to be understood in a "purely spiritual or symbolic" way (120). For Paul, baptism makes the believer actually and literally a participant in the death and resurrection of Christ. With Christ the baptized die to sin, to the law, and to the world; and with Christ they rise to a new existence (Rom. 6:3-11; 7:4-6; Gal. 2:19; 6:14; Col. 3:1, 3).

All of this is true in the present of the Christian. Of course the believer still bears a physical body and lives in the world. But a real, objective transformation has taken place, and only its "*outward realization . . .* is reserved for the future*" (104). All will be complete with the speedy coming again of Christ. Proof that the powers of the new age are already active among believers is found in the presence of the Spirit of God.

Justification by Faith

This broad understanding of redemption is the heart of Pauline theology. What is frequently regarded as its foundation—the doctrine of justification by faith—is quite secondary by comparison, a polemical doctrine developed out of, and intended solely for, Paul's controversy with Judaism and Jewish Christianity. Only in the context of this debate is the doctrine of justification by faith referred to in the epistles, and the references are few. To make the doctrine of justification the center of Pauline thought is to distort the whole picture.

According to the popular view, the doctrine of justification by faith arose full-blown out of Paul's conversion experience. His preconversion condition is interpreted in the light of Romans 7: "I do not do the good I want, but the evil I do not want is what I do" (v. 19). Hence it is commonly thought that Paul before his conversion was "continually and vainly wrestling for righteousness before God. Instead of moral progress he suffered defeat after defeat, and ever increasing despair" (143). His vision on the road to Damascus of the risen Christ marked a watershed. Now he realized that "only grace, and never human conduct, could lead to salvation" (144). Thus the doctrine of justification is taken to be the "immediate fruit" of Paul's conversion (144).

The truth of the matter is that "the soul-strivings of Luther have stood as model for the portrait of Paul" (146). Paul paints quite a different picture of his own preconversion experience in Phil. 3:6: his life under the law had been blameless. Nor should Romans 7 be taken as a "real personal confession" of moral failings (144). The "I" of this chapter is not Paul the individual; indeed, Rom. 7:9 simply cannot be taken as a true description of what Paul, personally, had experienced. Romans 7 is to be read as a typical, general statement of the human condition under the law before the redemption, seen from the perspective gained by one who has been redeemed. Finally, it is true that Paul's life was "cut clean in two" by his Damascus vision (6), that he became convinced that Jesus was indeed the Christ; but such a conviction by itself hardly implies that circumcision and other "works of the law" are useless. Paul later said they were. But this view was forced upon him, not by the vision of the risen Christ, but by developments in his mission to the Gentiles. Practice determined theory rather than the other way around.

The doctrine of justification was designed to meet a double challenge. First, a problem was created by those who insisted that Gentile believers should adopt a Jewish way of life. This was clearly impractical. After all, to pagans, circumcision and the laws about clean and unclean foods not only appeared "bizarre and childish"; they constituted "real burdens in the social life, exposed people to mockery, and made divisions in families" (64). It was therefore clear to Paul that Jewish customs simply could not be made a condition for Gentiles to enter the Church. Since, however, such a conclusion was anything but self-evident to others in the early Church, Paul was forced to define what in fact makes a person a Christian. Obviously, Christians are distinguished from others by their faith in Jesus Christ. Thus, out of the controversy that followed Paul's missionary endeavor, the formula arose: *"not the Law with its works, but faith"* (125). A further consequence was that Paul was then compelled to demonstrate "the superfluity, perhaps harmfulness, of the Mosaic ceremonial" (125).

Second, Paul was confronted by the Jewish alternative to Christian faith. It, too, claimed to lead to salvation, but the path to that goal was seen to lie in keeping the commandments. Paul was thus faced with the task of showing how the Jewish way of salvation was in error, and he did this through the formula: *"not the works of men, but grace"* (126). To be sure, the alternatives thus baldly stated involve a slight caricature of the Jewish religion, which, after all, was not ignorant of grace. But its dominant feature was nonetheless the observance of the law as a means to salvation, and this provided a sufficient base for the Pauline tenet.

The Law

The essential points in Wrede's view of Paul's understanding of the law have already been touched upon. According to Paul's view of redemption, the law is one of the hostile forces from which humanity must be redeemed. Deliverance from the law is granted to those who, by faith and baptism, are united with the Christ who himself died to the law. In Paul's polemical doctrine of justification by faith, the works of the law are seen as the opposite of faith, a false path taken by Jews in pursuit of salvation. Such a position was first developed by Paul in the course of his missionary endeavors.

Two further points require attention.

1. Paul's rejection of the law is radical and complete. "In the fullest sense 'Christ is the end of the Law'" (125, referring to Rom. 10:4). Not even the moral commandments of the law are exempted. "Certainly Paul never dreams that the *content* of the moral precepts, such as the ten commandments, is false. But he denies the right of the Law to *demand* their fulfilment; he declares that every 'thou shalt' is done away" (125-126). There is "something artificial" about all this, for "no

ethical religion can dispense with the thought that God gives commandments to men" (136). Paul himself repeatedly enforces the moral commandments on his readers. The directives he gives bear "splendid witness to the circumspection, sobriety, and tact of the apostle" (59)—but not to his logical consistency. Paul can even say—in spite of his doctrine of justification—that God will judge according to works. The contradiction is apparent to us, but Paul himself may not have perceived it. In the interest of polemics, he formulated a position impossible to maintain in all its implications.

2. Paul's view of the law bears no relation to Jesus' own. Here as elsewhere the judgment must apply that, "if we do not wish to deprive both figures of all historical distinctness the name 'disciple of Jesus' has little applicability to Paul, if it is used to denote an historical relation" (165). Paul never appeals to the practice of Jesus in his polemic against the law. He could not, for his view of redemption required that Jesus was born under the law and strictly fulfilled its demands. Paul's motives, too, are different. Jesus attacks the institutions of the law "when and because they slay the moral sense, rob the soul of piety, substitute appearance for reality. Where in Paul's work do we find such an ethical criticism of legalism? He fights against the Law as a missionary, and as the advocate of redemption in Christ. That is another matter" (160).

A hostile force enslaving men and women before their redemption by the Son of God; a false path to salvation in the polemical doctrine of justification by faith; a radically, though somewhat artificially, rejected element in Pauline ethics: such is the law in William Wrede's *Paul*.

ii. Albert Schweitzer

LITERATURE: The following abbreviations are used in the discussion (see Bibliography):

> Interpreters = *Paul and His Interpreters*
> Mysticism = *The Mysticism of Paul the Apostle*
> Quest = *The Quest of the Historical Jesus*

Albert Schweitzer—missionary doctor in Lambarene, philosopher, organist and musicologist, the "greatest man in the world" in the eyes of no less an authority than *Life* magazine, winner of the Nobel Peace Prize, and much more besides—wrote two books about Paul. Unaccountably, they are classics.

The first draft of *The Mysticism of Paul the Apostle* dates back to 1906, though pressures on Schweitzer's time prevented its publication for several decades. The delay meant of course that Schweitzer was able to take later literature into account, though its prime significance is perhaps as circumstantial evidence that Schweitzer's days may after all have been limited to twenty-four hours. In 1906, the thirty-one-year-old Schweitzer was just beginning medical studies after having served for three years as principal of a theological college in Strasbourg. He had already written a dissertation on Immanuel Kant, a fine study of J. S. Bach in French, a short work on organ construction, an important monograph on the Last Supper, and the German original of *The Quest of the Historical Jesus*. During his years in medical school, Schweitzer kept his hand in the activities of the Paris Bach Society (which he had helped to found), in organ performances, as well as in preaching and lecturing; he prepared a second, expanded edition of *The Quest* and an extended German version of his *J. S. Bach;* began editing the Bach organ works; and published the German original of *Paul and His Interpreters* (1911). Under the circumstances, if any justice prevailed among fallen humanity, Schweitzer's Pauline studies would neither bear scrutiny nor merit attention today. For once we may be thankful there is no justice.

Those familiar with *The Quest* will recognize the works on Paul at once as vintage Schweitzer: incisive, intimidating, and preoccupied with eschatology. His history of research on Jesus presented us with three inescapable choices: "*either* purely historical *or* purely supernatural," "*either* Synoptic *or* Johannine," "*either* eschatological *or* non-eschatological." Readers who thought the choices too sharply put were left in no doubt as to their place in the history of scholarship:

> Progress always consists in taking one or other of two alternatives, in abandoning the attempt to combine them. The pioneers of progress have therefore always to reckon with the law of mental inertia which manifests itself in the majority—who always go on believing that it is possible to combine that which can no longer be combined.... One must just let them be, till their time is over. (Quest 238-239)

The correct (read: Schweitzerean) answer to the third alternative, of course, is that Jesus can only be understood in terms of eschatology. Dogmatic eschatological convictions occupied Jesus' thinking and dictated his course of action: the cataclysmic end of this world was at hand, God's kingdom would replace it, and he—Jesus—would reign as Messiah and king. Schweitzer finds the rest of the world misguided when it "seeks . . . to find in the teaching of Jesus thoughts which force their way out of the frame of the Jewish eschatological conceptions and have the character of universal religion. . . . The Gospel is at its starting-point exclusively Jewish-eschatological" (Interpreters ix). Of course Christianity could not remain Jewish and eschatological. Somehow the transition to the outside world of Hellenism had to be made if the fledgling faith was to survive. "When and how the Gospel was Hellenised" thus becomes "the fundamental problem of the history of dogma" (Interpreters viii).

We cannot here trace Schweitzer's broader solution to the problem, but it is important to note his insistence that the process of Hellenizing did not begin with Paul. The alternatives, as always, are clearcut: "We must now consider either a purely eschatological or a purely Hellenistic explanation of his teaching" (Mysticism viii). The issue, as always, is not in doubt:

> Whatever views and conceptions are brought up for comparison, the result is always the same—that Paulinism and Greek thought have nothing, absolutely nothing, in common. (Interpreters 99)

Opposing views, as usual, are scarcely worth consideration:

> Since all [Paul's] conceptions and thoughts are rooted in eschatology, those who labour to explain him on the basis of Hellenism, are like a man who should bring water from a long distance in leaky wateringcans in order to water a garden lying beside a stream. (Mysticism 140)

The stage is now set for a typically Schweitzerean *tour de force:* every single aspect of Pauline thought will be explained as a consistent, logical deduction from early Christian eschatological convictions. Readers willingly suspend their disbelief as long as the master is at work, effortlessly fitting together the pieces of the intricate puzzle, providing an assured explanation for each apparent anomaly that arises. Never has Paul appeared more consistent.

> And how totally wrong those are who refuse to admit that Paul was a logical thinker, and proclaim as the highest outcome of their wisdom the discovery that he has no system! (Mysticism 139)

Schweitzer at least found a system.

What follows are the views of Schweitzer. The law is our main concern, but the presentation takes its structure from three different doctrines of redemption which, according to Schweitzer, appear side by side in Paul's epistles: eschatological, mystical, and juridical.

The Eschatological Doctrine of Redemption

Like Wrede, Schweitzer believes the Pauline doctrine of redemption consists in humanity's deliverance from the rule of angelic powers who dominate this world.

According to the view current in Jewish eschatology, evil in the world derives ultimately from the demons, who "have, with God's permission, established themselves between Him and mankind" (Mysticism 55). Since, in the eschatological timetable, this state of affairs is destined to end with the establishment of God's kingdom, the evil powers spend the final days of their hegemony wreaking their rage on those called to the kingdom. At the same time, this pre-Messianic suffering of the elect is the means by which the latter atone for their sins. It is a necessary precondition for the coming of the kingdom.

This Jewish eschatological worldview was shared by both Jesus and Paul. Indeed, Jesus deliberately brought on his own death in an attempt to hasten the drama, to turn the wheel of foreordained history. By dying he would take upon himself the suffering destined for the elect, atone for their sins, and thus force God to inaugurate the kingdom. After his death, he believed, God would elevate him to Messiahship; as Messianic king, and together with the heavenly angels, he would then overthrow forever those forces which opposed God. The earliest Christians lived in the expectation that the resurrected Christ would speedily return to complete this work of redemption.

With the advent of the kingdom, the law would no longer be valid. This conviction, too, was taken over by Jesus and Paul from Jewish eschatology. For Jewish thought it was "self-evident" (Mysticism 69), and that for two reasons. First, eschatology and law are by their very nature incompatible. The ethic of eschatology is "immediate and absolute" (Mysticism 189). Such an ethic was proclaimed by the pre-exilic prophets who created eschatology at a time when (according to Wellhausen's scheme) the law did not even exist. And, in truth, wherever there is a pressing sense of the nearness of the kingdom, no place is left for "a meticulous observance of the last detail of the Law" (Mysticism 190). Second, when the coming kingdom is conceived of as transcendental, "the Law, designed for natural men, becomes purposeless" since "no longer natural but supernatural beings are in view" (Mysticism 191). In Jesus' teaching, too, the law is represented as valid "till heaven and earth pass away"; that is, until the end of this age and the coming of God's kingdom (Matt. 5:18). Paul shares this understanding, but develops it in two important respects.

In the first place, the relationship between the law and the angels receives a novel definition from Paul. Not that Paul was alone in claiming that the law was communicated to Moses by angels (Gal. 3:19); while such a view is not found in the Old Testament, it was necessitated by the post-biblical Jewish understanding of God as so transcendent that direct contact with him becomes unthinkable. But Paul links this view of angelic mediation of the law with the Jewish eschatological worldview in an unprecedented way: "the Law was given by Angels who desired thereby to make men subservient to themselves"; hence "obedience rendered to the Law was rendered not to God but only to the Angels" (Mysticism 69-70; cf. Gal. 4:1-11).

Secondly, though there was nothing new in the idea that the law's validity would cease at the dawn of the Messianic age, Paul declared that, with the death and resurrection of the Christ, redemption had "already begun to come into operation" (Mysticism 64). As a result, believers are not subject to the angelic powers to the same degree as before, and Paul can represent the law itself as already done away by Jesus' death. In effect, Paul took the opposite course to the one ultimately chosen by Judaism: he "sacrificed the Law to eschatology; Judaism abandoned eschatology and retained the Law" (Mysticism 192).

Note, however, that it is only believers who have been set free from the law. Where the natural world retains validity, the dominion of angels is still in effect. Indeed, believers themselves, if they submit to the law, will in reality be returning to their bondage to the world-elements. This incredible situation is envisaged in Galatians 4:8-11:

> Formerly, when you did not know God, you were in bondage to beings that by nature are no gods; but now that you have come to know God, or rather to be known by God, how can you turn back again to the weak and beggarly elemental spirits, whose slaves you want to be once more? You observe days, and months, and seasons, and years! I am afraid I have labored over you in vain.

In saying that believers have been set free from the law, we are already bordering on Paul's mystical doctrine of redemption, by which he explains how the transformation takes place. Before we deal with

Paul's mystical doctrine, however, we must note Schweitzer's reaction to those who find the root of Paul's doctrine in considerations other than eschatological.

H. J. Holtzmann (*Lehrbuch der Neutestamentlichen Theologie, 1897*) is one of many to suggest that, whereas before his conversion Paul was distressed by his inability to fulfill the law, in the light of his Damascus experience, he became aware of a new way to salvation apart from law. For all its popularity, this suggestion, Schweitzer believes, leads nowhere.

> How do we know that Paul when he was still a persecutor of the Christians was suffering inward distress from his experiences of the powerlessness of the law? How did the vision of Christ bring about the resolution of this tension? How, exactly, did it reveal a way of salvation by which the abolition of the law was implied? (Interpreters 105)

At the time of his conversion, Paul became convinced that Jesus was Messiah. How did he draw from this conviction the conclusion that the law had been invalidated—a conclusion which neither Jesus nor the primitive Christian community (which also believed that Jesus was Messiah!) ever contemplated? The time has come when

> there must be no more talking about the "uniqueness of the event at Damascus" and psychologising about Paul's "religious experience." ... All explanations which represent the system of doctrine as something arising subjectively in the Apostle's mind may be assumed *a priori* to be false. Only those which seek to derive it objectively from the fundamental facts of the primitive eschatological belief are to be taken into consideration. (Interpreters 247-248)

Nor can Paul's understanding of the law be derived from the teaching of Jesus. Admittedly, Paul and Jesus shared alike in the common Jewish eschatological expectation. But for Paul "the hour in the world-clock" has advanced. Jesus has died and been raised. Consequently "the rule of the Angels is in process of being destroyed" and

> the transformation from the earthly state of existence to the superearthly is already going on. It is thus that [Paul] comes to regard what Jesus had said about the Law ... as no longer authoritative. Although Jesus had recognised the Law, and had never said anything against Circumcision, both must now be regarded as no longer valid, since they presuppose that rulership of Angels which is now being destroyed. (Mysticism 113-114)

Finally, the time has come to abandon all suggestions that Paul approached the law as a "purely practical question, which did not touch doctrine in the strict sense" (Interpreters 246). Even Wrede is guilty on this score. It is simply inconceivable that a Paul could have rejected the law in principle because of purely practical considerations (cf. Interpreters 137-138). What we find is rather that Paul reached his position on the law "by systematically thinking out to its conclusions the primitive Christian doctrine" (Interpreters 83).

The Mystical Doctrine of Redemption

We are always in presence of mysticism when we find a human being looking upon the division between earthly and super-earthly, temporal and eternal, as transcended, and feeling himself, while still externally amid the earthly and temporal, to belong to the super-earthly and eternal. (Mysticism 1)

Paul's mysticism consists in his conviction that "in Christ" he knows himself "as a being who is raised above this sensuous, sinful, and transient world and already belongs to the transcendent" (Mysticism 3).

"Being in Christ" means "having died and risen again with Him" (Mysticism 3), a process which begins with baptism (cf. Rom. 6:3-6). Paul's language here should not be interpreted as merely metaphorical. For Paul, the references to dying and rising with Christ express "a simple reality" (Mysticism 15). The result is that those who are "in Christ" have already begun to experience "the cessation of the natural world" through their participation in Christ's death; and, by sharing in his resurrection, they experience "the dawning of the supernatural world" (Mysticism 23).

How does this "mystical doctrine" affect Paul's understanding of the law? We have seen how Paul's *eschatological* convictions led him to believe that the law is no longer in force for the Christian, who already belongs to the Messianic age. Whereas outside of Christ, in the natural world, the law retains its power, its grip on the believer has been broken. Fully consistent with this, Paul's *mysticism* explains how Christians have passed from one sphere to another: with Christ, they "died to the law" (Rom. 7:4; Gal. 2:19), and were thus released from its fetters; with Christ they rose again, supernatural beings on whom the law has no claim.

What should the attitude of believers be toward the law which for them is no longer valid? Paul answers by applying here a comprehensive *status quo* theory: Christians are to remain in whatever external condition they were in when they became believers. This theory is stated in general terms in 1 Cor. 7:17, 20, and is applied to circumcision in verse 18. The result is that the one who believed as a Jew must continue to live by the Jewish law (Paul himself did so), whereas the non-Jew must not submit to its regulations.

While such a position may sound like a mere expedient, a compromise arrived at under the pressures of missionary experience, in fact we are dealing once again with a logical, "necessary inference" from Paul's fundamental convictions. Here it is his mystical doctrine of the believer's existence "in Christ" which is decisive.

> From the moment that a man is in-Christ his whole being is completely conditioned by that fact. . . . If in spite of this he begins to make alterations in his natural condition of existence, he is ignoring the fact that his being is henceforth conditioned by the being-in-Christ, and not by anything else connected with his natural existence. (Mysticism 194-195)

The theory at least is consistent. But if Jews and non-Jews were to enjoy table fellowship together, it became clear that Jewish believers would be required to make compromises in practice (cf. Gal. 2:11-14).

The Juridical Doctrine of Redemption

Paul's juridical doctrine of salvation is the familiar one of righteousness through faith. Strictly speaking "righteousness" in this context belongs to the future: to be "righteous" is to have "a claim to be pronounced righteous at the coming Judgment, and consequently to become a partaker in the Messianic glory" (Mysticism 205). Whereas in post-biblical Jewish theology such "righteousness" was acquired by keeping the commandments, for Paul the decisive factor was faith in the redemptive efficacy of Christ's death. But Paul's view differs in another important respect as well: Since believers are already "in Christ" (the mystical view of salvation), they possess already the state of existence which belongs to the Messianic kingdom, including righteousness. "There is therefore now no condemnation for those who are *in Christ Jesus*" (Rom. 8:1).

Thus, for Paul, the juridical doctrine of salvation is rooted in his mystical views of the believer's being in Christ. To be sure, this is not apparent from the expression "righteousness by faith" by itself, but the phrase must be understood as a convenient shorthand, adopted in a polemical setting in which Paul had to distinguish between this "righteousness" and that which is "by the law." But a more adequate summation of the doctrine would run "Righteousness, in consequence of faith, through the being-in-Christ" (Mysticism 206-207).

In Galatians, the connection between the juridical view and Paul's eschatological and mystical doctrines is clear. There Paul insists that the law cannot produce righteousness since it was not even designed to do so. On the contrary, the law comes (according to Paul's eschatological doctrine) from angel powers in order to keep humanity under their dominion. The promise of righteousness is made to the "seed" (singular) of Abraham, that is, to Christ (Gal. 3:16). Hence it belongs to those who, by faith, are "in Christ Jesus" (the mystical doctrine of salvation; v. 26). Thus we arrive at the doctrine of "righteousness, in consequence of faith, through the being-in-Christ." At least in Galatians the argument is not that Christ's death was an atonement made to God for sins; rather it was the means of setting free those who are subject to the angel powers (4:1-11).

In Romans, on the other hand, Paul attempts to develop the juridical doctrine of righteousness by faith in a different way. Aware that the church at Rome might have been prejudiced against him, he proceeds with great caution, exercising particular care in what he says about the law. Its connection with angel powers is not mentioned. Rather Paul explains the need for redemption on the basis of (1) human nature, which can do no good; and (2) the nature of the law, which forbids sin, but has no power to deal with it. From such a predicament redemption is brought by the atoning death of Jesus, bringing forgiveness of sin to those who believe in him (Rom. 3:21-28).

Such a view of redemption, however, must not be mistaken for the center of Paul's thought. On the contrary, it is utterly incapable of serving as a starting-point for the understanding of Paul, since it is rather "a fragment from the more comprehensive mystical redemption-doctrine, which Paul has broken off and polished" to suit the needs of a particular occasion (Mysticism 220). If "righteousness by faith" appears to stand on its own in Romans, Galatians clearly shows its dependence on notions derived from Paul's eschatological and mystical doctrines. In both Romans and Galatians, "righteousness by faith" is mentioned only

> where the controversy over the Law has to be dealt with, and—very significantly—even then only where a Scriptural argument is to be

based on the as yet uncircumcised Abraham. . . . Once Paul has left behind the discussion necessitated by his Scriptural argument, about faith-righteousness and Law-righteousness, it is of no more service to him. (Mysticism 220-221)

Paul made no effort to base his ethics on the doctrine of justification by faith, nor could he readily have done so if he had tried. "It would have been necessary to show how the man who previously was inherently incapable of producing good works received through the act of justification the capacity to do so" (Mysticism 295). And how can ethics be constructed out of the "idea of a faith which rejects not only the works of the Law, but works in general" (Mysticism 225)? The dilemma does not concern Paul, for "justification by faith" is not central to his thinking. Instead he bases his ethics on what is paramount, the mystical doctrine of dying and rising with Christ. "But those who subsequently made his doctrine of justification by faith the centre of Christian belief, have had the tragic experience of finding that they were dealing with a conception of redemption, from which no ethic could logically be derived" (Mysticism 225).

Furthermore, freedom from the law follows naturally from Paul's mystical doctrine, since those who died "with Christ" died to the law and to sin. But no case against the law's validity can be based on the atoning death of Jesus; in fact, the other early Christians, who certainly believed that Christ's death had secured for them the forgiveness of sins, continued nonetheless to live in accordance with the law. And why not? From Christ's death for our sins we may certainly deduce the inadequacy of our attempts to observe the law; but it does not follow from the atonement that the law is no longer to be observed. Paul's convictions on that score can scarcely have been derived from the doctrine of righteousness by faith in the atoning death of Jesus. "The doctrine of righteousness by faith is therefore a subsidiary crater, which has formed within the rim of the main crater—the mystical doctrine of redemption through the being-in-Christ" (Mysticism 225).

And so, there are three doctrines of redemption in Paul; he passes freely from one to the other. But they are not equally important. The juridical doctrine, justification by faith, is the least important of the three. The primary significance of the eschatological doctrine is that it served as the starting-point from which Paul developed his theology. But it is in his mystical views that we discover the heart of his theology and personal religion.

*   *   *

The significance of Wrede and Schweitzer for the Pauline debate is by
no means limited to their insistence that justification by faith was a pe-
ripheral concern of the apostle. The emphasis on Paul's eschatological worldview, on the "realism" of his language regarding human
bondage and deliverance, on the universal aspects of his scheme of redemption, on the perils of deriving Paul's views from those of Jesus
and the folly of tracing them to his preconversion psychological state:
all these themes have surfaced repeatedly in the subsequent debate.

Still, the best known phrase from Wrede's *Paul* remains his label
of justification as Paul's "polemical doctrine"; and, in Schweitzer's
case, his description of the same doctrine as a "subsidiary crater" rivals
the famous last words of *The Quest* in a bid for immortality. Perhaps
it is too much, perhaps even churlish, to ask of such deathless words
that they should also be true. Yet the impertinence must be permitted,
for to downplay justification is to challenge cherished notions of Paul.
In Part Two we will need to return to the question of the significance
of Paul's doctrine of justification by faith to his thought.

But first we must turn to other attacks on Luther's scheme.

Chapter Three

The Faith of Paul's Fathers: Montefiore, Schoeps, and Sanders

According to Luther, Christianity is set apart from the world by its insistence on justification by faith, not works, and the affinities of Judaism are with the world. This simple distinction has proven attractive to many Christian scholars and theologians, not least because it has relieved them of the tedious task of examining the sources of rabbinic Judaism for themselves. From his own experience, and with considerable acumen, Luther had described a religion of "works"; the pattern, it was supposed, would surely serve for Judaism as well. And, in fact, the correctness of the model was thought to be established by the efforts of one or two intrepid souls who culled from rabbinic writings quotations to illustrate each of its aspects. The hermeneutical circle was then made complete when these quotations were taken to provide background material for understanding Paul: the apostle was interpreted in contrast with Judaism, which itself was interpreted in the light of Catholicism, which in turn was interpreted by Luther's reading of Paul. Until recently, the cycle showed every sign of being self-perpetuating.

Such, in rough, is the picture given of the traditional view of Paul's relations with Judaism by those espousing a radical revision. Their most obvious point of attack has been the understanding of Judaism imposed by the scheme. What, after all, could be more damning than the simple demonstration that those who portrayed Judaism had very limited command of the primary sources, and that a misleading sixteenth-century analogy was the real basis for their depiction? It

33

is not surprising, then, that the latest stage in the debate about Paul and the Jewish law has been sparked by a large-scale attack on what are taken to be Christian caricatures of Judaism. The Judaism of our hermeneutical circle proclaimed that salvation was earned by human works. Sanders denies the accuracy of that description and suggests that a Paul detached from the "circle" will require reinterpretation as well.

In this chapter we will review the work of three Pauline scholars who have argued that Judaism is wrongly cast as a foil for the doctrine of justification by faith, not works. Montefiore and Schoeps see Paul himself as the source of the distortion, though they explain somewhat differently how he was misled. In Sanders's work the blame rests primarily with Paul's interpreters. Either way, the traditional understanding of Paul's rejection of the law is clearly in need of rethinking.

i. C. G. Montefiore

LITERATURE: Montefiore, *Judaism and St. Paul* (see Bibliography).

C. G. Montefiore is best known to students of the New Testament for his important work on *The Synoptic Gospels* (first edition, 1909). The world was young in 1909, and many Christian readers were surprised to find that a Jewish scholar was able not only to shed light on many aspects of the Gospels, but even to treat the figure of Jesus with obvious sympathy. That feat accomplished, Montefiore ventured upon the still more daunting task of understanding and fairly assessing the apostle Paul; in 1914 he published two essays under the title *Judaism and St. Paul*. Our attention will be limited to the first study, "The Genesis of the Religion of St. Paul."

Even in 1914, the questions Montefiore raised were not new. Still, he hoped that more satisfactory answers could then be given based on recent advances in the knowledge of the world in which Paul lived and—above all—on the contemporary spirit of impartiality which attempted to do justice to both Jesus and the Pharisees, Paul and the rabbis. The lack of sympathy which Christian scholars had customarily shown for rabbinic Judaism was self-evident. So, too, was their lack of firsthand knowledge. "Rabbinic Judaism seems to be the one department of learning about which many great scholars have been willing to make assertions without being able to read the original authorities, or to test the references and statements of the writers whom they quote" (7). The normal procedure had been to suppose that the Judaism Paul knew was rabbinic, to base one's understanding of rabbinic Judaism on polemical passages in Paul, and then to find support for such an understanding in quotations lifted, with no appreciation for their nature or context, from rabbinic writings. For his part, Montefiore attempts to show that the Judaism with which Paul was familiar was not rabbinic; he comments on the patent injustice of basing one's view of a religion on the polemical statements of an opponent and convert; and he notes that isolated quotations from the vast sea of rabbinic writings could be used to prove any thesis whatsoever.

The task which Montefiore sets for himself is to explain "Paul's religious antecedents—his religious history and opinions before his conversion," as well as "his relation to the Judaisms of his age and time" (13). The plural ("Judaisms") is deliberate: "several Judaisms, all more or less fluid and growing, existed in the first century" (3). Though the divisions "are not water-tight or cut and dry" (5), we may nonetheless speak of rabbinic, apocalyptic, and Hellenistic Judaisms in the world of A.D. 50 Montefiore's primary and, to some extent, apologetic concern is clearly to show that the Judaism Paul knew was *not* rabbinic.

He begins with a short account of rabbinic religion. To portray first-century "Rabbinic Judaism" is notoriously difficult, since rabbinic literature comes from a much later period, and Jewish writings closer to Paul's day were produced by "writers whose relation to Rabbinic Judaism is often doubtful and disputed" (15). Montefiore adopts a curious and, at first sight, unpromising procedure. Since the rabbinic Judaism of A.D. 300 or 500 is well known, he begins by simply asking: "What was the relation of Paul's religion before his conversion to *this* Rabbinic Judaism? How far was his religion, before the event at Damascus, the same as, or different from, that of any ordinary and average representative of Rabbinic Judaism?" (16) The justification for such a procedure is the obvious fact that Christian scholars have traditionally characterized rabbinic Judaism on the basis of Paul's first-century writings, simply assuming that the Judaism Paul knew was essentially the rabbinic Judaism of later centuries. A more accurate description of the later Judaism will suffice, Montefiore believes, to show the falseness of the assumption.

Here we may note three areas in which Montefiore finds differences between rabbinic Judaism as we know it from later sources and the religion of the apostle Paul.

1. We begin with the law. Rabbinic Jews regard the law as the gracious gift of a loving God to his people, designed to make them happy and good. Obeying God's law is the duty and the privilege which together distinguish Israel from the Gentile nations. Since the law was given for Israel's good, its observance brings life, happiness, and peace. Hence "the core and essence of the Rabbinic religion are contained in that one familiar phrase, 'the joy of the commandments'" (29-30).

It is simply false to suggest that the great number of commands represented an intolerable burden. For one thing, the imposition of the commandments was perceived as the granting of a privilege; thus, the more the commands, the greater the honor given to God's people. In an often cited prayer, Jewish men thanked God daily that they were not women because (note the reason!) "men have more commandments to fulfill than women" (29). Actually the number of commands to which any individual was required to conform was not that large in any case.

> The compulsion of the Law was chiefly felt in two directions—the Sabbath and food. There were very many things which you might not do upon the Sabbath, but you soon learnt what they were, and if there is one thing more certain than another it is that the Sabbath was a joy. There were numerous laws about food, but some concerned the butcher, others the women who cooked; those which remained were easily acquired and remembered. (32-33)

But what happened when the laws were transgressed? Did rabbinic Jews not believe that God was angered by the violation of his commands? And, since God's pleasure was thought to depend on obedience to his demands, did not the average Jew live in uncertainty and fear of the final judgment? Such dilemmas arise frequently in Christian portrayals of Judaism, but—it must be emphasized—they were not perceived as problems by the average Jew. Of course it was recognized that no one keeps the law perfectly, and that God is angered when his commands are broken. But the Israelite remembered "that the Law was given to men, and not to angels" (40); and it was given specifically to bring about improvement, purification, and increasing holiness in God's people. Perfection was not expected. If God is angered by transgression, his compassion certainly outweighs his anger; "and by the gracious gift of repentance He helps [the Jew] both to conquer his sin and to obtain its forgiveness" (42). Counting on God's love for

Israel and his willingness to forgive, the average Jew could be both "happy and hopeful: happy in the performance, within the limits of human frailty, of the divine commands in this world, hopeful in the belief of the sure inheritance hereafter of the finer and purer beatitudes of the world to come" (36-37).

All of this bears little resemblance to what we find in Paul. To be sure, Paul acknowledges that the law is holy. But, whereas for rabbinic Judaism the law was always thought to bring goodness and joy, for Paul it brought neither and was not intended to do so. "The Law was a curse. It evoked the knowledge of sin. It strengthened the desire to sin. By the works of the Law no man can win God's favour or be regarded by God as righteous" (70). One could understand if a rabbinic Jew, on becoming a Christian, were to argue that the law which, before Christ, had divided Jew from Gentile was now done away. It would be understandable, too, for Paul to say that the moral laws are now unnecessary, since their demands are met spontaneously by Christians who possess God's Spirit. But Paul goes much further.

> The important thing is that Paul does not content himself with saying that the Law was all very well, and did very well, up to Jesus Christ's day, but need not now, (and, therefore, should not now), be observed any more, but that he actually conceived the theory that the Law did definite and positive harm. . . . It made things worse than they were, or than they would have been, without it. And all this was its intention, the purpose for which it had been given. (106-107)

Montefiore finds it inconceivable that Paul could have arrived at such views after his conversion if his previous view of the law had been that of rabbinic Judaism.

2. Something has already been said of the role which repentance and divine forgiveness played in the thinking of the rabbinic Jew. Sin was taken seriously, no less seriously than by the apostle Paul; but God stood ready to forgive. "Let a man repent but a very little, and God will forgive very much. For He delights in the exercise of forgiveness far more than in the exercise of punishment." (42) Since God's mercy is so readily available, it is only "the deliberate and determined sinner" who fails to attain life. "For every decent Israelite there was a place in the future world" (44).

The contrast with Paul's position is, again, pronounced. "Nothing is more peculiar in the great Epistles than the almost complete omission of the twin Rabbinic ideas of repentance and forgiveness"

(75). Had Paul been brought up in rabbinic Judaism, he would at least have argued that the standard teaching on repentance was in some way inadequate. Instead it goes unmentioned, while Paul claims on the one hand that a single offense is sufficient to cause the curse of the law and the wrath of God to descend upon us (Gal. 3:10), and, on the other, that "only an amazing expedient and a terrific catastrophe" (70), the death of a "sinless divine being" (78), can redeem us. The need for such "a tremendous cosmic and divine event" as the incarnation and crucifixion was simply not felt by rabbinic theology, where "God was so good and near and kind," and where "man, through the Law and through repentance, had such constant, easy and efficacious opportunities of access to him" (74). It follows, surely, that Pauline soteriology is "impossible upon a purely Rabbinic basis" (77).

3. Finally, Pauline theology proves consistently more pessimistic than rabbinic thinking. The average rabbinic Jew perceived the world as good, created and governed by a loving God. "He has never allowed its government to fall into the hands of any lesser divine being than Himself, still less into the hands of some evil spirit or demon" (45-46). But for Paul, "the world is under the domination of demons and of Satan. Paul even goes so far as to call Satan the god of this world, an expression which, to the average Rabbinic Jew, would verge upon blasphemy" (69). As for the moral capacities of humanity, rabbinic Judaism was fully aware of human sin, but recognized that there was some observance of the law and righteousness in the world as well; human goodness is as real as human badness. God's help was of course thought essential, but it was "not supposed that human efforts count for nothing" (78), or that, apart from a new birth, man is completely powerless to overcome the "flesh." Hence there was no need of the cross. "Man could receive salvation, and get the better of sin, (for God was always helping and forgiving) even without so strange and wonderful a device" (78). By way of contrast, in the world of Pauline pessimism, those "in the flesh" simply cannot do good (Rom. 7:18; 8:7).

We are faced, then, with two alternatives: "Either the Rabbinic Judaism of 50 was not the Rabbinic Judaism of 500 (or 300), or Paul at the time of his conversion was no pure Rabbinic Jew" (68); for certainly the religion of Paul before his conversion was "poorer," "more sombre and gloomy than Rabbinic Judaism" (81). Montefiore notes that there are no indications of "any great improvement in the teachings of the famous Rabbis of the fourth century over those of the first"

(87). He is therefore "inclined to think that, even in 50, Rabbinic Judaism was a better, happier, and more noble religion that one might infer from the writings of the Apostle" (87). Paul's background, then, was not in rabbinic Judaism at all. We are to seek it rather in the Judaism of the Hellenistic world.

In Hellenistic Judaism, Montefiore finds a number of features which help to explain the apostle's thinking. Contact with pagan philosophy had resulted in a conception of God "more distant and less approachable . . . more august and majestic, but less gentle and kindly" (95). And "may we not also suppose that the general spiritual anxiety which was widely diffused in the later Hellenistic world had also infected the Jews? Some of them, too, may have begun to worry about their salvation and the 'state of their soul.' And as God had become more distant, so did sin seem, not more grievous, but less eradicable, than to their 'Rabbinic' brethren" (97).

The observance of the law came naturally to rabbinic Jews, and with little need for justification. Not so for Hellenistic Jews, living in the midst of pagans. They must have wondered often about the point of prohibitions which their neighbors did not observe. They could easily have come to think of the law "as something which restrained and forbade, rather than as something through which [they] gained ineffable joys and realised the presence of God" (100). Perhaps, too, a Hellenistic Jew would more readily be struck and troubled by the condemnation of Gentiles who did not observe, because they did not possess, the Jewish law. This, too, may have led to disaffection.

Along some such lines we may explain the development of Paul's theology. In any case, the foundation was not rabbinic. Of course a rabbinic Jew could become convinced that Jesus was the Messiah and convert to Christianity. But the Pauline theories of the law and soteriology, and the basic Pauline pessimism, cannot have grown from rabbinic soil.

ii. H. J. Schoeps

LITERATURE: Schoeps, *Paul* (see Bibliography).

Montefiore's study, stimulating though it is, remains brief and, at times, superficial. The task of assessing Paul's relations with the Judaism of his day was taken up again on a much larger scale by the Jewish historian of religion Hans Joachim Schoeps. His *Paul* has been widely acclaimed as one of the most significant contributions to Pauline scholarship in this century. Here we can only cast a brief look at the various subjects addressed before turning to the book's best-known argument: that Paul's reduction of the law to a sum of demands which cannot be kept represents a travesty of the Jewish position.

The book begins with a survey of "the main intellectual forces in the climate" (15) of Paul's day and evaluates their impact on Paul's thinking. Schoeps first reviews the work of scholars who believed that Paul's thought was heavily influenced by Hellenistic conceptions. Schweitzer, it will be remembered, attacked such a notion vigorously. For his part, Schoeps is willing to concede that much in Paul's thought-world was non-Jewish, and that in a number of ways Hellenistic ideas and vocabulary are evidenced in his writings. In particular, the influence of the pagan mystery cults is "unmistakable" in Pauline soteriology and "sacramental mysticism" (47). Nonetheless "pure Hellenism" is excluded as a source for Pauline theology (23). What Paul absorbed of Hellenistic thought would have reached him through the medium of the Hellenized Judaism of the Diaspora.

As we have seen, the position of C. G. Montefiore was that the Judaism Paul knew was Hellenistic, not rabbinic, and that this background explains many features of Paul's thought. Schoeps criticizes Montefiore's methodology on a number of counts. First, it is misleading to treat rabbinic Judaism as though it were a unified whole; indeed, some of the Pauline positions which Montefiore contrasts with rabbinic thought "also found exponents in Palestinian schools" (26). Second, Montefiore strictly distinguishes apocalyptic thought from rabbinic, when in fact the apocalyptic movement flourished throughout first-century Palestine. It cannot be considered a sectarian phenomenon apart from "normative Judaism." Nor, for that matter, are we to assume "an irreconcilable opposition between Hellenistic and rabbinic Judaism" (26). And what we know of the former is far too inadequate in any case to be used as a basis for explaining Paul's thought. Still, whatever the flaws in Montefiore's procedure, the fact remains that Paul was a Jew from the Diaspora; and, though we must bear in mind the complexity of Hellenistic Judaism, we do find many ways in which it proves an essential factor in a reconstruction of Paul's doctrine and faith.

According to Acts 22:3, Paul was educated in Jerusalem by Gamaliel (Rabban Gamaliel I). Schoeps believes that the influence of this school is apparent in Paul's argumentation and exegetical method. Paul was clearly a "rabbinist," and any explanation of a point in his theology which proceeds from rabbinic thought deserves from the outset "preference over all other explanations" (40). Most importantly, Paul's eschatological thought was shaped by the discussions of the Palestinian schools.

In short, none of the main intellectual forces of Paul's day can be discounted as an influence on his thought. Nor, on the other hand, should we reduce Paul's thinking to "the sum of its various component parts" (48). Paul was trying "to give expression to something quite new. This new element has dawned for him through his encounter with the risen Messiah, convincing him that the new aeon has already supervened" (40).

Schoeps's second chapter discusses "The Position of the Apostle Paul in Primitive Christianity." Paul's Christian experience began when he met the risen Jesus on the road to Damascus. Yet the question of the significance of Jesus for Paul is a difficult one. To judge by Paul's writings, the earthly Jesus played no great role in the piety or thinking of the apostle, though an exception must of course be made for Jesus' death on the cross. Central for Paul is simply the belief *that* the Messiah has come, and thus that "the times are now post-messianic" (58). The first church was convinced that it lived at the "end of the age." Paul made this common conviction the "point of departure for the structure of his own theology" (62).

As for Paul's relations with the early Church, we know that in the course of his ministry opposition arose on two basic issues: the practice to be followed in admitting Gentiles into the Church and the correct understanding of the apostolate. On the first issue, the differences between Paul and the prime apostles should not be exaggerated. Peter and James adopted what amounted to a mediating position between the extreme positions of Paul, who repudiated any claim of the Mosaic law on Gentile believers, and the Judaizers, who defended its complete validity for all Christians (Acts 15:20). We may certainly conclude from Galatians 2 and from the collection Paul gathered from his churches for the Jerusalem believers that his missionary procedure met with the approval of the leading apostles. The significant difference concerned the question of apostleship. Schoeps takes the oldest view of the apostolate to be that which limited the title to the twelve who accompanied Jesus throughout his earthly ministry. For Paul, however, the criterion of apostleship was not that of "knowing Jesus after the flesh, but only of witness to the Risen Lord" (72). But in this area too it was Judaizing extremists who attacked Paul's apostleship. The circle of the twelve was too impressed by Paul's missionary success to raise the issue.

After these introductory attempts to place Paul's work in the perspective of the first century, Schoeps discusses in turn Paul's eschatology (chapter 3), his soteriology (4), his teaching about the law (5), and his understanding of saving history (6). In each case he notes the roots of Paul's thinking in Jewish theology as well as areas where Paul goes beyond the bounds of what the latter could find acceptable.

Paul's *eschatology* has obvious links with the "tense Messianic expectation" (259) which pervaded Palestinian Judaism in his day. Not that there was any "unified scheme of thought about the last things" (97). Still the notion that Messiah would come at the end of time was simply adopted by Paul from current Jewish eschatology. For Paul, however, Messiah had already come—and yet the "end" had not followed. Hence the traditional understanding required correction, and the unexpected interval before the parousia required interpretation. Paul concluded that the boundary between "this age" and "the age to come" had broken down, giving way to a brief transitional period: the Messianic kingdom had begun, the age of salvation had dawned, the old aeon was in the process of passing away—and yet the old order remained somehow in place. None of these conclusions is acceptable in the eyes of Judaism, for which the world after its purported "transformation," that which Paul believed in, resembles nothing so much as its old, unaltered self. It is, of course, the fact that Paul looks *back* on the coming of the Messiah which has led to the different perspective.

Paul's *soteriology* has roots in at least three Jewish ideas.

1. The suffering of the righteous can have an atoning value. Such an understanding grows out of Biblical ideas of sacrifice as "expiatory and substitutionary" (130).
2. The "Servant of Yahweh" would suffer vicariously and surrender his life as an atoning sacrifice (Isa. 53). Schoeps believes that already in Judaism the Servant was "probably at an early period understood and personified as the Messiah" (135).
3. The "binding" of Isaac as Abraham prepared to sacrifice him (Gen. 22:9) was believed to have expiatory value. In Schoeps's opinion, this belief "provided the very model for the elaboration of Pauline soteriology" (141).

Yet despite these Jewish roots, Pauline soteriology becomes fundamentally un-Jewish when it views Jesus as God's incarnate Son, possessing "real divinity" (149). A Jewish source for this notion is simply inconceivable. If some derivation must be suggested, we should look rather to "heathen mythological conceptions, filtered through the Hellenistic syncretism of the time" (149).

Again, Paul's view of *salvation history* grew out of Jewish convictions. Before his conversion, Paul no doubt shared the belief that in the Messianic age the Gentiles would join Israel in worshiping Israel's God. Indeed, Paul may well have shared the missionary zeal of many Pharisees, who reasoned that they could hasten the coming of Messiah by converting the heathen. Such a task became even more urgent when Paul was convinced that Messiah had come and the Messianic age had begun. Now it was crucial that the prophetic promises which had not yet come to pass should be fulfilled in as short a time as possible.

On the other hand, what the traditional understanding did not foresee was that most Jews would not recognize their Messiah, but would crucify him, thereby "casting the promises to the winds" (220). Again, Paul was forced to rethink the traditional view; Romans 9-11 in particular shows him grappling with the problem. He came to distinguish between "the empiric-historical Israel" and the "eschatological Israel of the promise" (238). God's election of "Israel" does not include all (physical) Israelites, but only a remnant, a chosen few. Joining them in the "true Israel" of God were Gentiles who believed in Christ. Still, in the end, when "the full number of the Gentiles come in" (Rom. 11:25), the whole of (physical) Israel will be saved as well; "as the descendants of the patriarchs" they retain a "special sanctity in election" (242). For none of these speculations are we to seek Jewish parallels, since the problems which led to the revision of traditional views were the product of Christian faith.

In the matter of *the law* as well, Paul's theology amounts to "nothing other than the re-thinking of all received notions" (171) in view of the coming of the Messiah and his resurrection from the dead. Schoeps follows Schweitzer in thinking that Paul was guided by a common conviction that the law would lose its validity when the Messianic kingdom began. As support he cites rabbinic traditions which saw the age of the world as predetermined at 6000 years: 2000 years of chaos, a 2000-year era of the Mosaic law, then the era of the Messiah. Since, for Paul, the Messiah had come, it followed that the validity of the law had now passed (Rom. 10:4). What separates Paul's conviction from rabbinic views is simply the premise "that the Messianic age had begun with the death and resurrection of Jesus" (173).

Having arrived at this conclusion, however, Paul was led to reflect further about the purpose and nature of the law; and here his thinking proved in many respects incompatible with Judaism. We may note, for example, his suggestion that the law, far from limiting sinfulness (it had proven unable to do so before the coming of Messiah), must have been intended to make "sinfulness evident" and to pile "up the measure of sins" (174). Paul even views the law as leading inevitably to death, contrary to the Jewish conviction that its observance brings life. But Paul's conclusions are determined throughout by a "retrospective way of thought" (175). Starting with his faith in Jesus Christ, the Messiah and Savior, he is forced to rethink the function of the law. The result, not surprisingly, is that the law is seen as a "custodian until Christ came" (Gal. 3:24).

Other Pauline arguments share points of contact with rabbinic thought, but are developed in un-Jewish ways. Like Paul (Gal. 3:10; 5:3), the rabbis were concerned by the fact that no one fulfills the whole law; yet the problem never became for them a reason to dismiss the law as the basis on which life may be conducted according to God's will. The rabbinic tradition that angels were present at Sinai when the law was given was recklessly transformed by Paul into a notion that the law was given by angels hostile to the Jewish people (Gal. 3:19). This suggestion in particular, made by Paul "in the heat of the contest" (183), would have monstrous consequences when taken up by Simon Magus, Cerinthus, and Marcion.

Paul's argument in Romans 7 has interesting rabbinic parallels. For Paul, the human heart is the scene of a constant struggle between the spirit and the flesh, the human will and human moral capacities. The struggle, however, is an uneven one; actual conduct is inevitably determined by "sin" residing in the "flesh." This picture of inner moral conflict is related to the rabbinic doctrine of the struggle between the evil and the good "impulses" within us. And though usually the two are believed to have equal strength, there are certainly some rabbis who think, like Paul, that the evil impulse *(yēṣer hāra')* dominates. And still "other voices are raised which go farther and understand the *yeser hara* as an independently effective cosmic force, not merely as an impulse to evil but as an evil impulse conceived on almost daemonological lines, almost as an alien god dwelling in the body of man" (185). Here it is clear that Schoeps finds rabbinic parallels even to the

"Pauline pessimism" which, for Montefiore, must have had a Hellenistic source. For Schoeps, "Paul's doctrine of sin was not unusual but indeed typical of his time" (187). What Paul does not reckon with, however, is the power of repentance, "which according to Jewish belief of all ages is able to break the mastery of sin" (188).

Even this fundamental omission, however, does not mark the most radical difference between Paul and the rabbis with regard to the law. The Septuagint (the Greek translation of the Old Testament), by rendering Hebrew *torah* as *nomos,* brought about a shift in emphasis: whereas the Hebrew term "is best explained as instruction embracing both law and doctrine," the Greek equivalent comes to imply simply "a moral way of life prescribed by God" (29). Paul, whose thinking was guided by the Septuagint, understood the "law" as a "sum of prescriptions" to be kept (188). Righteousness and life would be granted if it was fully obeyed, but condemnation and death would follow if it was not. Here the notion of Torah has been effectively reduced to the ethical law, a body of demands which, Paul believes, have not been met because of the sinfulness of humankind. Thus "righteousness" cannot be attained by the "works of the law," that is, by human attempts to meet God's demands. Only faith in Christ brings salvation.

But such a view represents a "fundamental misapprehension" of what Jews mean by the "law." "Paul did not perceive, and for various reasons was perhaps unable to perceive, that in the Biblical view the law is integral to the covenant" (213). As the seal of God's covenant with Israel, the law is understood to bind Israel closely with her God. Through the law God intends to make his people holy.

Apart from its relation with the covenant, the law simply cannot be understood. It is not a mere "sum of prescriptions" against which human deficiencies can be measured and condemned. It is a token of God's love for his people, presupposing his relationship with them established in the covenant by his election-grace and intended to provide them with a remedy for the evil impulse within them. When Jews show a willingness to obey the law, God quickly comes to lend his aid so that sins may be overcome. That all the law's demands should be perfectly met is neither expected nor even an issue. What is important is the *intention* to obey, "because that intention is man's affirmation of the covenant, which precedes the law" (196). Israel's relationship with God is thus determined fundamentally by a covenant of divine grace. Observance of the law is not the basis, but the affirmation of that relationship.

We may go further. If obedience to the law is valued primarily as an affirmation of God's covenant, then it is scarcely just to regard such "works of the law" as an attempt to gain righteousness by human effort and an *alternative* to faith in the pursuit of justification. After all, "faith" in the Hebrew sense "connotes trust in the sense of fidelity" (202). A contrast between "faith" and the "works of the law" is thus unthinkable, for fidelity to the covenant can only be expressed by the affirmation implied in obedience to its demands. Furthermore even the ceremonial demands of the law can only be understood in the context of the covenant, for circumcision, sabbath observance, and the like have value only as symbolic acts pointing to, and affirming the reality of, God's special relation with Israel. For Israel to accept the abrogation of the law would be tantamount to renouncing the covenant on which its very existence was based.

A quotation from Schoeps's final chapter provides an eloquent conclusion:

> It must ever remain thought-provoking that the Christian church has received a completely distorted view of the Jewish law at the hands of a Diaspora Jew who had become alienated from the faith-ideas of the fathers—a view which ignores that side of it connected with the *berith* [covenant] as a sanctifying ordinance and which has reduced it to a matter of ethical self-justification and ritual performance. And still more astounding is the fact that church theology throughout Christian history has imputed Paul's inacceptability to the Jews to Jewish insensitivity, and has never asked itself whether it might not be due to the fact that Paul could gain no audience with the Jews because from the start he misunderstood Jewish theology. (261-262)

iii. E. P. Sanders

LITERATURE: Moore, "Christian Writers"; Sanders, "The Covenant"; *Paul and Palestinian Judaism* (Page references in the discussion which follows are from this book; see Bibliography).

Sanders's *Paul and Palestinian Judaism* has had its critics, but neither timidity nor smallness of vision have figured among the charges. Behind the simple proposal "to compare Judaism, understood on its own terms, with Paul, understood on his own terms" (xi) lurks an undertaking perhaps rivaled, within the purview of New Testament scholarship, only by the still more perilous enterprise of comparing Jesus with

Judaism. For our purposes, we will postpone our main review of Sanders's Paul until a later chapter. Here we will focus on his modest proposal "to destroy the view of Rabbinic Judaism which is still prevalent in much, perhaps most, New Testament scholarship" (xii).

Palestinian Judaism is discussed under the headings "Tannaitic Literature," "The Dead Sea Scrolls," and "Apocrypha and Pseudepigrapha." The careful delineations betray the modern awareness of the diversity which prevailed in Palestinian Judaism at the turn of the era. Yet it is among Sanders's most important conclusions that a fundamental unity underlies nearly every witness we possess to the Judaism of the period. (In his article "The Covenant as a Soteriological Category and the Nature of Salvation in Palestinian and Hellenistic Judaism," that basic unity is extended to Hellenistic Judaism as well.) Sanders describes the unifying concept as "covenantal nomism": the notion that the Israelite's place in God's plan is determined by the covenant which God established with Israel, and that obedience to the law is Israel's proper *response* to God's initial act of grace. While a Jew's intention to obey the law is thought necessary if the relationship with God is to be *maintained*, it does not follow that salvation is "earned" or regarded as a reward for human achievements. Since Sanders finds "covenantal nomism" to be the consistent pattern of religion in Jewish writings "from around 200 b.c.e. to around 200 c.e." (1), he concludes that this must have been the Judaism known by the apostle Paul. We will here pass over his discussion of the Dead Sea Scrolls, the Apocrypha, and the Pseudepigrapha. That "covenantal nomism" underlies the earliest rabbinic writings (the "Tannaitic Literature") is shown by Sanders both negatively and positively.

Obviously Sanders's definition of Judaism is designed to refute its depiction as a religion of "works." Among the simpler aspects of his assignment is the task of documenting in the work of New Testament scholars the notion that salvation, in Judaism, is earned by accumulating good works. On the basis of an important study by G. F. Moore, Sanders notes that the description of Judaism in these terms entered Christian scholarship in the nineteenth century through the work of Ferdinand Weber. In Weber's Judaism, the benefits of God's covenant with Israel were wiped out already in the wilderness when Israel worshiped the golden calf (Exod. 32). Thereafter individual Israelites can only gain acceptance before God by compiling a list of fulfillments of the law and other good deeds which will outweigh the list of their transgressions. In subsequent literature, Weber's theory of

Israel's fall from the covenant was ignored. Otherwise his account of Jewish soteriology was largely taken over in the work of Bousset and Schürer, Billerbeck and Bultmann. Repeatedly we find the view that, in Judaism, works "earn" salvation, that God weighs fulfillments of the law against transgressions to determine who will be saved, and that the result of such a soteriology was a despairing uncertainty of salvation on the one hand, or a self-righteous boasting on the other. A better foil for the Lutheran doctrine of justification could scarcely be conceived; but theological convenience is a hazardous guide to historical reality.

In fact, in Sanders's view, only a massive misunderstanding of the nature and intent of rabbinic sources could yield such a description of Jewish soteriology. The evidence requires a different interpretation.

1. Much of rabbinic literature is "halakic" in nature; that is, it is concerned to spell out the precise application of the many provisions of divine law. Outsiders to the system, confronted and confounded by endless definitions and distinctions, are liable to conclude that rabbinic religion never rises above a peculiar brand of petty legalism. Yet behind the legal endeavor lies the conviction of the rabbis, too self-evident to require continual articulation, that obedience to the commands marks the privilege and obligation imposed on Israel by the covenant with her God. Naturally it was important to define carefully Israel's covenantal responsibilities, for "Israel's situation in the covenant required the law to be obeyed as fully and completely as possible" (81). This conviction, not a belief that salvation was earned by keeping the laws they defined, was the rabbis' motive in formulating halakah.

2. God's commitment to the covenant with Israel was believed to be unconditional: he would remain faithful to his promises even when Israel disobeyed his laws. Such disobedience would of course be punished, and the *individual* Israelite who repudiated the covenant would fall from the sphere of its blessings. But the rabbis never suggested that the covenant itself might be revoked. It remained the framework which fundamentally determined Israel's relations with her God.

3. To the question why God chose Israel and granted Israel his covenant, different answers were given in different contexts. Sometimes a picture was drawn in which the covenant was actually offered to all the nations but only accepted by Israel. In other texts, Israel was said to be chosen because of some merit of the patriarchs or of the wilderness generation. Still elsewhere the laws were said to be given with a view to the obedience which Israel would yield to them in the

future. A final explanation found in the texts is that God acted simply "for his name's sake." Thus while some explanations stress the gratuity of the election, others suggest that merit was a factor. What is important to remember is that none of these answers can be taken to represent the definitive view of a supposed "systematic" theology held by the rabbis. In each case, the homiletic need of the moment determined the emphasis. We may safely conclude only that the election of Israel and the concomitant imposing of the commandments were convictions universally held by the rabbis, and that, for them, divine grace and human merit were not perceived as mutually exclusive.

4. Firmly entrenched in the rabbinic conception of God is the justice of his judgments: he rewards obedience and punishes transgressions. And, naturally, for homiletic purposes, the reward and punishment are frequently stressed in the literature. Two qualifications, however, must be borne in mind. First, divine justice was meted out to Israel within the framework of the covenant. As God's people through the covenant, the people of Israel were judged by their conformity to the covenant's laws. Their obedience was thus never seen as the means by which they *became* God's people, nor did they "earn" their salvation. Second, we are not to imagine that "a man's payment" was believed to be "strictly in accordance with his deserts" (119), for many statements are made to the contrary effect. Indeed, a rabbi might choose to emphasize the importance of obedience by saying that the fulfillment of a single "light" commandment brings very great reward. And, in general, the view prevails, not that merits and demerits are subject to strict measurement and recompense, but that God's mercy prevails and will be granted to all Israelites whose basic intent is one of obedience.

> What counts is being in the covenant and intending to be obedient to the God who gave the covenant. Rejection of even one commandment with the intent to deny the God who gave it excludes one from the covenant, while acceptance of a fundamental commandment, such as the commandment not to commit idolatry, may show one's intent to be obedient. (135)

5. That rabbinic soteriology did not involve the strict weighing of fulfillments of the law against transgressions is proven by the quite different view which is "totally pervasive" (147) in rabbinic literature. It is stated most clearly and concisely in Mishnah Sanhedrin 10.1: "All Israelites have a share in the world to come" (cited, 147). The only ex-

ceptions to the rule are the "worst individual sinners" and the "most unregenerate generations" (149). Not perfect, or even fifty-one percent fulfillment of the law's commands, but membership in Israel, the covenant community of God, is the basis of the Jew's standing before God.

6. That this, and not the theory by which merits are measured, constituted rabbinic soteriology is confirmed by the frequent claims made in the literature about the efficacy of repentance and atonement. "The universally held view is this: God has appointed means of atonement for every transgression, except the intention to reject God and his covenant" (157). If repentance can bring forgiveness for any number of sins, then God does not determine human destiny by weighing merits against transgressions.

7. The "righteous" Jew in rabbinic writings is thus not one who earns divine approval by compiling an impressive list of good deeds, but simply "one who accepts the covenant and remains within it" (204). Here we may anticipate our later discussion and note that, for Sanders, Paul and Palestinian Judaism are in substantial *agreement* as to the relationship between grace and works. In Judaism, as for Paul, salvation is by divine grace, since Israel gained its status as God's people by election and the gift of the covenant. On the other hand, works are necessary, for Paul as for Judaism, if that status is to be maintained. To be sure, Paul criticizes Judaism by saying that righteousness is by faith, not works; but the formula actually "misstates the fundamental point of disagreement" (551). When Paul talks about gaining "righteousness," he refers to how one gains one's standing before God— and his contemporaries in Judaism would have agreed that this was by grace. When Palestinian Judaism talked about being "righteous" by obeying the law, it meant that such works are required for one to *maintain* such a standing—and Paul too, according to Sanders, required works for that purpose. Hence the essential agreement is concealed by the different senses given to "righteousness."

8. Thus Pauline theology is *not* distinct from rabbinic thinking in its insistence that "justification" is by divine grace, not human works. The fundamental point of Paul's opposition was simply his conviction that salvation is only to be found in Jesus Christ. The inevitable consequence was that Israel's election, covenant, and law could not bring salvation. Paul's exclusive soteriology, and not a rejection of "works," is what sets his Christian faith apart from Judaism.

*   *   *

We are left, it seems, with the following alternatives. Either the traditional (Lutheran) view is correct, Pauline Christianity is distinguished from rabbinic thought by its doctrine of justification by faith, not works, and scholars such as Montefiore, Schoeps, and Sanders have misinterpreted Judaism; or these latter writers are correct in their depictions of Judaism, the traditional view is correct in maintaining that Paul opposed it as a religion of works, and Paul himself is the one who (for whatever reason) misrepresented the faith of his fathers; or the traditional view is wrong on both counts, and Paul's opposition to Judaism did not lie in a rejection of "works."

We will return to the issue below. But first we must note another area in which modern scholars have argued that there is a Lutheran distortion of Pauline thought.

Chapter Four

Paul's Robust Conscience: Kümmel and Stendahl

According to Protestant hagiography, the insights of the apostle Paul, which were hidden from ages and from generations, were discovered by Augustine and Luther. Krister Stendahl proposes a different model. The "hidden" insights were not Paul's, but those of Augustine and Luther themselves. Readers of Paul in the first Christian centuries and in Eastern Christianity of all periods have read Paul very differently for the simple reason that Augustine and Luther imposed on the Pauline texts concerns of the modern West. In particular, Augustine and Luther brought keenly sensitive, introspective consciences to their reading of the apostle, whereas Paul's own conscience was robust and untroubled. Nowhere is the resultant distortion greater than in Luther's understanding of the primary function of the law.

The argument is fascinating and instructive. Before we review it, however, we need to look at what Stendahl labels the "epoch-making study" of Kümmel on which it rests. No chapter in the Pauline corpus has aroused more controversy than Romans 7, and no question in that difficult chapter is more disputed than the identity of the "I" who speaks there. The chapter appears to reveal Paul's own inner struggles and his despair of keeping the law. Kümmel denies that this is the case. Perhaps the best indication of the impact of his study is the fact that Hübner, Sanders, and Räisänen, each of whom has written a major monograph on Paul and the law, do not feel the need to address this particular problem in depth. All refer their readers to Kümmel's work, and argue on the basis of the assumption that his results are fundamentally correct. This means, of course, that the current debate about the law in Paul's writings can scarcely be understood without some knowledge of Kümmel's *Römer 7.*

i. W. G. Kümmel

LITERATURE: Kümmel, *Römer 7 und die Bekehrung des Paulus* (Leipzig: J. G. Hinrichs, 1929), reprinted in *Römer 7 und das Bild des Menschen im Neuen Testament* (see Bibliography).

The interpretation of Romans 7 advocated in Kümmel's study was not in fact new. We have already seen a similar view in Wrede's *Paul,* and Kümmel amply demonstrates that the "rhetorical" understanding of the chapter which he espouses was widely held already in the patristic period and was common among scholars of the nineteenth and early twentieth centuries (87-88). Still it is his own statement of the case which has come to be regarded as all but definitive. It repays careful study. What follows is a restatement of Kümmel's arguments.

As noted above, the critical question for the interpretation of Romans 7 is the identity of the "I" who speaks in verses 7-25. Who is it who "was once alive apart from the law," but died "when the commandment came" (v. 9)? Who is it who cannot carry out his own good intentions, but continually finds himself doing the very evil he hates (vv. 15, 19)? Is Paul simply relating his personal experience? Or is he perhaps citing his own experience because it is typical of humanity as a whole, or of Jews outside of Christ, or, indeed, of Christians? Or is the "I" used rhetorically to portray the lot of humankind in general without necessarily reflecting the moral struggles in Paul's own life? The question is crucial; but it is best approached after the context and general trend of Paul's argument in Romans 7 have been established.

The Argument in Context

In the early chapters of Romans, Paul has made frequent side remarks about the Mosaic law without pausing to support them or even, in some cases, to make them comprehensible to readers not familiar with his thought (3:20; 4:15; 5:13, 20). Particularly noteworthy in this regard is Romans 6:14: "For sin will have no dominion over you, since you are not under law but under grace." The first part of the verse follows from the immediate context: Christians are not to "continue in sin" since, by dying with Christ in their baptism, they "died to sin," leaving the "sphere" of sin's influence. And, just as Christ was raised from the dead, so Christians are now to live a new life "to God in Christ Jesus" (6:1-13). The claim that Christians are not "under law," however, has not been demonstrated, nor how sin and the law are so closely connected that to be "under sin" is at the same time to be "under law." Substantiation for these claims is first offered in chapter 7.

The opening verses of Romans 7 explain the statement in 6:14 that Christians are not "under law." Only living people are subject to law—and Christians have died. In sharing Christ's death (cf. 6:2-11), they "died to the law" and may now "bear fruit for God" (7:4). This suggests, of course, that it was impossible to bear such "fruit" as long as they were "under" the law; and, indeed, a close connection between sin and the law was implied in 6:14. These latter implications are developed in 7:5-6. What the law arouses are "sinful passions," and these lead to death; release from the law, by way of contrast, is followed by new and effective service of God. The objections raised to Paul's position in 6:1 and 15 have now been answered: No, Christians are not to continue in sin, for a fundamental change in their condition has taken place. They have been set free from sin, and are to serve God in the Spirit (36-42).

But this answer raises new questions in turn. How can the law of God be said to arouse "sinful passions" (7:5)? Is this not tantamount to linking the divine law with sin? The suggestion is abhorrent, but to refute it is no easy task. In the remainder of chapter 7 Paul must demonstrate both the law's holiness *and* its close relationship with sin.

We may begin with verses 7-13. Though the law is "by no means" sin, the fact remains nonetheless (*alla,* v. 7) that it is linked with sin; for apart from the law "I" would have had no personal experience ("knowledge") of sin. Consciousness of sin is only possible where law exists to be transgressed. Indeed, without law, sin is "not counted" (5:13), it does not entail guilt, it has no effect on people. In the language of 7:8-9, "apart from the law sin lies dead" while "I" was truly "alive." The latter reference must mean something other than mere physical life, since the "life" here spoken of ended with the coming of the commandment (v. 9), though physical life remained (cf. vv. 14-25). Paul can only mean that true "life," in the full religious sense, was possible where there was no law and sin was inoperative. But all changed "when the commandment came." Sin then became active ("revived"). It incited "me" to disobedience, which was now conscious sin, entailed guilt, and brought "me" to ruin.

It is sin, not the law, which bears responsibility for what happened. The law remains "holy," its commandment "holy and just and good" (7:12). In that sense the law's holiness has been maintained. At the same time, it is clear that the law has come to be linked to sin, and that God has in fact used the law "in order that sin might be shown to be sin" (v. 13).

The commandment which Paul cites in this context is "You shall not covet" (7:7); perversely, it was when the "I" was confronted by this command that covetousness was roused and conscious sin followed. The prohibition is taken from the Decalogue (Exod. 20:17). This is confirmed by Paul's quotation of the same verse in the same abbreviated form in Rom. 13:9, where there is no doubt that the Decalogue is intended. Such an understanding is clearly to be preferred to that which interprets the "commandment" in Rom. 7:7-13 as an allusion to the prohibition of eating from the "tree of the knowledge of good and evil" (Gen. 2:17). The latter makes no reference to coveting, whereas this is precisely the prohibition spoken of in Rom. 7:7. Moreover, the whole argument in Rom. 7:7-13 is a defense of the Mosaic law. A part of the Decalogue could well stand for the Mosaic law as a whole and would make understandable Paul's use in this chapter of "commandment" and "law" interchangeably, which would not be appropriate if the "commandment" were the isolated prohibition given to Adam in Gen. 2:17 (42-57; cf. 85-87).

We have not yet considered the question of the identity of the subject ("I") in Rom. 7:7-13. Nonetheless, even a preliminary look at the passage in its context allows us to draw the following conclusions.

1. The passage is designed to show how the law remains holy while being related to sin. Paul accomplishes his purpose by showing the effect of the law on a subject ("I"): though its command was holy, it was misused by sin and resulted in the subject's ruin. The law is not responsible, though it proves to be the means by which the horror of sin is revealed.

2. Hence, even if what is said in 7:7-13 reflects Paul's own experience, the main point of the passage *in its context* is the defense of the law, not personal confession. Further, if personal experience is being related, that experience must at least be typical if others are to see it as establishing a valid basis for a general defense of the law.

3. Without yet attempting to identify the subject, we have seen that the following conditions must be met by any identification: the "I" knew true "life" witho... ...rsonal experience of sin at a time when

the Mosaic law either did not exist or had no bearing on him. When, however, the Mosaic law was introduced to the "I," sin and death were the result.

Paul's defense of the law continues in verses 14-25. He has described an event in which the law of God was used to bring death. He now sets out to explain how a good gift from God ("that which is good," v. 13) could lead to such a result. He does so by establishing the nature both of the law and of the one whom the law encounters. The defense of the law thus remains the primary concern (note especially vv. 16, 22), though it must be conceded that the discord within the subject who encounters the law takes on an interest of its own as the argument develops (note, e.g., v. 18).

Paul explains that the curious process described in the preceding verses is possible because of the contrasting natures of the law and humankind. While the law is "spiritual" (i.e., it comes from God, v. 14), the "I" whom it encounters is "carnal (*sarkinos,* "of the flesh"), sold under sin." "Flesh" *(sarx)* is frequently used in Paul's writings of all that resists what is Spirit (i.e., God and his activity), that is, of what is characteristic of a humanity which has turned from God (15-25). It follows, then, that a "fleshly" "I" will find it impossible to obey a "spiritual" law; what the "I" does is in fact evil (vv. 14-15). That the law is not responsible for this evil is clear from the admission that "the law is good" (v. 16). It is rather the responsibility of "sin which dwells within me" that there is a discrepancy between "the good I want" and "the evil I do" (vv. 17, 19). In the following verses, what is "within me" that vainly longs for the good is variously described as the "I" that wills, "my inmost self" (v. 22), and "my mind" (vv. 23, 25). Similarly, the "law of my mind" (v. 23) is clearly the same as the "law of God" (v. 22). Ranged on the opposite side are the "I" which is said to act, the "flesh" which contains no good (vv. 18, 25), and the "sin" which dwells in the "flesh" and determines actions (vv. 17-20). This "sin" is represented in verse 23 as "another law . . . in my members . . . at war with the law of my mind." The resulting discord is summed up in the "law" (or "rule") of verse 21: "When I want to do right, evil lies close at hand."

And so the total "I," made up both of impotent willing and sin-driven action, has been made a "captive" of sin (v. 23; cf. v. 14). It cries out for a deliverer from "the body of this death" (so the phrase should be rendered, v. 24), that is, from the whole desperate situation described in these verses. This is not, of course, a desire for physical death; release from "the body of this death" no more implies physical death than does the destruction of the "sinful body" in 6:6. The plea is not for deliverance from the physical body as such, but from the tyranny of sin over the body. Indeed, with such a deliverance the subject is already familiar, for the portrayal of the apparently hopeless dilemma is interrupted by a cry of thanks in verse 25, anticipating the victory described in 8:1-4: "Thanks be to God through Jesus Christ our Lord!" (57-68).

It is essential to see the claims of Rom. 8:1-4 in their context, where they provide the answer to the cry of 7:24: "Who will deliver me from the body of this death? . . . The law of the Spirit of life in Christ Jesus has set [you] free from the law of sin and death." (Kümmel defends the reading "you" found in the oldest manuscripts.) Curiously, however, the liberation spoken of in 8:1-2 is said to *follow* from what precedes ("There is *therefore* now no condemnation . . ."). It can hardly follow from 7:25b, which has summed up the dilemma of 7:14-24 without establishing the solution. And though the cry of 7:25a may anticipate the deliverance spoken of in 8:1-2, it is too brief, and its terms are too general, to provide a logical basis from which 8:1-2 might follow. The "therefore" of 8:1 must hark back to the whole train of thought begun in 6:1 and, in particular, to the Christian's deliverance from sin and the law spoken of in 6:14 and 7:6. The emphatic "now" of 8:1 (as in 3:21) underscores the fact that the deliverance is a feature of the new age in salvation history. Those who are "in Christ Jesus" have been delivered from the bondage to sin described in 7:14-25. They have been set free "from the law of sin and death."

How has the deliverance been made possible? Paul explains in 8:3-4. Note again that the reference in verse 3 to "what the law, weakened by the flesh, could not do" echoes the situation of impotence described in 7:14-25, where the "I" which is in the "flesh" encounters the law but cannot carry it out. But God has done what the law could not do. He has condemned "sin in the flesh" by sending his Son in that very "flesh of sin" which has been described in chapter 7 (cf. 7:5, 17-20). Since God's Son has vanquished sin, Christians have been set free from its power and condemnation. They are now able to fulfill God's demands as they walk "not according to the flesh but according to the Spirit" (8:4; 68-73).

Again, without resolving the question of the subject's identity in 7:14-25, we may draw the following conclusions.

1. The logic of the passage requires that the subject ("I") of 7:7-13 be maintained in verses 14-25: the latter passage, by portraying the

nature of the "I," shows how the law and sin can have had the curious effects on "me" described in 7:7-13.

2. The main purpose of 7:14-25 remains the defense of the law. Even if personal experience is being related, what is said must be capable of general application if it is to have any force in a general defense of the law.

3. We may reach the same conclusion by another route. The readers of chapter 8 are themselves said to have experienced the deliverance spoken of in 8:2. If the deliverance is thus a general one, this presupposes that the dilemma portrayed in 7:14-25 as preceding the deliverance must also be capable of general application.

4. It is clear from 7:25a and 8:1-4 that the subject of 7:14-25 knows not only the dilemma of discord within, but victory through Jesus Christ.

5. Chapter 8 returns to the perspective of chapter 6. In both chapters deliverance from the power of sin and death is described and made the basis for an appeal to let that victory have consequences in Christian living. Rom. 7:7-25 is crucial to Paul's argument, explaining as it does the nature of the relationship between sin, the law, and the flesh which is otherwise presupposed in 6:14; 7:4-6; and 8:3. Nonetheless, in the context between Romans 6 and 8, it is a parenthesis; and it must at least be conceded that the lot of hopeless bondage to sin described in 7:14-15 is far different from the description in chapters 6 and 8 of the practical lives of Christians, over whom "sin will have no dominion," since they are "not under law but under grace" (6:14; cf. 6:2-4, 6, 17-18, 22; 8:4, 13).

The Subject of Romans 7:7-25

We begin with Romans 7:7-13. Since the passage is in the first person singular, it is natural to interpret it of Paul's own experience. But such an explanation runs into difficulties (74-84).

1. Certainly Paul could never have written these verses of anything in his *Christian* experience. He did not *first* encounter the commandment against covetousness as a Christian (cf. "the commandment came," v. 9). Above all, it was not part of his Christian experience that sin first then became active through the commandment, *and he died!*

2. But it is also difficult to see how what is said in these verses can be true of Paul's life before his conversion. To be sure, many interpreters have understood the passage to refer to the transition from

Paul's childhood innocence to his consciousness of the law's demands, which was followed by lust, leading ultimately to spiritual death. But such an interpretation does not fit Paul's language.

a. How could Paul have said that he was truly "*alive* apart from the law" if he meant the "relative innocence" of his childhood? "Alive" is here used in its full religious sense, as the contrast with (spiritual) death in verse 9 shows.

b. How could a Jew ever say that he once lived "apart from the law"? Paul would have learned the commandments from his earliest years. Nor can he be thinking of a period before his *bar mitzvah* when he was not yet responsible for obeying the commands: partly because the institution of the *bar mitzvah* is much later than the time of Paul, partly because even before the age of full responsibility Jewish minors are responsible for obeying some of the commands.

c. Paul speaks of a time "apart from the law," then a time "when the commandment came" (7:9). The latter is surely a strange way of saying "when I became conscious of the commandment."

3. The passage is Paul's defense of the law; to relate a purely personal experience would not have served his purpose. And if we argue that Paul is citing his own experience as typical of every Jew, the problems remain: how could Paul write that he (or any Jew) once "lived" in a state "apart from the law," and that then "the commandment came"?

If, then, Paul is not speaking of his own experience, can he be speaking of that of Adam, understanding Adam as a representative of all humanity? After all, Adam was without sin before he encountered a divine commandment. And certainly the narrative of the "fall" in Genesis 3 is a story of "deception" (Gen. 3:13; cf. Rom. 7:11) followed by "death." The difficulty here, as we have already seen, is that the commandment which Paul quotes ("You shall not covet," 7:7; cf. 13:9) comes from the Decalogue given to Moses on Mount Sinai; it is thus not a summary of the prohibition spoken to Adam in Genesis 2:17. In fact, "commandment" is used throughout the passage interchangeably with "the (Mosaic) law," and the whole illustration is part of a defense of the Mosaic law. That the "I" who encountered the Mosaic law could be Adam is thus out of the question. The fact that the subject is said to be "deceived" (Rom. 7:11) is natural enough in the context. It need hardly be an allusion to Genesis 3:13.

The only alternative to these interpretations would seem to be the "rhetorical" understanding of the "I": the first person is used, not of

Paul personally, but rhetorically, as a way of depicting what happens to men and women under the law (85-89). A number of passages in the Pauline epistles illustrate such a usage (121-123). When Paul writes, for example, in 1 Corinthians 13: "If I speak in the tongues of men and of angels, but have not love, I am a noisy gong or a clanging cymbal" (13:1; see also vv. 2-3), he is not making a statement of personal application only; the statement is general, and its meaning would not change if second person pronouns were substituted for the first. Similarly, Paul writes in the first person, "When I was a child, I spoke like a child . . . ; when I became a man, I gave up childish ways" (1 Cor. 13:11; see also v. 12); but his words are meant to express the common experience of humanity. Other examples may be given as well (Rom. 3:5, 7; 1 Cor. 6:12, 15; 10:29-30; 11:31-32; 14:11, 14-15; Gal. 2:18). Note especially that in Romans 3:7, a rhetorical question is put in the first person from which Paul dissociates himself in verse 8; and in 1 Corinthians 11:32, Paul makes a general statement in the first person, though he would not have thought of himself as one to whom it applied (he was not among those who came unprepared to "the Lord's supper"!). Hence the fact that Paul speaks in the first person in Romans 7:7-13 by no means proves that he is relating personal experience.

But if Paul is using the first person rhetorically to picture the lot of humanity under law, then it is clear that the portrayal has a place in a general defense of the law. Similarly, there is force in the words, "I was once *alive apart from the law,* but *when* the commandment came . . . I died" (Rom. 7:9). Not that Paul is describing a specific incident; he is portraying, theoretically and pictorially, the fact that the law and sin together bring death to humankind. Apart from the law, sin would have no effective power, and people could be said to "live." When they encounter the commandments of God, however, sin becomes operative and the result is "death."

The question that remains, of course, is whether such an understanding of the "I" can be maintained in verses 14-25 as well; for, as we have seen, the logic of the passage requires that the same subject be found throughout 7:7-25.

This latter consideration in itself would seem to rule out the possibility that Paul is speaking of his own experience in 7:14-25, for we have already noted what difficulties such an interpretation of 7:7-13 encounters. Nonetheless, we will first consider whether Paul could have written 7:14-25 of his *Christian* experience (97-104). The answer must be an emphatic, No!

1. Paul has just declared that Christians have been set free from the law, indeed, that they have "died to the law," in 7:1-6; as a result, they are not to be ruled by sin but are to serve God. But the law to which Christians are said to have died in 7:6 is precisely what encounters the subject of 7:7-25, and it brings the subject into that same hopeless bondage to sin from which (as Paul has just argued) Christians have been delivered.

2. According to 7:25a; 8:1-4, all who are "in Christ Jesus" have been set free from the dilemma of 7:14-24, 25b (specifically, from the "law of sin and death") in order that they may "walk not according to the flesh but according to the Spirit." How, then, could Paul describe himself as a Christian as being merely fleshly *(sarkinos),* "sold under sin" (7:14), and sin's "captive" (7:23)? How could Paul say that, as a Christian, he *could* only do what is evil (7:18), when he will claim in 8:4 that God's Son was sent "in order that the just requirement of the law might be fulfilled in us"? And how could Paul the Christian cry out in despair, wondering *who* would deliver him from his bondage to sin and death (7:24)?

3. It is clear from Paul's letters that he reckons with the possibility of sin in his own life (1 Cor. 4:4; 9:26-27; Rom. 14:10; 2 Cor. 5:10), though he seems not to be aware of specific sins (1 Cor. 4:4), claims that he does not live according to the flesh (2 Cor. 10:3; 13:6), and feels fit to serve as an example for others (1 Cor. 4:16; 11:1; Phil. 3:17; 4:9). All of this excludes the possibility that Romans 7:14-25 is a description of Paul's present experience. Who could set himself up as an example for others to follow, or claim, "I am not aware of anything against myself," and cry out at the same time for deliverance from bondage to sin? This is not to say that Paul never experienced ethical struggles within himself. But ethical struggles are not the same thing as being hopelessly overpowered and enslaved by sin, and it is the latter of which Romans 7:14-25 speaks.

4. Nor will it do to say that Romans 7:14-25 is true of Paul's experience as a Christian *apart from the help of the Spirit,* or *when left to himself.* Romans 7:25 in particular has led to such an interpretation, for *autos ego* is taken to mean "I on my own" (cf. RSV "I of myself"). But that Paul could conceive of Christian experience apart from Christ, or apart from the Spirit, is incredible. For Paul, either a person has the Spirit or he does not; and the Christian does, else he is not a Christian (Rom. 8:9). Besides, *autos ego* can scarcely be translated "I on my own." The words mean "I myself" (and no other); that is, the very "I"

who has been speaking throughout the passage here sums up his experience.

5. Finally, it cannot be said that the vividness of the portrayal means that Paul must be describing his present experience. Even the dramatic question of 7:24 belongs at best to Paul's past, since what follows shows that Paul's present experience is one of deliverance, not impotence and discord.

But if the passage cannot refer to Paul's experience as a Christian, neither can the "I" be understood rhetorically of the ethical condition of Christians in general (104-109). The first, second, and fourth arguments just given exclude this possibility. Here we may add the following considerations.

1. Paul is fully aware that Christians are not sinless, that they are in need of constant admonition. But all the ethical imperatives which he writes presuppose the possibility of obedience. The norm for the Christian is to live "according to the Spirit"—the Spirit which every believer possesses (Rom. 8:9) and which makes it possible to "put to death the deeds of the body" (8:13). But the subject of Romans 7:14-25 knows no such possibility. He is the slave of sin, and does not know who can deliver him. He is of the flesh (7:14), and nowhere is it suggested that he possesses the Spirit with which he might oppose the flesh.

2. Galatians 5:17 is often cited as a parallel description of the ethical struggles of the Christian; but it is no parallel. The whole passage in Galatians presupposes that the Christian need not give in to the flesh, that victory is possible for those who "walk in the Spirit." The opposite is true of the subject of Romans 7:14-25, who finds himself the impotent slave of the flesh. The explanation of this is simple. The Christian of Galatians 5 has the Spirit; the subject of Romans 7 does not. The point of Galatians 5:17 is not (as is supposed) that Christians are the helpless battleground of opposing forces, for verses 16 and 18 presuppose that the Spirit will enable them to triumph over the flesh. The point of the verse is simply that, since the Spirit and the flesh are opposing forces, Christians may not do as they please, but must obey the one or the other. Precisely this choice is not open to the subject of Romans 7:14-25.

3. Those who are anxious to preserve Romans 7:14-25 as a witness to Christian experience emphasize the inner struggle there depicted as an essential part of Christian living. But Romans 7:14-25 speaks not merely of a struggle, but of utter helplessness, slavery to

sin, and despair of deliverance. To downplay or ignore these features while emphasizing the struggle is to misrepresent the text.

4. Similarly, to object that Christians must recognize their own experience in the description of 7:14-25 is to distort the exegetical task. Exegetes may not disregard the context of a passage while interpreting it in the light of their experience. Experience must be exluded while the exegete listens to what the text is saying. Only so is the authority of the text preserved. If, after all, there is a question which needs to be asked, it is rather this: Why is it that our Christianity departs so widely from Paul's that we recognize ourselves in his description of non-Christians?

It is thus incredible that Paul could be depicting Christian experience in the terms of Romans 7:14-25. Is he, then, rhetorically describing in the present his personal experience of moral impotence before his conversion? (109-117).

1. The possibility would seem to be excluded from the start, since the "I" of Romans 7:7-13 did not refer to Paul, and the logic of the passage requires that the same subject be maintained throughout.

2. Romans 8:2 is intended to describe the deliverance effected by the "law of the Spirit of life" from the dilemma of 7:14-25. But the original reading of 8:2 is that this "law . . . has set *you* free from the law of sin and death." Since the deliverance is not stated of Paul himself, it is not likely that the dilemma was merely his own.

3. Above all, we have Paul's own testimony in Galatians 1:13-14; Philippians 3:4-6 to the nature of his pre-conversion piety; and it tells not of moral impotence, but of a "blameless" life according to the law. Paul clearly believed he had lived up to the Pharisaic ideal. And that ideal was one of joy in the law of God, not despair at the hopeless task of fulfilling it. Philippians 3:6 and Romans 7:14-25 are simply irreconcilable—*if* the latter is interpreted of Paul's pre-conversion experience.

This leaves us, again, with the rhetorical understanding of the "I" as depicting the condition of humanity in general under the law (117-126). Paul is using the first person pronouns, as he does elsewhere, to depict the lot of humankind. The perspective from which the portrayal is drawn is that of Paul the Christian: it was first "in Christ" that Paul became convinced of the impotence of moral strivings outside of Christ; and clearly the cry for deliverance in 7:24 is placed on the lips of the sinner by one who has experienced redemption. The purpose of the passage, as our study of the context has made clear, is to show the relationship between sin and the law, and the effects that sin and law have on those "in the flesh." That the tense shifts from the past tense in Romans 7:7-13 to the present in verses 14-25 is easily explained. Paul first describes in the past tense the "event" in which sin used the law to bring death. But when he then comes to describe the nature of the law, the nature of humanity, and the state of affairs which prevails for men and women under the law, the present tense comes naturally. The passage as a whole demonstrates the utter moral impotence of humanity under the law, a gloomy contrast to the glorious picture of redemption in Romans 6 and 8.

Finally, we must note an objection which is frequently raised to such an interpretation (134-138). How can Paul ascribe to non-Christians an agreement with, and even delight in, the law of God (7:16, 22)? While it is true that such statements go beyond what Paul says elsewhere of humanity outside of Christ, in the context of Paul's argument here they are understandable. First, Paul's primary purpose in the passage is not to portray the human condition, but to defend the law; and it is clear that the statements of 7:16, 22 are meant to underline that the law itself is good and bears no responsibility for the fact that people do not obey it. Second, the lot of humanity under the law is here seen from the perspective, not of the non-Christian, but of the Christian. It is thus possible that Christian experience of the Spirit's resistance to the flesh has colored Paul's picture of the struggle between the "mind" and the flesh. But, most importantly, it must be noted that the agreement between the "mind" and the law of God in this passage merely serves to emphasize the hopelessness of the human situation. Certainly there is discord within the subject of the passage. But it is not true that Paul is here depicting the co-existence in the Christian of a sinful flesh and a renewed "mind." Such an understanding would require that the "I" who is spoken of as "fleshly" and "sold under sin" in verse 14 merely referred to one *part* of the Christian while another part represented the believer's new life in Christ apart from sin. But the "I" of verse 14 must be the whole person; for verse 15 shows that this "I" includes *both* the willing of the good and the doing of the evil. Again, in verse 23 it is the whole person who has been made sin's "captive"; and it is the whole "wretched man" who cries out for deliverance from the tyranny of sin and death in verse 24. In the light of Romans 8:2, this can only be a picture of the non-Christian.

The Conversion of Paul

Here we may be brief. If the interpretation advocated for Romans 7 is adopted, then the chapter offers no basis for speculation about Paul's psychological condition before his conversion. We cannot conclude from Romans 7 that Paul the Pharisee despaired of ever fulfilling the law; in fact, the evidence of Galatians 1 and Philippians 3 indicates the contrary. Consistent with Galatians and Philippians is the evidence of Acts, for there is no suggestion in Acts of psychological preparation preceding Paul's conversion. That he was vainly "[kicking] against the goads" (Acts 26:14) can hardly refer to a struggle on his part to repress an inner attraction to Christianity! It is simply a proverbial expression for senseless opposition. In this case, as the context makes perfectly clear, the reference is to Paul's persecution of Christians. Such opposition is useless, for Christ will direct Paul, as an oxdriver his ox, where he pleases. That Acts wants to portray a Paul struggling against the attraction of Christianity is incredible in the light of Acts 9:1-2; 22:4-5; and especially 26:9-12. It was only the appearance of Jesus to Paul near Damascus that convinced him that the Christians who proclaimed Jesus' resurrection were right, and turned the enemy of Christ into his missionary and apostle (139-160).

Such is Kümmel's argument. If true, it would mean that Romans 7 should not be read as Pauline autobiography, that it provides no evidence of inner turmoil or pangs of conscience felt by Paul. It is this conclusion that led Stendahl to distinguish sharply between what we know of the apostle's experience and that of Luther.

ii. Krister Stendahl

LITERATURE: Stendahl, *Paul among Jews and Gentiles* (see Bibliography).

We may begin our summary of Stendahl's argument where it most clearly overlaps with that of Kümmel.

The Conscience of Paul

In Stendahl's view, traditional pictures of Paul's inner struggle with sin are based on the misleading analogy of Luther and on faulty interpretations of Pauline texts. A fresh examination of Paul's writings shows that his conscience was remarkably "robust" both before and after his Damascus encounter with the risen Christ.

Our best evidence for Paul's piety before his Christian calling is found in Philippians 3. Nothing in the passage suggests that he had found it difficult to keep God's law—his performance, he says, was "blameless" (v. 6). Clearly he suffered no pangs of conscience on that score! To be sure, his values shifted when he met Christ, but it was "his glorious achievements as a righteous Jew" (80), not painful shortcomings and a plagued conscience, which he left behind. What once occasioned pride seemed worthless when compared with the treasure of knowing Christ. But the insight was a new one. It reflects no previous dissatisfaction.

Nor does the evidence suggest to Stendahl that Paul's Christian conscience was burdened by besetting sins. While Paul harbored no illusions that believers were without sin, he never intimated that his own conscience was troubled by personal wrongdoing. The confident assertion of Acts 23:1 ("Brethren, I have lived before God in all good conscience up to this day") has a number of parallels in the epistles. According to 2 Cor. 1:12, Paul's conscience agreed with the assessment that his conduct was marked by "holiness and godly sincerity." Paul's hope, according to 2 Cor. 5:11, was that his conduct would meet with the Corinthians' approval just as it met with God's. Most telling is Paul's frank confession in 1 Cor. 4:4 that he was "not aware of anything against" himself. Though Paul was not averse to acknowledging "weakness," what he meant by the term was physical handicaps (2 Cor. 12:7; Gal. 4:13) and sufferings (2 Cor. 12:10), not sin. Thus it would be completely incompatible with the evidence elsewhere if we were to read Romans 7 as a confession of Paul's inability to cope with sin. And, in fact, Kümmel has shown that Romans 7 must not be understood as autobiography. It is a defense of the law.

The Concerns of Paul

Interpretation of Paul has gone astray because we have lost sight of his central concern: his role among Jews and Gentiles and relations between Jewish and Gentile believers. On what terms were Gentile converts to be admitted to the Messianic community? How were they to be made heirs to the promises God gave to Israel? These were issues that engaged the apostle to the Gentiles. He wrestled with the problem of Israel's law, not because his conscience was tormented by a failure to keep its commands, but because it appeared to bar the access of Gentiles to the people of God. His solution, and the central conviction of his ministry, was the doctrine of justification by faith *apart from the works of the law;* that is, that Gentiles would "become part of the people of God without having to pass through the law." This was "Paul's secret revelation and knowledge" (9).

The Distortion of Paul

But the problem which so occupied Paul's thinking was no longer an issue after the end of the first century. Christianity had become largely a Gentile faith. If the specifically Pauline teaching on faith and the law finds few echoes in Christian writings before Augustine, the reason may well be that it had lost its immediate relevance. "The early church seems to have felt that Paul spoke about what he actually spoke about, i.e. the relationship between Jews and Gentiles—and that was no problem during those centuries" (16). Paul's writings only took on new importance when they were used by Augustine to address a problem which Paul himself never faced: the "Western development" and the "Western plague" of the "introspective conscience" (17).

Augustine himself may well have been among the first to give expression to the dilemma. In a sense he may be called "the first modern man" since "his *Confessions* is the first great document in the history of the introspective conscience." Paul's treatment of the Gentile question was now "applied in a consistent and grand style to a more general and timeless human problem" (85): How is a conscience tormented by its sins ever to be set free? Can we ever find assurance of salvation? The introspection which could lead to such despair became more and more refined in late medieval piety. The rigors of penance, the self-examination characteristic of monastic life, the soul-searching which followed in the dreaded path of the Black Death—all these played a role. Luther, "a truly Augustinian monk" (83), was but one of many who practiced introspection with the utmost intensity.

For Luther and subsequent Protestant tradition, Paul's doctrine of justification by faith provided solace from the tormenting question, "How can I find a gracious God?" This was not, however, the issue which the doctrine was designed to meet, and its reapplication led to distortions of Paul's meaning.

1. In his epistle to the Galatians, Paul was concerned to show that "Gentiles must not, and should not come to Christ *via* the Law"

(87). The law referred to was, of course, that of Moses, given to the Jews 430 years after God's promise was made to Abraham (Gal. 3:17). Paul insists that the law cannot save, and warns the Galatians in the strongest possible terms against complying with its requirement of circumcision (5:3). As part of his argument, he stresses the limitations of the law's validity and function. It was only in force until Messiah came (3:19), and it created the possibility of "faith" in him (v. 23). The role of the law until that time was that of "Custodian for the Jews," a kind of "waiting room with strong locks" (86). In its context, then, Paul's claim that "the law was our custodian until Christ came" (v. 24) is designed to show why Gentiles need not submit to its rule: the Mosaic law was intended only for Jews (*"our* custodian"), and served its purpose only "until Christ came."

But the context of Paul's argument—the relation between Jews and Gentiles—was later lost to view, the problem of the introspective conscience was forced upon the text, and the point of Paul's words was reversed. "Law" came to be used in a general way for the divinely imposed imperative. And whereas Paul's words were designed to *exclude* the (Mosaic) law as a path to salvation, they were read to mean that the law (now in the sense of a confrontation with God's moral demands) was a *necessary precondition* for faith: it was now our "schoolmaster (or tutor) to bring us unto Christ" (KJV; ASV). Here the (redefined) law is understood as given "to make man see his desperate need for a Savior" (87). True faith is thought to be impossible unless human self-righteousness has been crushed by the law. Thus what Paul depicted as a once-for-all transition from the age of the law to that of Christ has become a necessary process in the life of each believer. "The only door into the church" becomes "that of evermore introspective awareness of sin and guilt" (96)—in spite of the fact that Paul, "a rather good Christian" (96) himself, showed little such awareness!

2. A similar transformation took place with regard to the opening chapters of Romans. Paul's concern was to place Jew and Gentile on the same footing before God. Both are equally culpable; the path to justification by faith lies equally open to both; thus Abraham "is the father of us all" (Rom. 4:16). When the first-century context was forgotten, however, Romans came to be read as "a theological tractate on the nature of faith" (5), prescribing a path through awareness of sin to faith in Jesus Christ, and thus providing a solution to the human predicament. In the same way, at a time when the status of the Mosaic law was no longer the issue as it was for Paul, his argument in defense

of the law in Romans 7 became distorted and the chapter was read on the one hand as a statement of human nature and the power of sin, and, on the other, as a testimony that Paul himself had been "shattered" by the law before coming to faith!

3. Finally, the current emphasis on "forgiveness" is but another indication of the shift brought about by the introspective conscience. Terms related to forgiveness are "spectacularly" absent from the Pauline writings (23). Today they serve to define the sum and substance of what Jesus Christ is thought to provide. The reason is no doubt that "forgiveness" suits our psychological bent and the quest of the West for relief from sin and guilt. Our concern is more centered "in ourselves than in God or in the fate of his creation" (24).

For Stendahl, then, the "use" of the law as "God's mighty hammer" bringing complacent sinners to despair has little support in Paul. The roots of the notion are rather in problems peculiar to the modern West. Hence the function and, indeed, the definition of the law need reexamination. Does the same apply to Luther's explanations of why "works" cannot justify?

Chapter Five

The "Righteousness of the Law": Bultmann, Wilckens, and Sanders

Paul's conviction *that* no one can be justified by means of the law is expressed in the epistles too frequently and too explicitly to leave any scope for argument. On the other hand, it is not so readily apparent *why* Paul finds the "righteousness of the law" inadequate, and scholars have made the most of the ambiguity. As we have seen, Luther was ready with a barrage of explanations, ranging from the belief that our best efforts are offset by transgressions to the view that our best efforts, apart from faith, are themselves misdirected, presumptuous, and even blasphemous. The range of explanations represented in contemporary scholarship is equally diverse, but the debate has been enhanced immeasurably by a marked trend toward advocating one of the possibilities while downplaying or excluding the others. The juxtaposition in the present chapter of the work of three prominent scholars will give some picture of the state of the debate: it remains unsettled whether Paul saw the "righteousness of the law" as something good (Wilckens), bad (Bultmann), or indifferent (Sanders).

i. Rudolf Bultmann

LITERATURE: The following abbreviations are used in the discussion (see Bibliography):

Anthropology = "Romans 7 and the Anthropology of Paul"
End = "Christ the End of the Law"
Jesus = "Jesus and Paul"

70

Mythology = *Jesus Christ and Mythology*
NT = "New Testament and Mythology"
Paul = "Paul"
Problem = "Das Problem der Ethik bei Paulus"
Setting = *Primitive Christianity in its Contemporary Setting*
Theology = *Theology of the New Testament,* Vol. I

If we are to trace Rudolf Bultmann's understanding of the "righteousness of the law"—or, for that matter, of most other subjects as well—we must begin with his view of Pauline anthropology. For Paul, in Bultmann's view, man is fundamentally *creature,* a created being who has nothing that he has not received, who lacks any possibility of security in himself or in the transitory, visible world he inhabits, and who is totally dependent on his Creator. It is only as man acknowledges this that he is "at one with himself" and "achieves his authentic Being" (the phrases were current when Bultmann wrote). Thus the possibility of being good or evil, of finding life or death, confronts man in the choice whether or not he will acknowledge and obey his Creator. To fail to do so, to live as though one were independent and autonomous, is sin, rebellion against God, and at the same time a missing of man's true existence, since man is fundamentally creature (cf. Theology 228-229, 232).

Man lives in the "flesh," that is, in the sphere of things visible and tangible, subject to corruption and death (NT 18). Life "*in* the flesh" does not in itself necessarily imply sin. On the other hand, it does open for man the possibility of living "*according to* the flesh," of trying to derive one's life from, and base one's security on, the created sphere. But this is "sin, because it is a turning away from the Creator, the giver of life, and a turning toward the creation—and to do that is to trust in one's self as being able to procure life by the use of the earthly and through one's own strength and accomplishment" (Theology 239).

In principle, then, good and evil, life and death are equally options within man's reach. In fact, however, Paul is of the opinion that "*man has always already missed the existence that at heart he seeks,* his intent is basically perverse, evil" (Theology 227). Through his self-assertion, man has become a totally fallen being (NT 31). The perverse desire to gain recognition for one's achievement is universal and, at the same time, "the root of all other evils" (Setting 183). In Judaism this common "human striving has . . . taken on its culturally . . . distinct form" in the desire to win recognition in God's sight by obedience to God's law; hence zeal in fulfilling God's law becomes the typically Jewish sin (End 43)! How has this paradoxical state of affairs come about?

What one encounters in the Old Testament law is, of course, the demand of God. The human attitude demanded by the law is that of obedience, the genuine obedience which acknowledges the Creator and refuses to seek life and security anywhere but in him. If met with such obedience, the law would lead to life. Indeed, the intent of God's commandment "is to snatch man out of his self-reliant pursuit of life, his will to rule over himself," and so set him again on the path to true life (Theology 250; cf. 259, 315). But in the very fact that the law promises "life" for those who submit to God and obey his commands there lies the possibility of misunderstanding. Man, knowing that to transgress God's law is sin, and that life is promised to those who obey it, may conclude that he can secure his *own* life and establish his *own* righteousness by doing what the law requires. But such apparent conformity with the law is really its perversion. It is merely a refined, highly deceptive expression of the universal desire to gain recognition by one's own accomplishment. To be sure, there is an apparent renunciation of self in the willingness to do what God's law demands. In fact, however, the self has not been renounced, for it is using its very "obedience" as the basis on which to claim recognition (cf. Theology 246, 267, 315-316). Hence "according to Paul the person who fulfils the law needs grace as much as the one who trespasses against it—indeed it is he most of all who needs it! For in seeking to establish his own righteousness, he is acting *fundamentally* against God" (End 46).

Jewish zeal in fulfilling the law is thus no less an expression of life "according to the flesh" than Gentile sensuality (cf. Gal. 3:2-3). Nowhere is this more apparent than in Philippians 3, where the basis for Paul's erstwhile "confidence in the flesh" is given. The prerogatives of Israel are listed since they belong to the sphere of the earthly and visible. So, too, are Paul's efforts in fulfilling the law (Phil. 3:6). Such efforts are expressions of an attitude oriented toward the "flesh," "the self-reliant attitude of the man who puts his trust in his own strength and in that which is controllable by him" (Theology 240). The sin of self-reliance reaches its culmination in "boasting"—and, again, both Jew and Greek are guilty. The Jew boasts of God and the Torah (Rom. 2:17, 23), the Greek of his wisdom (1 Cor. 1:19-31). Both forget that they have nothing which they have not received (1 Cor. 4:7). And God for his part insists that all human pretensions must be shattered "so that no human being might boast in the presence of God" (1 Cor. 1:29).

We are now in a position to answer why, in Bultmann's view, Paul rules out "the works of the law" as a path to salvation. Two reasons may be cited.

First, *"there is no true fulfilment of the Law"* (Theology 263). This is implicit in Gal. 3:10 and is the point of the argument in the opening chapters of Romans. No one can be justified by the "works of the law" because no one fulfills them in their entirety. All are transgressors (cf. End 50). This is as true of Jews as it is of Gentiles. Indeed, the purpose of Rom. 2:17-24 is to remind Jews who may "suppose that in God's eyes they are superior to the Gentiles . . . that as transgressors of the law they are not a bit better" (Anthropology 149; cf. End 40).

But the fundamental reproach which Paul brings against "the way of the law" is not that it is "wrong because, by reason of transgressions, it fails to reach its goal . . . , but rather that the *direction* of this way is perverse and, to be sure, because it intends to lead to 'one's own righteousness' (Rom. 10:3; Phil. 3:9)" (Anthropology 149). The "real sin" of Jews is thus not their violation of God's law but their intention to become righteous in his eyes by keeping it. *"Man's effort to achieve his salvation by keeping the Law* only leads him into sin, indeed this effort itself in the end *is already sin."* This conclusion follows from "the insight which Paul has achieved into the nature of sin" as "man's self-powered striving to undergird his own existence in forgetfulness of his creaturely existence, to procure his salvation by his own strength" (Theology 264). Since such striving leads to boasting, the ultimate reason why "works" do not justify is simply that "man must not have any boast before God (Rom. 3:27; 4:2)" (Theology 283).

Bultmann's understanding of what Paul means by redemption follows naturally from this interpretation of sin. The cross of Christ gives expression to God's judgment on the world and its illusions. In light of the cross, what is required of man is that he "subject himself to God's judgment, i.e., to the judgment that all of man's desires and strivings and standards of value are nothing before God, that they are all subject to death. . . . All of man's accomplishments and boasting are at an end; they are condemned as nothing by the cross" (Jesus 197). Faith, on this understanding, amounts to a willingness to submit to God's judgment, to renounce all boasting and every attempt to find security in oneself, and to find one's security only in God (Mythology 40; cf. NT 19-20). The believer is one who comes to recognize that righteousness is a gift which cannot be gained by anything he does; his "achievements" establish no claim on God (Theology 281). Thus the choice with which the sinner is confronted by the gospel is "whether or not he is willing to understand himself anew and to receive his life from the hand of God" (Theology 269). Conversion inevitably involves the "resolve to surrender [one's] whole previous self-understanding . . . and to understand [one's] existence anew" (Paul 115: cf. 122; End 45; Theology 187-188).

And what, finally, is the will of God for the believer? "Christian morality is simply the fulfilment of the Old Testament commandments (Rom. 13.8-10; Gal. 5.14)" (End 36; cf. Theology 262). Even though the law cannot serve as the basis for gaining favor with God by one's achievements, its content remains a valid statement of God's will (End 60). The ethical demands placed upon believers are thus no different from those made of all persons (cf. Problem 51). Two qualifications to these statements must, however, be added.

1. Though the substance of the moral demand remains the same, the manner of fulfillment is critical (cf. Theology 283, 341). Christian "fulfilling of the law" is no longer "'work' in the sense of meritorious accomplishment" (Theology 344). The one who "works" may obey the law outwardly, but his obedience only extends to the content of what he does; he does not submit *himself* to God, but rather "stands side by side with what he does," thinking he "has a right to be proud of [his] accomplishment" (Theology 316; cf. Setting 69). The believer, however, has radically renounced any claim to "accomplishment," and thus in his acts of obedience submits himself as well as his deed to the demand of God. He is set free from sin (the Pauline indicative) only as the self-renouncing decision of faith is constantly renewed in fresh acts of radical obedience to the commandment of God (the Pauline imperative; cf. Mythology 76-77; NT 21; Paul 142).

2. Though Paul does not work out the distinction, it is clear that when he speaks of the abiding validity of the law he is thinking of its ethical rather than its ritual or cultic commands. Thus "freedom from the law" implies the freedom to distinguish between what is valid and what is not valid within the law. Paul speaks of this task as proving "what is the good and acceptable and perfect will of God" (Rom. 12:2, RSV margin), as approving "what is excellent" (Phil. 1:10; cf. Theology 341).

We conclude: for Bultmann's Paul, the pursuit of the "righteousness of the law" is the typically Jewish expression of man's universal striving for recognition on the basis of his accomplishments. Faith is the renunciation of such striving as one recognizes one's utter dependence on God. It is expressed in genuine, radical obedience to God's demand in the law.

ii. Ulrich Wilckens

LITERATURE: The following abbreviations are used in the discussion (see Bibliography):

Bekehrung = "Die Bekehrung des Paulus als religionsgeschichtliches Problem"

Christologie = "Christologie und Anthropologie im Zusammenhang der paulinischen Rechtfertigungslehre"

Entwicklung = "Zur Entwicklung des paulinischen Gesetzesverständnisses"

Resurrection = *Resurrection*

Review = "Zum Römerbriefkommentar von Heinrich Schlier"

Römerbrief = *Der Brief an die Römer*

Werken = "Was heisst bei Paulus: 'Aus Werken des Gesetzes wird kein Mensch gerecht'?"

Much of what Ulrich Wilckens has written about the "righteousness of the law" has been formulated in deliberate, at times almost diametric opposition to the views of Rudolf Bultmann. Yet the criticisms raised represent only the negative side of what is in its own right an impressive counter-understanding of Paul. In what follows, we will for the most part allow the criticism of Bultmann to remain implicit, focusing rather on Wilckens's own reading of the relevant aspects of Paul's thought.

We may begin with Romans 2. Wilckens is one of the few scholars who believe Paul means what he says in Rom. 2:13: "For it is not the hearers of the law who are righteous before God, but the doers of the law who will be justified." Admittedly, the verse restates what is a basic principle of Judaism. But for Wilckens this does not mean that Paul here adopts his opponents' point of view for the sake of argument, that he reasons from a position which he himself regards as inadequate, superseded, misleading, or even perverted (cf. Römerbrief I, 145). On the contrary, the radical demand for works-righteousness in Rom. 2:13 is precisely *Paul's* position in opposition to contemporary Jewish thought (cf. Review 853-854). In current

Jewish theology, all sins were not equal. Heathen sin might damn, but the sins of Jews were countered by their membership in the covenant people of God. Hence the "righteousness" of all Jews who did not apostatize was ultimately guaranteed (Römerbrief I, 150-151). This is the position, such is the "boasting" which Paul is opposing in Romans 2; the passage says nothing of the supposed self-righteous claims of Jews to have kept the law and earned their salvation. It is against Jewish boasts of salvific privileges that Paul here insists on a righteousness demonstrated in deeds, contending that the sins of Jews leave them no better off than pagans. God will judge all according to their works, with no regard for membership in the people entrusted with his law. A Paul who insists on works-righteousness against Jews who rely on God's favor: the contrast with Bultmann's Paul could hardly be more dramatic (cf. Römerbrief I, 177)!

If Paul means what he says in Rom. 2:13—God does promise salvation to those whose works show them to be righteous—he also takes seriously the claim of the law that those who do its demands will live (Lev. 18:5, quoted in Rom. 10:5; Gal. 3:12). The law was given for "life" (Rom. 7:10). Paul's gospel is in no way opposed to works as such (Römerbrief I, 145). On the contrary, the full validity of the demand for righteous deeds in Rom. 2:13 is the presupposition behind Paul's judgment in 3:9 that all are under sin, and forms the basis for the dilemma from which, according to Paul's gospel, only Christ can deliver.

For Paul, according to Wilckens, there is one reason—and one reason only—why no one can be justified by the works of the law (cf. Werken 79-94): all have sinned, and where works are the decisive criterion by which righteousness is assessed and humankind is judged, then the sins of all bring all humankind under the wrath of God. This is the point of Rom. 1:18–3:20. The heathen are guilty of concrete sins (1:28-32)—and so are Jews (2:21-22). Throughout the passage Paul consistently maintains the position that actual deeds of righteousness are what God requires (cf. 2:14, 26-27). Nowhere does Paul suggest that Jews are wrong in attempting to keep the law; they are judged because they transgress it. Similarly 5:12-21 is concerned to show the universality of sin as transgression. And in Romans 7, "I" am "sold under sin" (v. 14) not because "I" try to keep the law (that, after all, is what "I" am supposed to do!), but because, for all my noble desires, "I" do what the law prohibits.

Such is Paul's position in Romans—and the picture is in this respect no different in Galatians. There too we read that "by works of the law shall no one be justified" (2:16) because Jews as well as pagans are found to be *sinners* (v. 17); distinctions based on the privileges of salvation history have thus become irrelevant. Since, according to Gal. 3:10, the law pronounces a curse on *all who do not obey* its commands completely, those subject to the law are said to be under its curse. Salvation by keeping the law is no longer a possibility. To be sure, the law promises life for those who carry out its demands (v. 12); yet it has no power to *create* life (*zōopoiēsai,* v. 21) for transgressors, but must simply curse them (Entwicklung 172-173). Thus salvation can only come apart from the law; indeed, it must include the removal of the law's curse upon transgressors (v. 13).

In Wilckens's view, Paul's understanding of the human dilemma is thus more radical and more pessimistic than that of his Jewish contemporaries. As a result, it requires a solution quite outside the salvific institutions granted to Israel. The latter are real enough in themselves, but powerless to cope with the problem posed by human sin (Römerbrief I, 222). The sacrificial system outlined in the priestly code of the Pentateuch could atone for "unwitting" sin, but it made no provision for deliberate, radical wrongdoing (Num. 15:30-31). Justification of sinners is thus not possible by means of the Jewish cult (cf. Römerbrief I, 238). To agree that works of righteousness are required and conclude that therefore only a few can be saved, as the Jewish apocalyptic tradition tended to do, is, again, to fall short of Paul's radical view of the dilemma that *none* is righteous when deeds are the criterion (Römerbrief I, 84, 152-153). To say that the election of Israel in itself guarantees Jewish participation in God's salvation, or that concrete observances of the law can offset transgressions, is to view the effects of sin less seriously than Paul does (cf. Christologie 71, 74; Römerbrief I, 240-241; II, 99-100). Thus whereas Bultmann's Paul differs from (Bultmann's) Judaism in condemning any attempt to establish one's own righteousness by fulfilling the law, according to Wilckens's understanding Paul differs by his more radical view of the consequences of transgression.

If we are to grasp Paul's thinking both in this respect and in the matter of how sin's consequences are cancelled by the death of Christ, Wilckens believes we must reckon with Old Testament notions of sin and atonement. The Israelites shared with much of the ancient Near East the idea that what one experiences is directly related to what one does. This relationship is misunderstood when it is thought of purely in judicial terms (i.e., God the judge measures deeds by the standard of the law and rewards or punishes accordingly). Such a view of the process is too abstract, whereas the Israelites regarded deeds, once committed, as having a kind of concrete existence of their own, as creating a sphere of power about them for good or evil which then works itself out on the doer: "He who digs a pit will fall into it, and a stone will come back upon him who starts it rolling" (Prov. 26:27). Yahweh is thought of not as assigning retribution, but as overseeing the process, directing the consequences of deeds so that they return, for good or ill, to the doers (cf. Prov. 24:12). And atonement, properly understood, is not a human attempt to placate a God bound by his righteousness to punish, but *God's* way of delivering sinners from the consequences of their sins by providing a substitute victim on whom those consequences can work themselves out (cf. Römerbrief I, 128, 236-238, 243; Resurrection 78-79). When sin and its effects are viewed so concretely, it follows that neither a simple pardoning of transgressions nor compensating for them by deeds of righteousness is adequate for solving the dilemma; both "solutions" leave untouched the pernicious process begun by sin. Only when the evil which has been set in motion has been allowed to work itself out, either on the doer or on a substitute provided by God, is it effectively done away.

Concrete *sin,* then, and not a perverted self-understanding, is the cause of the human dilemma; and the solution must be suited to the dilemma. Not faith *per se,* in the sense of a correct self-understanding, reverses the human predicament, but the death of Christ as the atoning sacrifice for sin provided by God (Römerbrief I, 89, 200-201, 232, 247-248). If Paul contrasts the righteousness of faith with that of the law, he does so in order to make the point that *sinners* cannot be justified by works of the law and that, since all are sinners, only faith *in the crucified Christ* can avail (Werken 92; Christologie 75). It is because of its christological content that faith can be said to justify (Werken 108). Neither in what Paul says about the righteousness of God nor in his view of faith are *anthropological* considerations central. The decisive convictions are christological: that God has intervened in the death and resurrection of Christ for the salvation of sinners (Römerbrief I, 92, 211-212).

Hence faith *per se* must not be seen as opposed to works, nor does it deliver the believer from the obligation to do deeds of righteousness, to "fulfill the law." The deliverance it brings is rather from the consequences of sins committed in the past and, indeed, of the believer's failures to live up to the law in the present: all have their atonement in the death of Christ (Römerbrief I, 145-146). The law's role of condemning the sinner is thus ended. And the law as a means to life, which, because of universal sin, was already inoperative, is now replaced by the saving act of God's righteousness in Christ (Römerbrief II, 22; Christologie 68). Nonetheless the law as a statement of God's will remains, and believers are intended to fulfill it—through love (Werken 109).

That the law as a path to salvation has been done away with has important consequences for its adherents (cf. Römerbrief I, 178; Werken 98-104). Whereas, for (Wilckens's) Paul, the "works of the law" are good in themselves, and the law was originally given to be obeyed and to bring life, the latter possibility has now and forever been closed. For Jews *now,* after the crucifixion of Christ, the attempt to establish righteousness by keeping the law is a vain pursuit in defiance of the righteousness revealed in Christ and available to faith (Rom. 9:31-32; 10:3; Phil. 3:9). It must be noted, however, that such a pursuit is vain, not because there is anything inherently wrong in attempting to do what the law commands, but because, with Christ, the period in which the law could lead to righteousness reached its end (Rom. 10:4).

For the believer in Christ, on the other hand, it is important to define in what respect the law has been done away with and in what sense it remains valid. Believers are free from the *condemnation* of the law—not that the sentence of the law is evaded, that God in his mercy has decided to dispense with the law's verdict, for the curse of the law is allowed its full force; Paul means rather that since that curse has been exhausted on Christ, believers are delivered from its effects (Römerbrief I, 186; II, 70). On the other hand, they are to fulfill "the whole law" by carrying out the single command to love one's neighbor (Gal. 5:14; Rom. 13:8-10). Practically, of course, this involves a massive reduction of the law's demands. The concentration on the command to love means that, at least where Gentile Christians are concerned, even basic commandments like that of circumcision, and, in general, the cultic and ritual demands of the law are abrogated (Gal. 2:14; 4:10). Furthermore it should be remembered that it is as Christians are guided by the Spirit that they are able to fulfill the law (Entwicklung 176). But the principle of judgment by works set forth in Rom. 2:5-11 remains valid for Christians. Their acquittal is assured by the death of Christ which frees them from the consequences of their failings (Römerbrief I, 146). But the law as such is not done away.

Finally we may ask how Paul arrived at his views of the law. Other Jews who believed that Jesus was the Messiah still maintained their confidence in the status of Israel as God's chosen people and in the abiding, salvific force of Israel's covenant law; hence, for example, they required circumcision of non-Jewish believers. Why did Paul adopt a different position? Why did he see—from the very moment of his conversion (Bekehrung 14-15)—the law and Christ as exclusive alternatives?

Wilckens suggests that the pre-Christian Paul must have belonged to one of the Hellenistic synagogues in Jerusalem (Entwicklung 154-155). There he encountered and came to persecute Christians who claimed that the temple cult and the sacrifices prescribed in Torah were done away with by the atoning death of Christ (cf. Römerbrief I, 174, 241). Thus even before his conversion Paul would have regarded Jesus and Torah as exclusive alternatives. His conversion would have simply meant that he now championed the former alternative.

Paul's radical assessments of the universality of sin and of the law as cursing sinners are clearly the *consequences* drawn from his Christian conviction that Christ died for sins (cf. Entwicklung 166-167). Indeed, apart from a belief in the justification of sinners through Christ, Paul's depiction of the universality of sin and the powerlessness of the law would amount to an outright denial of the righteousness of God (cf. Römerbrief I, 179-180). Only Paul's belief that the "righteousness" of God has been revealed in the atoning death of Christ can explain his depiction of the human dilemma.

As we have seen, Wilckens understands Paul's doctrine of justification as fundamentally the justification of *sinners* through the atoning death of Christ. In his early (postconversion) thinking, Paul's soteriology was founded on his christology in a traditional way: the forgiveness of sins, the "justifying" of sinners, was proclaimed on the basis of the atoning death of Christ (1 Cor. 1:30: 6:11; 2 Cor. 5:21; cf. Christologie 69-72). The necessary human response was of course always seen as "faith in Christ," but it was first in contesting the views of his Galatian opponents that Paul used the phrase polemically, contrasting it with the works of the law. In Romans Paul attempted to work out the positions he had arrived at polemically in Galatians in a more positive, general way (Christologie 69). It should be clear, however, that on Wilckens's understanding the basic christological structure of Paul's doctrine of justification remained constant throughout and, in fact, was fully consistent with traditional, pre-Pauline theology. In confronting proponents of the law, Paul drew radical consequences about the dilemma posed by human sin and the impotence of the law to save. But the basis of those consequences was the universal Christian conviction that "Christ died for our sins" (1 Cor. 15:3).

We conclude: for Wilckens's Paul, the pursuit of the "righteousness of the law" was positively enjoined on the Jews, who, however, failed to attain their goal because they transgressed the law. Salvation is by faith in the death and resurrection of Jesus, who thus provided atonement for transgressions. But the demand to fulfill the law, now seen as summed up in the love commandment, remains valid for believers.

iii. E. P. Sanders

LITERATURE: The following abbreviations are used in the discussion (see Bibliography):
Law = *Paul, the Law, and the Jewish People*
Paul = *Paul and Palestinian Judaism*

Even before Sanders, in *Paul and Palestinian Judaism,* begins his discussion of Paul, his study of Palestinian Judaism (reviewed in Chapter 3 above) has given reason to doubt that the "boasting" of Jews in their own righteousness can be the basis on which Paul rejects the "righteousness of the law." Had that been Paul's charge, his picture of Judaism would have been a distorted one; but, though the existence of such a distortion in Paul has frequently been asserted, Sanders does not think this is what we find. "The supposed objection to Jewish self-righteousness is as absent from Paul's letters as self-righteousness itself is from Jewish literature" (Law 156). Certainly Paul opposed boasting in anything other than the cross of Christ. But there is in the epistles "no indication that Paul thought that the law had failed *because* keeping it leads to the wrong attitude or that his opposition to boasting *accounts* for his saying that righteousness is not by law" (Law 35). Implicit in such a statement is, of course, a rejection of Bultmann's interpretation of key passages in Paul. Sanders's alternative interpretations are, briefly, as follows.

1. The Jewish "boasting" rejected in Rom. 3:27 is not (Sanders believes) that which expresses pride in human achievement but rather that which assumes and relies on the special privileges granted to Jews. The term thus has the same significance as in 2:17, 23. And while the

opening verses in Romans 4 establish that Abraham was justified by faith, not works, there is no hint of the view that the attempt to gain righteousness by observing the law is itself the fundamental Jewish sin and Paul's reason for objecting to the law (Law 33). The argument of 3:27–4:25 simply does not address the attitude of self-righteousness. Its subject is God's plan of salvation announced in the Abraham story and now made available to both Jew and Gentile on the same terms: faith in Jesus Christ.

2. In its context, the statement in Rom. 9:32 that Israel sought righteousness not by faith but by works cannot mean that Jews failed because they observed the law in the wrong way. Their problem, as the immediate sequel shows, is their lack of faith *in Christ,* who is the "stumbling stone" over whom they "stumble" (Law 37). Nor does the claim in 10:3 that Jews try to "establish their own" righteousness refer to a self-righteousness based on personal achievements in keeping the law. In the immediate context (v. 2) Paul even commends the "zeal" of Jews. But the Jews are seen to be wrong in pursuing a kind of righteousness available only to themselves ("their own," i.e., that which follows from observing the *Jewish* law) rather than recognizing that God's righteousness is available to Jew and Gentile alike on the same basis. Not Jewish self-righteousness, but the equality of Jews and Gentiles is the point of the argument.

3. Nor does Phil. 3:9 condemn any supposed "self-righteousness" on the part of Jews. Paul does reject the righteousness of the observant Jew, but, again, this is not because there is anything inherently wrong in such righteousness—on the contrary, it is regarded *in itself* as "gain" (v. 7). Rather, since Paul has come to believe that true righteousness is found only in Christ, he necessarily looks upon any other righteousness as "loss" *by comparison* (Law 44-45); hence the rejection of the "righteousness of the law."

When these critical passages are interpreted in this way, we are left with no textual support for the view that Paul regarded the "righteousness of the law" as wrong because it leads to self-righteousness and boasting. That in itself might seem to rule out Bultmann's interpretation. Sanders notes as well the complete absence of any suggestion that law observance leads to boasting in Galatians (Paul 482); and even in Romans, the variety of ways in which Paul uses the word "faith" *(pistis)* in the opening chapters suggests that his goal can hardly be to establish faith as specifically the abandonment of boasting; his concern is simply to do away with any requirement to keep the law

(Paul 490-491). But the primary criticism which Sanders brings against Bultmann, the "principal fault" which he finds in the latter's treatment of Paul, is that he "proceeded from plight to solution and supposed that Paul proceeded in the same way" (Paul 474). It is wrong to think that it is "Paul's analysis of the nature of sin which determines his view" (Paul 481-482). What Paul begins with is the conviction that only belonging to Christ brings salvation. "For Paul, the conviction of a universal solution preceded the conviction of a universal plight" (Paul 474). If this, as Sanders argues, is the case, then the *starting-point* of Paul's thought can hardly be any sense that the effort to keep the law was misdirected. Whatever the criticisms Paul may bring against the law, they all *presuppose* his faith in Christ.

Sanders's arguments against Wilckens's position follow similar lines. Obviously "the common observation that everybody transgresses" is found in Paul as well, and, to be sure, in the opening chapters in Romans Paul uses it as an argument "to *prove* that everyone is under the lordship of sin. But this is only *an argument to prove a point,* not the way he actually reached his assessment of the plight of man" (Paul 499). Transgressions do not constitute the problem, the real plight of humankind. The problem, perceived by a Paul who is already convinced that Jesus is Savior and Lord, is that people are under a different lordship and need Christ to be their Savior (Paul 443). That we are dealing with an argument "based on the conclusion" rather than the other way around is clear from the "remarkably inconsistent" nature of Paul's "statements of universal sinfulness" (Law 35). Romans 2 actually "holds out the possibility of righteousness by the law as a real one" (Law 35), contrary to what we find elsewhere in Paul. Even the different ways in which Paul regards transgressions—as the *cause* of sin's dominion in Romans, or "as the *result* of being in the flesh (Gal. 5.19-21)"—indicate that this was not Paul's starting-point (Paul 501). Moreover, it is important to note "that Paul does not cite human inability to fulfill the law in his principal arguments against his opponents, Galatians 3 and Romans 4, when he undertakes to prove that righteousness *cannot* be by law" (Law 25). Thus, while we cannot "say that Paul never thought that everybody sins," it remains true that "that view is not put forward as the ground of his own view that righteousness must be by faith, to the exclusion of doing the law" (Law 25).

Other attempts at explaining why Paul rejected the "righteousness of the law" may be dealt with more briefly. Some think, on the basis of Gal. 3:13, that Paul inevitably rejected the law when he came to believe that Jesus, on whom the law pronounced a curse, was really the Messiah. This seems logical, but in fact no one in the first century seems to have reasoned that way. In its context, Gal. 3:13 explains why Christians are no longer under the law's curse. It is "not actually an argument against righteousness by the law," nor does Paul reason in the way suggested anywhere else when he "recounts his own rejection of the law" (Law 26). Many scholars ("especially of an earlier period") have argued on the basis of Romans 7 "that Paul had become frustrated in his attempt to find righteousness under the law and therefore denounced it" (Law 48, n. 2). Yet Romans 7 represents, not Paul's reason for rejecting the law, but one of his several attempts to explain the relationship between the law and sin. Paul shows elsewhere that he believes that Jews can do what the law requires—and that he himself had done so (Law 77)! Romans 7 is quite unique in Paul, suggesting as it does that "humanity without Christ cannot fulfill the law at all" (Law 78). Thus it can scarcely be made the basis of his rejection of the law. Finally, the suggestion that Paul's views were determined by a supposedly common scheme which saw the validity of the law ending with the dawn of the Messianic period may be rejected if for no other reason than that Paul "*never appeals to the fact that the Messiah has come as a reason for holding the law invalid.* . . . If such reasoning governed his view, he kept it completely to himself" (Paul 479-480).

Paul's real *reason* for excluding the law has already been suggested. It followed from his conviction that salvation is available only in Christ. "If salvation comes only in Christ, no one may follow any other way whatsoever" (Paul 519). In other words, it is primarily Paul's "exclusivist soteriology" which ruled out the "righteousness of the law" as a path to salvation. Admittedly, Paul produces many *arguments* against the law. He cites scripture to prove that righteousness comes only by faith. He claims that the law provokes transgressions; or that, while good in itself, it has become an agent in the service of "Sin"; or that it is powerless to cope with the weakness of the human "flesh" (Law 26, 65-76). Yet the very diversity which characterizes Paul's portrayals of the human plight under law demonstrates that he "did not begin his thinking about sin and redemption by analyzing the human condition, nor by analyzing the effect of the law on those who sought to obey it. Had he done so we should doubtless find more consistency" (Law 81). Paul's actual thinking is more clearly reflected in 2 Cor. 3:4-

18 and Phil. 3:3-11, where the Mosaic dispensation is described in positive terms ("glorious," "gain"), but where it is abandoned because of the surpassing splendor of the new dispensation. Paul "came to relegate the Mosaic dispensation to a less glorious place *because* he found something more glorious. . . . Once a greater good appears, what was formerly good is regarded not just as second best, but as 'loss.' . . . The only thing that is wrong with the old righteousness seems to be that it is not the new one" (Law 138, 140). "This logic—that God's action in Christ alone provides salvation and makes everything else seem, in fact actually *be* worthless—seems to dominate Paul's view of the law" (Paul 485).

There is, however, another consideration, a further "primary conviction" of Paul's, which governed his thinking: Paul believed that he was called to be the apostle to the Gentiles. Christ has been appointed Lord of the whole world and Savior of all believers—including Gentiles. Hence righteousness cannot come by keeping the Jewish law, because that would exclude Gentiles. "The salvation of the Gentiles is essential to Paul's preaching; and with it falls the law; for, as Paul says simply, Gentiles cannot live by the law (Gal. 2.14)" (Paul 496).

It is, then, these Christian convictions about God's solution in Christ which, in Sanders's judgment, lead Paul to reject the law rather than any deficiency he perceived in the law itself. Paul's thinking was not determined by a view that the "righteousness of the law" is itself bad because it leads to boasting, or that it is good but unattained; it is merely indifferent when compared with God's righteousness in Christ—though, admittedly, in Paul's black-and-white thinking, this led to its outright rejection as "loss."

And what of the law in the life of the Christian? Here we encounter the surprising fact that, when Paul "was asked, as it were, the question of what was the necessary and sufficient condition for membership in the body of Christ, he said 'not the law.' . . . When, however, he thought about behavior, he responded, 'fulfill the law'" (Law 84)! To be sure, without making any theoretical distinction between aspects of the law which remain binding and those which do not, Paul never in fact enforced the provisions regarding circumcision, dietary restrictions, or the observance of special days and seasons (Law 100-101). And, admittedly, it is the leading of the Spirit which enables Christians to do what the law requires (Law 105). The fact remains, however, that when Paul is not dealing with the polemical issue of the basis for membership in the people of God, he can speak quite positively of the role of the law in Christian behavior (Law 114). This again suggests that his critique of the law is not the starting-point of his thought.

* * *

The positions reviewed in this chapter demonstrate—if little else—the lack of a scholarly consensus on Paul's view of the law. Not surprisingly, some scholars have suggested that the problems of interpretation are the result of a lack of consistency or coherence in Paul's own statements on the subject. We turn now to a consideration of three forms in which this proposal has recently been argued.

Chapter Six

The "Hobgoblin" of Consistency: Drane, Hübner, and Räisänen

The novice who wishes to pass unsuspected at a gathering of New Testament scholars needs only to wait for an appropriate moment to utter the axiom: "But, of course, Paul was no systematic theologian!" That, with an otherwise steadfast adherence to the principle of Prov. 17:28, should ensure acceptance.

Like a number of the axioms of the discipline, this one contains a grain of truth. Paul's writings have been preserved for posterity in the Christian Bible, but this unanticipated development should not be allowed to conceal their original, occasional nature. He wrote letters, not theological treatises, designed to deal with concrete situations in contemporary Christian communities rather than as a vehicle for the ordered presentation of his thought. The epistle to the Romans has long been regarded as the exception which proves the rule; but even this concession to the devotees of system may not be necessary. Recent studies have stressed that Romans too is a response to peculiar conditions prevailing at a crucial point in the life of Paul and in the history of the early Church.

Paul did not write systematic theology. Yet this in itself does not mean that such theology cannot be constructed from his piecemeal responses to particular issues. Several of the scholars we have considered have attempted to do just that, and Schweitzer's denunciation of those who refuse to admit the logic of Paul's positions was noted. Still, doubts have persisted, nourished in part by the patent discrepancies that exist between the numerous systems proposed as Pauline. Do

Paul's diverse claims about the law really yield a single, coherent picture? Do we not rather find a development in his views from one epistle to the next? Or perhaps we should simply admit a total lack of coherence?

While Luther's interpretation of Paul has served as a starting-point for other chapters in our review, the perspectives on Paul discussed here represent a challenge not so much to Luther's interpretation per se as to any understanding of Paul which supposes that his various statements on the law can be reduced to a coherent scheme. Drane and Hübner believe that a significant shift in Paul's thinking on the subject can be traced between the writing of Galatians and that of Romans. Räisänen maintains that Paul's thinking on the law is characterized throughout by contradictions. To many readers, such a menu no doubt portends an unpalatable meal; the proof—one way or the other—can only be found "in the pudding."

i. John W. Drane

LITERATURE: Drane, *Paul: Libertine or Legalist?* (see Bibliography)

In the title of his monograph, Drane asks whether Paul should be considered a "libertine" or a "legalist." In the substance of the book, he argues that the answer depends on which epistle one is considering. A libertine (of sorts) when he wrote Galatians, a legalist (of sorts) when he wrote 1 Corinthians, Paul finally developed in his thinking to the point where his views are expressed in a more balanced form in 2 Corinthians and (especially) Romans. For our purposes, a brief summary of the proposed development from Galatians to Romans via 1 Corinthians will suffice.

The Galatians to whom Paul wrote were under pressure from "false teachers" to become circumcised and observe the Jewish law. Only so, it was argued, could they be "incorporated into the true People of God" (84). In responding to an insistence that the Old Testament law be observed, Paul was naturally concerned to demonstrate the inferiority of the law to the Christian gospel. The result is a series of "devastating denunciations of the Old Testament Law and all that it stood for" (5). By its very nature the law is inferior to God's promise, according to Gal. 3:18. The law's divine origin is denied in 3:19. In 3:21, Paul claims that the law is too weak to give life. The law does indeed serve as a revealer of sin and a "custodian" (vv. 19, 24), but these positive aspects of its function are stated quite baldly. No attempt is made to show the law as a benevolent gift of God.

Does the rejection of the law mean a rejection of morality? Not at all, argues the Paul of Galatians. It is only morality of the purely external kind—the only morality which law can dictate—that has been done away with. The precepts of the Jewish law are no longer relevant, but in their place the Christian has been given the Spirit of God, who provides them with sufficient guidance and strength for moral behavior. It is consistent with this conviction that Paul gives no specific instructions in Galatians on Christian conduct in particular circumstances. Such instructions are unnecessary and run counter to the principle of Christian liberty, which knows no limits in this epistle.

At the time when he wrote Galatians, however, Paul did not anticipate the problems to which such views could lead. His own opposition to legalism in Galatians came back to haunt him in Corinth, where Paul was confronted with Gnosticizing libertines whose pursuit of unrestrained liberty led to intolerable consequences. And so, the Paul who writes 1 Corinthians now appears in the guise of a quasi-legalist. The Old Testament law as such is not a subject for discussion. But when Paul claims that "keeping the commandments" is essential (1 Cor. 7:19), "he reintroduces the *form* of legal language, which in turn leads him into an ethical position in 1 Corinthians not so very much different from the legalism he had so much deprecated in Galatians" (65). No longer does Paul simply rely on the guidance of the Holy Spirit. Rather he "[defines] in very precise terms the ways in which the principle of Christian ethics should be applied, and by bringing in himself as an authorized example, and his own teaching as a kind of universal moral code, he moves a considerable distance in the direction of the 'law ethics' which he had so much deplored in the Galatian situation" (64). As for Christian liberty, 1 Cor. 6:12 introduces deliberate limitations on Paul's earlier position; the rules given at various points in the epistle "constitute a substantial modification of the original principle of Christian freedom" (69); and the plea that Christian liberty should be restrained by a consideration of the needs of weaker brethren represents something of a discovery for Paul himself, who showed no compunction on that score in his encounter with Peter at Antioch, related in Gal. 2:11-14.

What we find in the letter to the Romans is Paul's attempt "to give a completely balanced exposition of his theological position, which would be susceptible of misunderstanding by neither Judaizers nor Gnosticizers" (124). In essence he returns to many of the things he had said in Galatians, but with modifications necessitated by his Corinthian experience. In Romans as in Galatians, the law cannot save, and its precepts are not binding on Christians. On the other hand, the law is no longer despised: it is described as God's law (8:7), as spiritual (7:14), holy, just, and good (v. 12). Its positive role in preparing for salvation through Christ receives an emphasis lacking in Galatians (cf. Rom. 3:21), and Christians are even said to fulfill its demands (8:3-4). While the Holy Spirit's role in Christian ethics is maintained in Romans as in Galatians, in the later epistle Paul "goes on to describe in some detail the ways in which the Christian ought to behave" (134).

In the final analysis, Paul should not be considered a libertine or a legalist. He was first and foremost a servant of Jesus Christ, prone to blunders "in his enthusiasm for his vocation" (135), but willing to take whatever risks seemed necessary "for the sake of the gospel" (1 Cor. 9:23).

ii. Hans Hübner

LITERATURE: Hübner, *Law in Paul's Thought* (see Bibliography).

Hübner's study of development in Paul's thought focuses on perceived shifts between Paul's positions on the law in Galatians and those we encounter in his letter to the Romans. Hübner speculates that Paul's very negative view of the law in the earlier epistle may have become known to the Jerusalem apostles, and that it was their severe criticisms which forced Paul to reconsider the matter. The primary concern of the book, however, is not with historical reconstruction, but with the interpretation of the Pauline texts. Though Hübner treats Galatians and Romans separately, the (not to be despised) voice of convenience suggests that we simply note the relevant points on which Hübner sees significant differences between the epistles.

1. We may begin with the origin and purpose of the law. Like Drane, Hübner interprets Gal. 3:19-20 as indicating that angels were the actual source of the law, not merely its mediators. Since the purpose of these angels is said to have been "to promote transgressions" (so we may understand *tōn parabaseōn charin* in v. 19), the character of the angels must be that of hostile demons. This interpretation allows verse 21a to appear in its full force: since the law was given by demons, the question whether such a law is "against the promises of God"

becomes indeed acute! As for the law's purpose in Galatians, the discussion must be conducted on three levels. The "immanent purpose" of the law is found in what the law itself promises: it gives life to those who carry out its commands (3:12). The purpose of the demons who gave the law was to provoke transgressions (v. 19). Overriding both is the purpose of God, who made of the law a "custodian until Christ came" (v. 24).

The picture in Romans is much simpler, largely because there is no suggestion that the law came from hostile angels. Here the law is divine, its purpose that of bringing the knowledge of sin (Rom. 3:20; 7:7). Whereas in Galatians, the law was said to provoke transgressions, in Romans it is explicitly exonerated of any such responsibility. Sin itself is to blame—though it uses the law to achieve its ends (Romans 7).

2. A dominant feature of Galatians first discovered by Hübner is the contrast between a quantitative and a qualitative understanding of the law. The former requires obedience to each of Torah's individual demands; the law's curse is thought to strike those who transgress a single one, though (on the normal quantitative view) full compliance with the law is considered a manageable proposition. This, Hübner believes, was the view of Torah held by Beth Shammai, one of the schools within the Pharisaism of Paul's day. In Galatians, Paul himself expresses such a quantitative view—a case, according to Hübner, of not yet shaken adherence to the tenets of his alma mater: "only total obedience to the Law is obedience to the Law at all. . . . If just a single prescription of the Law is transgressed against, the effect is as if the entire Torah had been disregarded" (24). Paul assumes, however, that no one fulfills the law in all its requirements; hence the law brings a curse to all rather than life (Gal. 3:10, 13).

But for the Christian, the "law" is defined in a new, qualitative way. No longer is it a totality of individual commands; the "whole law" valid for the believer is simply the command to love (Gal. 5:14). It is crucial to Hübner's argument that this "whole law" is *not* to be identified with the law of Moses; rather it represents a radical reduction of its demands to a single commandment binding on believers.

The contrast between the two views of the law is not maintained in Romans. On the one hand, Paul does not argue here, as he did on the basis of the "quantitative" view of Torah in Galatians, that a curse strikes those who do not keep *each* of Torah's precepts. On the other hand, whereas in Galatians the Christian is not bound by the Mosaic law itself, but only by a radically reduced form of it (the qualitative view), in Romans the actual law of Moses (when correctly understood) remains valid for believers. The love commandment which alone survives the radical reduction of Torah in Galatians is seen in Rom. 13:8-10 as simply a summary of the still binding demands of the Mosaic law.

3. From the preceding distinction it follows that Romans allows for a dialetic in the Christian's relation to the law on which Galatians is silent. In Galatians, Christians are "free" from the law. No limitations are placed on their freedom, though they are warned not to abuse it (5:13). In Romans, however, the law is rehabilitated, and Hübner insists that a distinction must be drawn between Torah as it has been *perverted* into a law of works and Torah as it is perceived from the standpoint of faith (cf. Rom. 3:27). Properly interpreted, the law is on the side of faith, not works: "the Law in so far as it is 'scripture' testifies of itself that in so far as it is a divine demand its intention is not to be a 'Law of works'" (143, emphasis removed). It is thus a distortion of the law to imagine that it demands works as the basis of righteousness; such a distortion leads one to see one's existence as based on one's own activity, thereby forgetting that one "owes one's being to God" (121). It is from this distortion of the law, "from the dominion of the perverted Law" (135), that Christians are set free. They remain subject to God's law. *"Freedom from the perverted Law is the dominion of the Law of God"* (135), which still states the will of God for believers (Rom. 7:12; 13:8-10). As a result, in Romans (but not in Galatians) Paul can say "We uphold the law" (3:31); that is, we allow the law to serve its intended function by showing the misunderstanding involved in interpreting it as a "law of works." In Galatians, Christ is the end of the law. In Romans, he is "the end of the misuse of the Law" (so Hübner interprets Rom. 10:4, 138).

4. Finally, according to Hübner, Galatians lacks the prohibition of boasting in one's own works before God which in Romans is such an essential part of the Christian's self-understanding. Indeed, Gal. 6:4 appears to allow for Christian "boasting": not, of course, for "works of the law" which have been performed, but for one's "work" as a Christian.

In Romans, however, such boasting is excluded, largely because Paul has now thought through the implications of a righteousness based on "works."

> If the Law is defined as the sum of commandments which when complied with make man righteous, and if furthermore being righteous means being righteous in the presence of God, then the whole point for the man who understands the Law in this way is that he claims recognition in the sight of God for the works he has achieved. Yet more: he is in fact dependent on so doing, he must claim recognition for them in the sight of God. But this means no more nor less than boasting in the presence of God. If *righteousness through works* is legitimate . . . then it *implies the legitimacy of self-glorying or boasting.* (116)

Such boasting, such elevating of oneself in the sight of God, Paul now perceives, is fundamentally evil. Hence the Paul of Romans is led both to denounce the view of the law (as a "law of works") which leads to such a result and to exclude boasting of one's works from Christian experience (Rom. 3:27; 4:2). In place of such boasting, Paul says in the paradoxical statement of 5:2-3 that Christians "boast in the hope of God's glory, but that this coincides with our boasting also of suffering or distress" (122).

Such, in brief, are the major developments which Hübner detects by comparing Galatians with Romans. The (Lutheran!) Paul who opposes human works and boasting of their performance is the Paul of Romans, not Galatians. As in Drane's study, the impressiveness of Paul's theology is granted, but its blossom is considered late, not perennial.

iii. Heikki Räisänen

LITERATURE: Räisänen, *Paul and the Law* (see Bibliography).

If, as Ralph Waldo Emerson would have it, "a foolish consistency is the hobgoblin of little minds," then Räisänen's *Paul and the Law* bids fair to prove that Paul was never so afflicted. For Räisänen, it is not enough to say that Romans betrays shifts in Paul's thinking from what we encounter in the earlier epistles. On the one hand, the interval between the writing of Galatians and Romans was scarcely sufficient to allow major developments in Paul's thought, nor is it likely that, after twenty years of missionary work, Paul's thinking suddenly matured. On the other hand, Paul's statements about the law are not consistent even within the limits of single epistles. In short, "contradictions and tensions have to be *accepted* as *constant* features of Paul's theology of

the law" (11); the exegete should "take them very seriously as point-
ers to Paul's *personal theological problems*" (12) requiring "a historical and psychological explanation" rather than resolution in terms of
"theological dialectic or theories of interpolation or development"
(14). Under five headings, Räisänen explores Paul's thought with this
agenda in mind.

1. On two counts, Räisänen finds inconsistencies in Paul's very
concept of law. In the first place, Paul sometimes speaks as though
Jews alone were given the law, in other texts as though Gentiles, too,
are subject to its demands. Secondly, Paul speaks of the law as a unity
and never explicitly distinguishes between its moral and ritual parts;
but his argument in several places presupposes a reduction of Torah to
its moral demands.

a. If "*nomos* in Paul refers to the authoritative tradition of Israel,
anchored in the revelation on Sinai, which separates the Jews from the
rest of mankind" (16), then there is nothing surprising in those passages which speak of Jews as living "under law" and Gentiles as being
without it (Rom. 2; 1 Cor. 9:20-21; cf. Gal. 2:15). The distinction is
clear, and its basis in the traditions of God's unique revelation to Israel
on Mount Sinai is obvious.

Curiously, however, when Paul speaks of the human dilemma
from which Christ delivers, the power and curse of the law appear to
be universal, affecting Gentiles as well as Jews. According to Gal.
3:13-14, "Christ redeemed *us* from the curse of the law . . . that *we*
might receive the promise of the Spirit through faith": the first person
pronouns can hardly refer to Jewish believers alone (cf. also vv. 23-
26). Gal. 4:5-6 assumes that the (Gentile) Galatians were redeemed
from bondage "under the law" so that they might be "adopted" as
"sons." The Roman believers addressed in Rom. 7:4-6 are said to have
"died to the law"; yet the Roman church included Gentiles as well as
Jews. Thus, "apparently without noticing it," Paul oscillates "between
the notion of a historical and particularist Torah and that of a general
universal force" (21).

b. Though some scholars have suggested that Paul rejected only
the ritual elements of the law, such a view does not withstand scrutiny:
Paul can speak positively of Israel's cult (*latreia,* Rom. 9:4) and negatively about the moral law (Rom. 4:15; 7:5, 7-11; 2 Cor. 3:6-7). Nowhere, in fact, does he consciously distinguish between the cultic and
the moral aspects of the Torah.

Nonetheless, when Paul speaks in Romans 2 of Gentiles who

"keep the law" (2:27; cf. vv. 14, 26), the statement is patently untrue if Israel's ritual law is included. Paul can only be thinking of moral standards recognized by Jews and non-Jews alike. Similarly, when Paul claims that believers fulfill the law (8:4; cf. 13:8-10; Gal. 5:14), it is obvious that he has tacitly reduced Torah to its moral requirements. Paul never articulates such a distinction, and, presumably, he himself is unaware of the oscillation in his concept of the law; yet his argument depends upon it.

2. Räisänen finds in the apostle's writings evidence that Paul believed that the law both is and is not still valid. The force of the latter statements is sometimes evaded by claims that Paul repudiated Jewish misunderstandings of the law rather than the law itself. But Galatians 3 clearly states that the law as given on Mount Sinai was intended to be a temporary measure. Similarly, in 2 Corinthians 3, Paul speaks of the Sinaitic law and the ministry of Moses as inferior and transient without suggesting that such liabilities resulted from Jewish legalistic misunderstandings. And why, if the human dilemma was one of misunderstanding the law, was the death of Christ and even of Christians to the law the necessary path of deliverance (Gal. 2:19; Rom. 7:1-6)?

Paul's sweeping statements about Christian freedom further substantiate the view that he believes the law has been set aside. No one for whom the Mosaic law remained the valid statement of God's will could claim that "nothing is unclean in itself" (Rom. 14:14), that the propriety of eating food offered to idols depends on the circumstances (1 Cor. 8; 10), that "all things are lawful" when sexual license is under discussion (1 Cor. 6:12). Passages such as Rom. 12:1-2; Phil. 1:10 and 4:8 make it clear that Paul relied on no ready code for discovering the will of God. Moreover, in a context where the righteousness based on the law is contrasted with that of faith, Paul declares that Christ marks an end to the former (Rom. 10:4). Paul's varied attempts to explain how the law was set aside (it was temporary by design; believers somehow died to the law; believers have been liberated from the law through the vicarious death of Christ) at least confirm that freedom from the law was one aspect of the apostle's thought. Finally, the evidence of the epistles shows that Paul himself did not scrupulously adhere to the law. In 1 Cor. 9:20-21, he notes that he behaves differently ("as one outside the law") in the presence of Gentiles than he does among Jews; nonobservance of the "ritual" Torah must be meant. Gal. 4:12 refers to the apostle's abandoning of ritual observance in the course of his activity among the Galatians. Gal. 2:17 probably indicates that Paul and, at one time, Peter lived in a way which made them "sinners" from the perspective of Torah. And how could Paul have written Gal. 4:10 if he himself had kept the sabbath in Galatia? Is he likely to have observed Jewish dietary laws when he emphatically claims that *all* foods are clean (Rom. 14:14)?

Yet Paul was not a consistent antinomist. Occasionally he cites demands of Torah as though they were still binding (1 Cor. 9:9; 14:34 [?]; 2 Cor. 8:15). More importantly, he sees the Christian's task as one of "fulfilling the law" (Gal. 5:14; Rom. 8:4; 13:8-10), claims that "keeping the commandments of God" is essential (1 Cor. 7:19), and insists that he himself "[upholds] the law" (Rom. 3:31). "Paul thus wants to have his cake and eat it": Christians are free from the law, yet "now as before the law is justified in putting a claim on man, even on the Christian" (82).

3. Is it possible to keep the law? Again, Räisänen's Paul comes down hard on both sides of the issue. In Gal. 3:10, the curse of the law, which strikes "every one who does not abide by all things written in the book of the law," is said to fall on all those subject to the law: the implication, clearly, is that none of the adherents of the law "abide" by all its commands.

That everyone transgresses the law is Paul's explicit point in Rom. 1:18–3:20: all have sinned (3:20) and are under sin's power (3:9). Yet Paul's argument in support of his point is neither convincing nor coherent. In the course of his argument, Paul accuses Jews and Gentiles alike of serious transgressions. His conclusions would follow only "if the description given of Jews and Gentiles were empirically and globally true—that is, on the impossible condition that Gentiles and Jews were, *without exception,* guilty of the vices described" (99). Even if judged by the coherence of its own statements, Paul's argument fails. In the context of his denunciation of Jews, Paul contrasts Jews with *Gentiles who keep the law* and are approved by God (2:14-15, 26-27); but Gentiles, like Jews, are universally condemned in chapters 1 and 3. The attempts which have been made to reconcile these statements are implausible. The Gentiles praised are not "casual" observers of a few commands, for Rom. 2:27 credits them with observing (the totality of) the law; in any case, "Gentiles fulfilling just a few requirements of the law could hardly condemn the Jew (as v. 27 states), for undoubtedly he has fulfilled a few things as well!" (103). Nor will hypothetical but nonexistent Gentile observers of the law serve Paul's

purpose of condemning Jews! That Gentile *Christians* are meant is
simply impossible. Throughout the passage (beginning with 2:9) Paul
contrasts Jews with Gentiles, circumcised with uncircumcised; in this
context *ethnē* (2:14) must mean simply "non-Jews." And Paul would
never say that Christians do not know the law, that they keep the law
"by nature" rather than by the Spirit, that they "are a law to themselves"
(2:14). The contradiction must stand: "when Paul is not reflecting on
the situation of the Jews from a certain theological angle he does not
presuppose that it is impossible to fulfil the law" (106, emphasis removed). Paul's testimony to his own "blamelessness" according to the
law (Phil. 3:6) supports this conclusion. Arguments for universal sinfulness occur only when Paul wants to support the position that "the
death of Christ was a salvific act that was absolutely necessary for all
mankind" (108).

The inadequacy and, indeed, unfairness of Paul's argument become even more apparent when we compare his statements about non-
Christian behavior in Romans 7 with his claim about Christians in 8:4.
According to 7:14-25, those living "under the law" are "not able to do
any good at all" (110). Here Paul draws on Hellenistic traditions about
the discrepancy between human intentions and actions in order to support his thesis that those living "in the flesh" and "under the law" are
morally impotent and incapable of pleasing God. Christians, by way
of contrast, can and do fulfill God's requirements in the law (8:4; cf.
2:29; 13:8-10; Gal. 5:14-23). They have died to sin, so that sin will not
reign over them (Rom. 6:14); freedom from the law allows them to be
led by the Spirit, an existence characterized by the Spirit's fruit (Gal.
5:22-23) and by the possibility of overcoming the desires of the flesh
(v. 16). Yet such idealized pictures of Christian behavior stand in stark
contrast with the way Christians actually behaved in some of Paul's
own congregations. Paul "compares Christian life at its best (if not an
ideal picture of it) with Jewish life at its worst (if not a pure caricature). Paul thus uses different standards for Christians and Jews respectively" (117).

Theological theory has forced Paul into a corner. "His point of
departure is the conviction that the law *must not* be fulfilled outside of
the Christian community, for otherwise Christ would have died in vain.
Among Christians, on the other hand, the law *must* be fulfilled; otherwise Christ would be as weak as the law was (Rom. 8.3)" (118). The
actual conduct of Christians proves the "'doctrinaire' character" of
Paul's assertions (118).

4. Not even with regard to the origin of the law does Paul speak with one mind. Normally, to be sure, Paul assumes that the law is divine (Rom. 7:22; 8:7; 9:4; cf. 7:12; 1 Cor. 9:8-9). Even in Galatians, it is apparent that Paul "at bottom" (132) continues to link God with the giving of the law: it is still an expression of God's will, and God's intentions with the law are still a subject for discussion. Nonetheless, Gal. 3:19 leaves open the possibility that angels were the actual originators of the law, and the context shows that Paul was indeed "toying" with the idea (133). In 3:17 he uses the bald expression "the law . . . came" with no indication of a divine source, whereas the "covenant" is explicitly said to have been "ratified by God." In Paul's analogy, the law's relation to God's promise is paralleled with the additions which an outsider might want to make to the will of a testator. Finally, according to 3:20, a mediator is said to be unnecessary when God communicates with humanity, for God is "one"; that a mediator was involved at the giving of the law thus implies that "God was *not* involved" (130). Paul himself never returned to the idea. The suggestion that angels were the source of the law marks a momentary overreaction in a polemical context, revealing the "latent resentment" which Paul must have felt toward the Mosaic law (133).

Hopeless confusion results when Paul attempts to explain God's purpose with the law.

a. Was the law intended to give life to those who observe it? The answer, according to some passages in Paul, is clearly Yes. The argument of Romans 3 is that God provided the free gift of salvation as a remedy after men and women had sinned; at least theoretically the law could have been observed and led to life. Similarly, in Rom. 7:10 Paul insists that the law was intended to give life, though, as the sequel shows, it was too "weak" to carry out this function (8:3). But this line of thought is contradicted by other passages which exclude in principle the notion that the law could convey life (cf. especially Gal. 3:21). The first position provokes the question why God would bother giving a law too weak to serve its purpose; the second, why, if God did not intend to provide life through the law, did he give a law which promises life (Lev. 18:5; cf. Gal. 3:12; Rom. 10:5).

b. In discussing the role actually performed by the law, Paul consistently links it with sin. It is difficult, however, to be more precise. Rom. 3:20 suggests that the law brings an awareness of sin. This is straightforward enough, but is not Paul's characteristic emphasis. A second suggestion is that the law "defines sin as 'transgression,'"

making "sin a conscious and wilful activity" (141). This seems to be
the argument of Rom. 5:13 (cf. 4:15), where Paul says that only in the
presence of law is sin "counted." The statement is strange in the light
of 2:12-16 ("All who have sinned without the law will also perish
without the law" [v. 12]!) and in view of the actual fate of sinners between Adam and Moses: were Noah's contemporaries, for example,
not held accountable for their sins?

Paul's third suggestion is both his most characteristic and most
problematic response. The law actually "brings about sinning" (141).
This is probably the point in Gal. 3:19 (cf. also 1 Cor. 15:56) and is
certainly Paul's thesis in Rom. 5:20; 7:5, 7-13. At times, Paul suggests
that the presence of the law is actually "necessary to induce man to
sin" (142, referring to Rom. 7:7-11); elsewhere sin, already present (cf.
Rom. 5:20; 7:13-14), is merely the reason why the law cannot "effect
what it ought to have effected" (143). At the root of this proposal is
the everyday experience that "prohibitions sometimes incite people to
transgress them" (149). But Paul transforms a common experience into
a sweeping generalization with a "vigorous theological emphasis"
(149)—an emphasis, however, which does not do justice to the empirical reality of Judaism (did the law really promote sin among Jews?)
and which, if it is to be made at all, could be made equally well of
Paul's own apostolic commandments (do his commands, like the law's,
incite to sin?).

5. Finally, Räisänen discusses Paul's famous contrast between
"works of law" and faith in Christ. For Paul, the two are rival principles of salvation: the former is that pursued by Jews, whereas the latter represents a new soteriological system replacing the old one.

The Pauline texts have given rise to a desolate picture of Judaism
among Christian exegetes; but Räisänen follows Sanders in thinking
that much of the common caricature has no real basis in Paul's words.
For Paul, "the Jews err in imagining that they can be saved by keeping the law rather than by believing in Christ" (176); he does not speak
as though smugness, self-righteousness, and boasting in one's achievements were characteristic sins of Jews.

Nonetheless, Paul distorts Judaism by the very suggestion that
the law was its "way of salvation." Again, following Sanders, Räisänen
believes that salvation in Judaism was perceived "as *God's* act." God
had chosen his people and entered a covenant with them. "Salvation,
i.e. a share in the age to come, was based on God's faithfulness in his
covenant." The observance of Torah was, for the Jews, an expression

of "gratitude and obedience to its Giver" (178). Thus "the theme of *gratuity* with regard to salvation is conspicuously present in Judaism" (179), and Paul's contrast between salvation by grace in Christ and the Jewish path centered on the "works of the law" lacks foundation.

Nor is Paul himself consistent in propounding salvation by grace. Like the rabbis, he "speaks of right behaviour as *necessary* for salvation" (184), of judgment as according to *deeds*. Grievous sins lead to condemnation even for Christians. The pattern is precisely what we find in Judaism. Paul's doctrine of grace differs only from the Judaism of his own distorted representation.

At this point, a reader may be inclined to ask how a reasonably intelligent man like Paul could have managed to contradict himself on so many counts within the limits of time imposed by our common mortality. Räisänen proposes an explanation, but with some diffidence, noting that it is necessarily hypothetical, and warning that the analysis of the problems in the Pauline texts must not be thought to depend on the plausibility of his proposal as to their origin.

Räisänen shares with Kümmel and Stendahl the conviction that Paul's critique of the law was not spawned by frustrated attempts at keeping it. Still, Paul's repeated depictions of life under the law as bondage must have some basis in his personal experience. Perhaps before his conversion Paul's compliance with Torah was marked either by fear of punishment or by doubts as to the point in observing precepts for which no motive was supplied.

At his conversion, Paul came in contact with Hellenistic Christians who displayed a "liberal" attitude toward the Torah, were "*somewhat* relaxed" in their "attitude to the observance of the ritual Torah," and perhaps were inclined to neglect circumcision "as part of the missionary strategy" (254). No theological foundation had yet been established for such laxity; the new way of life flowed spontaneously from the experience of ecstatic gifts and the sense of eschatological fulfillment in the community. At first Paul, too, "simply adopted this 'liberal' position" (255): the tentative, inconsistent nature of his arguments in the later epistles forbids us to think that he had reflected on the issues for twenty years or more.

When, however, a reaction came, and Jewish Christians urged that Gentile believers submit to the law, Paul was forced to defend his position. "Over the years Paul had become internally alienated from the ritual aspects of the law," had "fully internalized the Gentile point of view and identified himself with it" (258). Now he was not able to "retrace his steps" (261). "He thus came upon several *ad hoc* arguments for the termination of the law . . . and its allegedly sin-engendering and sin-enhancing nature etc. The numerous problems and self-contradictions in his statements expose the overall theory as more or less artificial. It would seem that the difficulties can best be explained if the whole theory owes its origin to a polemical situation" (261-262).

In his conclusions, however, Räisänen goes further: Paul's real problem is that he is attempting to defend the indefensible position "that a *divine* institution has been *abolished* through what God has done in Christ" (264-265). Either Paul "must attribute to God an unsuccessful first attempt to carry through his will . . . or else he gets involved in the cynicism that God explicitly provides men with a law 'unto life' while knowing from the start that this instrument will not work" (265). In fact, "if something is truly divine, it is hardly capable of being abrogated! . . . The only reasonable way to cope with the Torah theologically . . . is to admit that it was *not* a direct divine revelation to Moses" (265-266). But that, of course, was an option which Paul did not consider.

Räisänen's monograph brings us forcibly back to the issue raised in the introduction to our study—the issue ignored by the epistle to Diognetus: how can Christians dispense with a law they believe to be divinely ordained? In a book which, perhaps more than any other, shows an awareness of earlier attempts to answer the question, Räisänen concludes that Paul has no satisfactory solution; indeed, in the terms in which it is posed, the question is simply unanswerable. Inevitably such conclusions will provoke further studies. Yet, if not the last word on the subject, Räisänen's work makes the task of those who would advance beyond it a daunting undertaking.

PART TWO

Chapter Seven

Matters of Definition

What the law was meant to do, what it does and cannot do: the debate on Paul's view of these matters is endless. Yet relatively little attention has been paid to what Paul meant by the "law." Repeatedly we are informed in an almost casual way that *nomos* in the epistles refers to "the Old Testament law." The ambiguity of the phrase goes apparently unnoticed, questions of definition are apparently thought resolved, and, with little further ado, discussion is launched into the more enticing topics mentioned above.

That haste makes waste is, however, one of those rare truths equally applicable to the diverse worlds of biblical scholarship and reality. In the course of a protracted yet inconclusive debate we constantly stumble upon reminders that our subject needs better definition. Too late we learn that *nomos* sometimes means not the Old Testament law itself, but its perversion, "legalism"; that Paul's notion of "law" may or may not have formed a contrast with the gospel as he saw it; that Paul's "law" is emphatically based on "works" for some, as emphatically based on "faith" for others, while still other scholars deny that he posed the question in these terms. Moreover, even the casual reader cannot but notice that the debate on the relation between Christian conduct and the "law" flounders in part because the term is used differently by the various antagonists. For the moment, then, we must postpone response to the principal questions raised in Part One of our study and confine our attention to matters of definition.

The notion is widely and ably represented in recent studies that, to Paul's mind, the law's basic demand is for faith, not "works." The

Judaism of Paul's day, by way of contrast, is believed by those hold-ing this view to be characterized by its interpretation of the law as demanding "works" and hence by its perversion of the law's true na-ture. Paul's polemic, it follows, is directed against this "legalistic" mis-understanding of God's law. Underlying the following discussion is my own conviction that such a reading of Paul not only misrepresents Judaism, but also distorts Paul's arguments as to its shortcomings and renders inaccessible both his doctrine of justification by faith and his understanding of Christian ethics. The latter issues will be dealt with in subsequent chapters; but the error or those scholars who dissociate the law's demands from deeds begins already with a failure to define adequately what Paul means by the "law" and its "works." To matters of definition, then, we turn our attention in this introductory chapter.

The argument proceeds by the following points.

1. Paul sometimes uses *nomos* to mean the Old Testament scriptures, or, more specifically, the Pentateuch. But according to his most frequent usage, "law" refers to the Sinaitic legislation.

2 Though Paul certainly believes that the Old Testament scriptures point to Christ and witness to the "righteousness of faith," he un-derstands the Sinaitic legislation as comprised of commandments which need "doing," and hence as based on "works" rather than "faith."

3. It is thus fully consistent with this usage to see "law" and "gospel" as standing in contrast with each other. This conclusion is sup-ported, not contradicted, by an examination of the Pauline phrase "*nomos* of faith" in Rom. 3:27 and of Paul's argument in Rom. 9:30-32.

4. Paul does not use *nomos* by itself to mean a *perversion* of the law held by Jews of his day. Indeed, the notion that the law demands works is a Pauline thesis, not a Jewish misunderstanding.

5. Paul's usage of *nomos* is fully in line with Hebrew usage of *torah*.

i. The Meaning of "Law"

We begin with the uncontroversial. Both Hebrew *torah* and Greek *nomos* had long been used to denote the first part of the sacred scrip-tures of the Jews (the Pentateuch), and Paul uses *nomos* ("law") in this sense as well. The sacred writings could then be said to be made up of "the law and the prophets" (Rom. 3:21; cf. Matt. 7:12; John 1:45; Acts 13:15, etc.). Moreover, when Paul speaks of a passage in Isaiah as coming from the "law" (1 Cor. 14:21, of Isa. 28:11-12), and provides a series of quotations from the Psalms and Isaiah (Rom. 3:10-18) as evidence of what "the law says" (v. 19), his extension of the term "law" to include the sacred scriptures as a whole can be paralleled in both Greek and Hebrew sources.[1] On this, at least, there is agreement.

In the same verse in which Paul refers to the testimony of "the law (= the Pentateuch) and the prophets," he claims that the "righteousness of God has been manifested *apart from law*" (Rom. 3:21). The wordplay is no doubt deliberate: God's righteousness is both "apart from law" and supported by "the law" (and the prophets). In the former case, a different meaning than the Pentateuch, or the sacred scriptures as a whole, is required. For its definition, we turn to Paul's usage of "law" in Romans 2, which provides the context for Paul's claim.

According to Romans 2, non-Jews do not "have" the law (v. 14), whereas Jews both have it (v. 20) and rely on it to provide instruction in God's will (vv. 17-18). So much could, of course, be said of the Jewish scriptures. But other verses show that "law" is used here in ways inappropriate of the sacred text as a whole. The "law" is something that can be "done" (cf. "doers *(poiētai)* of the law," v. 13), "obeyed" *(prassein,* v. 25; literally, "done"), or "kept" *(telein,* v. 27). Conversely, one may be a "transgressor" of the law *(parabatēs nomou,* vv. 25, 27; cf. v. 23). Such usages presuppose that the "law" in this narrower sense is made up of requirements which may be kept or broken by those subject to them. Again, in verse 14, the components of the law *(ta tou nomou)* are the object of "doing" *(poiein);* presumably they are equivalent to "the precepts of the law" *(ta dikaiōmata tou nomou)* which, according to verse 26, are to be "kept" *(phylassein).*[2] Similarly,

---

1. Cf. John 10:34; 15:25; Bacher, *Terminologie,* 197.

2. In a fine discussion of Pauline usage, Moo suggests that *nomos* in Rom. 2:26-27 (and in v. 15) may refer to "the will of God, without regard to any definite, historical form in which that will is expressed" (Moo, "Law," 80). But surely the "law" which is fulfilled in verse 27a is the same law of which the Jew, according to verse 27b, is a transgressor; and this, as the whole context shows clearly (cf. vss. 17-23), is the Mosaic code. It is indeed paradoxical that Paul could speak in verses 26-27 of the Mosaic law as being observed by *uncircumcised* Gentiles; but Rom. 8:4; 13:8-10; Gal. 5:14 present an analogous problem, so that this in itself is no reason to suggest that a different law must be meant. No doubt Paul is thinking in all these passages primarily of the law's moral demands. Cf. Grafe, *Lehre,* 9; Sanders, *Law,* 135, n. 45; Räisänen, *Law,* 23-28. That Paul uses *nomos* with and without the definite article with no shift in meaning has been demonstrated by Grafe, *Lehre,* 5-8 and Bläser, *Gesetz,* 1-23.

to ergon tou nomou (literally, "the work of the law," v. 15) is correctly paraphrased "what the law requires" (RSV). In fact, Paul supplies in this context several examples of the law's requirements: the prohibition of stealing, adultery, and idol-worship are among the demands with which Jews are familiar because they possess the "law," but which, according to Paul, they nonetheless transgress, thus "breaking the law" (vv. 20-23). The particular commands listed are, of course, all taken from the Decalogue (Exod. 20:1-17).

Evidence that, for Paul, the "law" is frequently used in this narrower sense of a particular collection of divine requirements is not confined to Romans 2. According to Gal. 6:13, Paul's opponents "do not themselves *keep (phylassein)* the law." If those who are circumcised are "bound to *keep (poiein;* literally, "do") the whole law" (5:3), then "the whole law" is obviously a collection of demands to be "done." Returning to Romans, we find that the introduction of the "law" at the time of Moses (Rom. 5:13-14; cf. Gal. 3:17) is what made "transgression" possible (Rom. 4:15): demands must be made before they can be broken! Rom. 7:7-12, a most revealing passage, uses "law" and "commandment" interchangeably: "I was once alive apart from the *law,* but when the *commandment* came, sin revived and I died. . . . So the *law* is holy, and the *commandment* is holy and just and good." Here the prohibition of coveting (v. 7; cf. Exod. 20:17) is given as one of the law's requirements. Other commandments from the Decalogue, together with the requirement of neighbor-love, are listed as demands of the "law" in Rom. 13:9-10.

All of these texts indicate that the "law" in Paul's writings frequently (indeed, most frequently) refers to the sum of specific divine requirements given to Israel through Moses.[3] This usage of the term must be carefully distinguished from instances in which the Pentateuch or the sacred scriptures as a whole are meant. That ambiguous cases—such as the notorious Rom. 3:31[4]—occur is not surprising, since the divine legislation ("law" in the narrower sense) is contained within the sacred scriptures ("law" in the broader sense). But such instances are few and do not justify the general claim that Paul normally means by *nomos* "the Old Testament Law (without distinguishing between the legal parts and the rest of the Pentateuch)."[5] The law which can be

3. Cf. Maurer, *Gesetzeslehre,* 82.
4. See the discussion of possible meanings for *nomos* here in Rhyne, *Faith,* 27, 31-32, 71-74.
5. Cranfield, "Law," 44.

"kept," "done," "fulfilled," or "transgressed" is clearly "the legal parts" of the Pentateuch. The law which was given four hundred and thirty years after the Abrahamic promise (Gal. 3:17, 19) was not the Pentateuch as a whole, but the Sinaitic legislation, the substance of the *nomothesia* ("the giving of the law") mentioned in Rom. 9:4.

The Sinaitic legislation was accompanied by sanctions, and Paul includes these when he speaks of the "law." Thus the law promises life to those who perform its commands (Rom. 10:5; Gal. 3:12; cf. Rom. 2:13, 25; 7:10), while it pronounces a curse on transgressors (Gal. 3:10, 13). When the law has been transgressed, its curse becomes operative, so that the law of God, like sin and death, can be personified as a hostile power from which people need deliverance (Gal. 4:5; cf. Rom. 5:20; 7:6). In a later chapter we will need to examine the passages in which Paul speaks of people being "under the law." Here we may anticipate that discussion by saying that the basic meaning of the phrase appears to be "bound by the demands of the Mosaic law code and subject to its sanctions."

ii. The Law and Works

That the Old Testament scriptures "[predict] the sufferings of Christ and the subsequent glory" (1 Pet. 1:11) was the universal conviction of the early Christians; but Paul's use of the witness of scripture goes much further. He finds the "righteousness of faith" itself to be announced in scripture (Rom. 3:21; Gal. 3:8), noting scripture's declaration that Abraham was justified by faith (Rom. 4:3-5), its pronouncement of blessing on those counted righteous "apart from works" (vv. 6-8), the promise it contains for Abraham and his offspring (v. 13; Gal. 3:16), and so on. In a discussion of Rom. 10:4,[6] Räisänen disputes (rightly, I believe) the view that *telos* in this verse means "goal"; he adds, however—what no one will dispute—that it is at least fully consistent with Pauline thought to say that Christ is the "goal" of the Old Testament "law" in this sense: the scriptures point to the Savior.

But, as we have seen, "law" in Paul most often means the Sinaitic legislation; and *it is not legitimate to apply what Paul says of the scriptures in general to the Sinaitic laws without further ado.*[7] It does not follow, for example, that because Paul thought the scriptures witness to faith, or contain the divine promise, he could not have con-

6. Räisänen, *Law,* 53-56; cf. Sanders, *Law,* 38-39.
7. Cf. Moo, "Law," 88.

trasted the Sinaitic legislation with faith and God's promise. Such a
stricture seems self-evident, but examples of its violation in the
scholarly literature could be supplied by the truckload. Two illustra-
tions must suffice.

Cranfield argues that Paul uses "law" in Gal. 3:15-25 to mean
something less than "the law in the fullness and wholeness of its true
character"; it is "the law as seen apart from Christ."[8] His reason for
suggesting that Paul must be speaking of a distorted form of the law
is that "Paul here distinguishes the promise from the law (verses 17
and 21), although the promise in question is contained in the Pentateuch."[9] Räisänen has shown that such an interpretation makes non-
sense of the passage: if Paul meant by the "law" in verses 17 and 19
what he is supposed to have meant by the "law" in verse 18, it would
follow that, four hundred and thirty years after the promise was given
to Abraham, the angels gave Israel a distorted form of the law on Mount
Sinai; and, in that case, one wonders when the true law arrived![10] But
Cranfield's error is apparent: certainly the Pentateuch (the "law" in a
broader sense) contains the "promise"; but Paul here means by "law"
the Sinaitic legislation (and hardly a distorted form of it). And in this
sense the Mosaic law and the Abrahamic promise are not only distinct,
but are even said to be mutually exclusive as ways for granting the "inheritance" (v. 18). We will return to this contrast below.

George Howard argues that Gal. 3:12 cannot mean what it is usually taken to mean, that the law does not rest on faith. "Is it proper to
ascribe such an argument to the apostle when it must have been clear
to all that faith was the very warp and woof of the law? The whole law
and the Prophets were fundamentally and primarily concerned with
faith in God and all that that implied, including loyalty, trust, commitment and absolute submission to his sovereignty."[11] Howard is of
course correct in insisting on the prominence of faith in *scripture* ("the
whole law and the Prophets"). But, as we have just seen, the "law" in
the context of Gal. 3:12 is not scripture as a whole, but the Sinaitic
legislation. And what Paul says of scripture must not be transferred automatically to "law" in this narrower sense.

To repeat: according to Paul's most frequent usage of *nomos*, the
term refers to the sum of specific divine requirements given to Israel

8. Cranfield, "Law," 63, followed by Schnabel, *Law,* 274.
9. Cranfield, "Law," 62.
10. Räisänen, *Law,* 43-44.
11. Howard, *Crisis,* 63.

through Moses. They are intended to be "done" *(poiein, prassein)* or "kept" *(phylassein, telein)*, though the placing of concrete demands of course makes possible the "transgression" *(parabasis)* of the law as well. With this in mind, we return to the passage at which Howard takes offense.

In Gal. 3:11, Paul finds it "evident that no man is justified before God by the law; for 'He who through faith is righteous shall live.'" One need not introduce subtleties where there are none: Paul is simply saying that since, according to the scriptures, righteousness comes "by faith," any alternative path is excluded. Thus it is "evident" that one cannot be "justified . . . by the law." "Faith" and the "law" are treated as alternative paths, only one of which the scripture allows.

Interestingly enough, however, Paul did not leave the argument at that. Apparently he sensed that his readers then (or anticipated that his readers now!) would not readily see "faith" and the "law" as alternatives which exclude each other. Such mutual exclusion is in any case the subject of his insistence in verse 12: though justification is based on faith (v. 11), the law is based on a different principle (v. 12): "But the law does not rest on faith, for 'He who does them shall live by them.'" To make his point, Paul introduces a quotation (actually a paraphrase) of Lev. 18:5 as illustrative of the nature of the "law." In the cited passage, the things to be "done" *(poiein)* are God's "statutes" and "ordinances." Paul is saying (or quoting Leviticus as saying) that the "law" promises life to those who "do" its statutes. He does not imply— and could hardly have meant to imply—that "doing" what the law commands is wrong. What he says is simply that a law which demands deeds is based on a different principle than that of faith.

The point is both obvious and crucial that what Paul means by "law" in this passage does not differ from his usage in the other passages we have considered: the "law" refers, not to the Pentateuch, but to the divine requirements imposed upon Israel at Mount Sinai and intended (need it be said?) to be "done." But whereas in other passages it was regarded as self-evident that the law was to be "done" or "kept," that it was not to be "transgressed," here the axiom is made the basis for a fundamental claim about the nature of the law: since the law requires "doing," it "does not rest on faith." Faith[12] and "doing" are con-

12. I.e., the "faith" of believers. This is contested by Howard ("End," 335; "Faith," 459-465; *Crisis,* 46-65) and Hays (*Faith,* 139-224) who, wary of reading the Reformation's contrast between human faith and works into Paul, suggest that *pistis* here refers to the divine "faithfulness." This interpretation is closely

trasted in a way which shows that, for Paul, in some contexts at least
they are exclusive alternatives. And the "law," the Mosaic legislation,
is aligned on the side of "doing."

Gal. 3:12 may reveal the basic Pauline contrast most clearly; yet
it is hardly an isolated statement. Romans 4 makes a similar point: "If

---

linked with their reading of the *pistis Christou* formulas (which are contrasted
with "works of the law" in Gal. 2:16; cf. v. 20; 3:22; Rom. 3:22, 26) as "the faithfulness of Christ" rather than (human) "faith in Christ." Such an understanding
makes good theological sense, but the evidence is clear that it is not what Paul
had in mind:

a. Gal. 3:11-12 together make up Paul's argument here: justification cannot be attained by the law since Habakkuk says it comes by faith ("he who through
faith is righteous shall live," v. 11) and "the law does not rest on faith" (v. 12).
"Faith" in verse 12 must have the same meaning as in verse 11. Yet when Paul
quotes Hab. 2:4 in Rom. 1:17, the verse is understood as referring to human faith
rather than divine faithfulness. Presumably the verse is understood similarly when
quoted in Gal. 3:11; hence human faith is discussed in verses 11-12.

b. The main argument raised in support of the view that the *pistis Christou* formulas mean "the faithfulness of Christ" (subjective genitive) is that Paul's
other uses of a genitive with *pistis* are subjective rather than objective. But this
should not occasion surprise, since the list of possible objects of one's faith becomes all but depleted when "Jesus" (Rom. 3:26), "Christ" (Gal. 2:16), "Jesus
Christ" (Gal. 2:16; 3:22; Rom. 3:22), and "the Son of God" (Gal. 2:20) have been
removed from it. "God" remains, to be sure; but in the context of Paul's mission
it is natural that faith in Christ receives an emphasis which is not required for faith
in God, and Mark 11:22 at least shows that "God" may stand as an objective genitive with *pistis* (cf. also Acts 3:16). Furthermore, Hultgren ("Formulation," 253)
correctly notes that *pistis* in Paul appears consistently with the article when used
with a subjective genitive, but does not have the article in the *pistis Christou*
formulas.

c. Paul's thesis that one is "*justified* by *faith (pistis)* in Christ, and *not by
works* of the law" (Gal. 2:16; cf. Rom. 3:20, 28) is surely being restated in Rom.
4:5, where the "faith" is explicitly human: "To one who does *not work* but *trusts*
(verb: *pisteuein*) him who *justifies* the ungodly, *his faith* is reckoned as righteousness." Similarly, it would be perverse to interpret "justified by faith" in
Rom. 3:28 differently than in 5:1; but the latter verse is drawing a conclusion
from 4:22-24, where righteousness is said to be "reckoned to *us who believe*" as
Abraham believed. Human faith is meant. Nor should the "faith" which justifies
according to 3:28 be different from the "faith" of the circumcised and the "faith"
of the uncircumcised, the basis of justification according to verse 30 (cf. the similar insistence on the faith required of Jews and Gentiles alike in 1:16; 4:11-12;
10:11-12). And the "righteousness based on faith" (10:6) is expressed in the message "Man believes with his heart and so is justified" (v. 10). These references
leave no doubt that when Paul speaks of "faith" as essential for justification, he
is thinking of human faith.

it is the adherents of the law who are to be the heirs, faith is null and the promise is void. . . . That is why it depends on faith, in order that the promise may rest on grace . . ." (Rom. 4:14, 16). Two alternatives are envisaged: Abraham's "heirs" are either the adherents of the law or those who have faith (cf. v. 13). That Paul would opt for the latter occasions no surprise, nor does it require comment here. Note again, however, how the "law" is contrasted with faith, God's promise, and grace. The latter are all excluded from a process where obedience to the law is a requisite.[13] The reasoning appears to be the same in each case.

1. We may begin with *"grace."* For many moderns, a contrast between "law" and "grace" is unthinkable.[14] But there can be little doubt that Paul intends such a contrast in Rom. 4:13-16 (cf. also 6:14-15; Gal. 5:4). The "inheritance" is given either "through the law" *(dia nomou)* or "through the righteousness of faith" *(dia dikaiosynēs pisteōs,* Rom. 4:13). And one of the reasons, according to Paul, that it had to "[depend] on faith" rather than the law was "in order that the promise may rest on grace" *(hina kata charin,* v. 16). Had the granting of the inheritance depended on law, it could not have been given *kata charin,* "by grace."

How are we to understand Paul's claim? The context supplies the answer. In Rom. 4:4, *kata charin* is contrasted with *kata opheilēma:* the one who works does not receive wages *kata charin,* "as a gift" (literally, "according to grace") but *kata opheilēma,* "as his due." Similarly, "grace" and "works" are opposed in 11:6: "If it is by grace, it is no longer on the basis of works; otherwise grace would no longer be grace" (cf. also 9:16). Clearly, if the "inheritance" is to be granted on the basis of divine "grace," then, on Paul's understanding, "works"— whether they are good or bad—simply cannot be a factor. But this, for Paul, means that the "law" is excluded, not because it is sinful to adhere to the law, but simply because law by its very nature demands "deeds" of its subjects, and thus is incompatible with "grace."

2. As in Gal. 3:12, so in Rom. 4:14, 16, *faith* is contrasted with the law. The point is the same. The "law" requires that its subjects

---

13. Cf. Räisänen, "Legalism," 72: "Grace, faith, promise, and Spirit are, according to [Paul], something diametrically opposed to the law. The entirety of Paul's argument is, indeed, little more than a constant reiteration of this axiom."

14. E.g., Davies, *Studies,* 95, 117-118; Moule, "Obligation," 394-397; on the Pauline opposition between law and grace, see van Dülmen, *Theologie,* 176, 190-191.

comply with its commands. And just as "faith" and "doing" are opposed in Gal. 3:12, so in Romans 4 faith *(pistis)* is the mark of one who *"does not work* but trusts *(pisteuein)"* God (Rom. 4:5; cf. also 9:32). In both passages "faith" indicates a reliance on God and an openness to his bounty which does not involve human "doing." Thus, for Paul, if adherence to the law (by "doing" its demands) is required, then "faith" (which "does not *work*") is ruled out.[15] "If it is the adherents of the law who are to be the heirs, faith is null. . . ." On the other hand, whereas a law which demands deeds stands in contrast with God's grace, a faith which merely accepts what God offers is its natural complement: "that is why it depends on faith, in order that the promise may rest on grace" (4:16).[16]

3. The law requires that its subjects comply with its commands. *God's promise* to Abraham, however, cannot be made conditional upon what humans do. Therefore, if adherence to the law is required of Abraham's descendants, "the promise is void" (Rom. 4:14). The same point is made in Gal. 3:18: "If the inheritance is by the law, it is no longer by promise." For Paul, God no longer acts solely to fulfill his own sovereign promise *if* his granting of the "inheritance" is dependent on human obedience to the demands of the law. Thus the law, which by its very nature demands "works," by that same nature excludes the promise, and *vice versa*. Since faith in God, however, does not involve human "work" (Rom. 4:5), it does not compromise, but properly complements, God's sovereign promise.[17]

With this in mind, it becomes clear as well why Paul can equate the righteousness which is "based on law" with one's "own" righteousness, and contrast both with the righteousness of faith (Phil. 3:9; Rom. 10:3, 5-6). According to Sanders,[18] the righteousness based on law is a pursuit open only to Jews (to whom, after all, the law was given). Hence, "their own" righteousness (Rom. 10:3) means the righteousness available only to Jews, not Gentiles. And the point of the contrast with the "righteousness of faith" is that the latter is open to Jews and Gentiles alike. But Paul's insistence in other passages that

15. Paul's view here is that the very nature of the law stands in contrast with faith; the contrast does not depend on the view that trying to keep the law leads to self-righteousness (so Gundry, "Grace," 13).

16. Cf. Bläser, *Gesetz*, 188-189.

17. Ibid., 149, 167-169, 188.

18. Sanders, *Law*, 36-45; cf. also Wright, "Paul," 82-83; Dunn, "Works," 530-531.

the law is based on "works" as opposed to faith suggests that the usual and, I think, simpler explanation of these texts is the correct one: the righteousness of the law is one's "own" righteousness in that it is the product of one's own righteous deeds in compliance with the law's commands. This is contrasted with a righteousness which comes "from God" as a gift (cf. Phil. 3:9).

In Phil. 3:3-6, Paul attempts to document his protestation that he can match and even surpass the claims of those Jews whose "confidence" is "in the flesh." Some of the privileges he lists were his by birth, others by the piety of his parents. But he emphasizes in particular the evidence of his own strict compliance with the demands of the law: "as to the law a Pharisee, as to zeal a persecutor of the church, as to righteousness under the law blameless." But all these "gains" he now finds worthless; knowing Christ far outweighs them (vv. 7-8). His desire is to be found in Christ, "not having a righteousness of my own, based on law, but that which is through faith in Christ, the righteousness from God that depends on faith" (v. 9).

Here Paul's "own" righteousness is that which is "based on law," and it is contrasted with the righteousness which "depends on faith." We have already noted in other passages how Paul contrasts the "law" and "faith," insisting that the former demands deeds of its subjects whereas the latter is the mark of those who "do not work." The same contrast is surely intended here. If the "righteousness of the law" is that which is expressed by human deeds in compliance with the law, and *Paul has documented his claim to that righteousness* (cf. "as to righteousness under the law," v. 6) *by citing his acts of zeal for the law,* then Paul's "own" righteousness is the result of his personal zeal in fulfilling the law's demands. Such righteousness is contrasted with the righteousness "from God that depends on faith"; that is, with a righteousness where (as in other Pauline statements about faith) one's own works are not a factor.

In Rom. 10:3, it is unbelieving Jews who "[seek] to establish their own" righteousness, a righteousness which is again contrasted with "the righteousness that comes from God." Without entering into the discussion of a much disputed passage at this point, we can simply note that verses 5-6 appear to carry the contrast further, now in terms of "the righteousness which is based on the law" and "the righteousness based on faith." Certainly Phil. 3:9 strongly supports the identification of "their own" righteousness with that which is "based on the law." But Rom. 10:5 in fact carries us back to the starting-point of this discussion: with a paraphrase of Lev. 18:5, it argues (as does Gal. 3:12) that the righteousness "based on the law" is one which requires "doing" *(poiein);* and this is then contrasted with the righteousness of faith (Rom. 10:6-13). Again, we find Paul using "law" of the divine commands, and contending that its righteousness is one of "works."

Finally, we should note that this understanding of "law" confirms the traditional understanding of the Pauline phrase *erga nomou* ("works of law") as "deeds demanded by the law" (Rom. 3:20, 28; Gal. 2:16; 3:2, 5, 10). The phrase is thus a close parallel to the Johannine *ta erga tou theou,* i.e., deeds demanded by God (John 6:28).[19] Similarly, the "works of the Lord" *(ta erga Kyriou)* in Jer. 31:10 (LXX) are tasks he assigns, and *ta erga autou* in Baruch 2:9 are explicitly said to be "works which he commanded us."

But this natural reading of the phrase, which coheres perfectly with Paul's well-attested view of the "law" as a sum of demands for deeds to be done, is repeatedly challenged in contemporary Pauline scholarship. And, repeatedly, the challenges are accompanied by attacks on the "Lutheran" contrasts of law and gospel, works and faith. Certainly it is the task of scholars to reexamine constantly the received wisdom of the past.[20] But in this instance the alternatives proposed do not commend themselves.

1. Lloyd Gaston suggests that the only natural way to understand the phrase, according to the rules of Greek grammar, is to take *nomou* as a subjective genitive: "works which the law does."[21] A number of passages in Paul refer to effects which the law is said to bring about: it brings the knowledge of sin (Rom. 3:20), deception (7:11), death (7:10-11), wrath (4:15), and so on. Thus Paul is claiming that the law itself cannot effect salvation in stating that "by works of the law shall no one be justified" (Gal. 2:16).

But the parallels cited above surely demonstrate that *erga nomou* can mean "works demanded by the law." And though Gaston's proposal is an interesting one, it does not explain why Paul supports his claim that one cannot be justified by "works of law" (Rom. 3:28) by showing that Abraham was not justified by "works" (4:2), where Abraham's own deeds are meant. Paul then proceeds with a reference to the "one who works" and receives his due (v. 4) and the "one who

19. Cf. John 6:29; also 4:34; 9:4. See von Wahlde, "Faith," 304-315.
20. Cf. the remarks of Kuss, "Nomos," 173-175.
21. Gaston, "Works," 39-46.

does not work" but believes (v. 5). If his argument has any relevance for the claim that justification is by faith, not by "works of law," then the latter must refer, not to the law's effects—the illustration of Abraham says nothing on that score—but to deeds done by humans.

2. A second counter to the traditional understanding is represented by James D. G. Dunn, and springs from what he calls "The New Perspective on Paul."[22] While conceding that "'works of the law' denote all that the law requires of the devout Jew,"[23] Dunn argues on the basis of the context in Galatians that "Paul intended his readers to think of *particular observances of the law like circumcision and the food laws*" and perhaps "special days and feasts" as well;[24] he has in mind such observances as "were widely regarded as characteristically and distinctively Jewish,"[25] the "identity markers" which demonstrated the Jew's commitment to the covenant. Paul is thus not attacking "'good works' in general, 'good works' in the sense disparaged by the heirs of Luther."[26] Nor is a supposed contrast between "faith" and "works" at stake, since Paul is only concerned to deny that the particular works which set Jews apart are "the necessary expression of faith."[27] Paul is attacking Jewish exclusivism, which had "taken over" and distorted the law.[28]

That Paul opposed Jewish exclusivism is not in question. Moreover, that the specific issues raised in Paul's letter to the Galatians are circumcision, food laws, and festival observances is also clear. But in rejecting "works of law," Paul moves the discussion onto another level.

a. Dunn criticizes Sanders for "taking the phrase 'works of the law' as though it was simply a fuller synonym for 'law.' So far as Sanders is concerned, 'no man shall be justified by works of law' is just the same as saying 'no man shall be justified by the law.'"[29] The criticism is a strange one, since a comparison of Gal. 2:16 with 2:21; 3:11; and 5:4 shows that Paul could indeed state his thesis either way with no

22. Dunn, "Perspective," 95-122; "Works," 523-542; cf. Sanders, *Law,* 46; Tyson, "Works," 430.
23. Dunn, "Works," 531.
24. Dunn, "Pespective," 107.
25. Ibid. (emphasis removed).
26. Ibid., 111.
27. Ibid., 115.
28. Ibid., 122.
29. Ibid., 117-118.

apparent shift in meaning. Synonymous usage seems apparent in Romans as well (compare "apart from law," 3:21, with "apart from works of law," v. 28). Indeed, Paul's thesis in Romans 3:20a that no one is justified by "works of the law" is supported in v. 20b by a statement of what the "law" *does* accomplish (it brings "knowledge of sin"). "Works of the law" and "law" are clearly coterminous here. And Paul's insistence in Romans 3:31 that he does not "overthrow the law" is intended to counter an objection to his claim that justification takes place "apart from works of law" (3:28).[30] That Paul could use "law" and "works of law" interchangeably makes it highly unlikely that, with the latter phrase, he has in mind only a few specific statutes or, indeed, a distortion of the law.

b. We may concede that the letter to the Galatians represents Paul's response to the demand that his Gentile converts be circumcised. But it is equally clear that Paul placed the particular issue in the broader context of a discussion of the origin, nature, and function of the Mosaic law as a whole. The point requires no elaboration with regard to Galatians 3 and 4: the law which was given four hundred and thirty years after Abraham (3:17), which served as a "custodian until Christ came" (v. 24), which cannot justify because it "does not rest on faith" (v. 12)—this law cannot be restricted to the three or four issues explicitly mentioned in Galatians. But the same can be said of 2:16-21. Paul claims that "through the law" he "died to the law" (v. 19)—neither a fragment nor a perversion of the Mosaic law can be meant in both phrases. And *since Paul's thesis in Gal. 2:21; 3:11-12, 15-18, 21-22; and 4:21-25 is that the nature of the law is such that it cannot justify, and that, according to 3:19, 23-24, its function is more limited, there is no reason to restrict the similar statement about the "works of the law" to a few of the law's demands, or to a distortion of its purpose.*

c. Nor do the occurrences of the phrase in Romans (3:20, 28) support Dunn's contentions. Dunn claims that, since Paul has just refuted "Jewish presumption in their favoured status as the people of the law, the 'works of the law' must be a shorthand way of referring to that in which the typical Jew placed his confidence, the law-observance which documented his membership of the covenant."[31] But the only commandments of the law mentioned by Paul before his reference to "works of the law" in Rom. 3:20 are taken from the Decalogue (2:21-22), and do not refer to Jewish "identity markers." Circumcision has

30. Cf. Rhyne, *Faith,* 59.
31. Dunn, "Works," 528.

been touched upon, but it is treated (rather curiously) as though it were not a part of the law to be observed (2:26-27); in this context at least it can hardly serve as a prime referent of the phrase "works of the law" in 3:20. The focus of Paul's statements about the law is not Jewish presumption based on observance of some of its statutes (here Jews are credited with no such observance), but Jewish transgressions of its demands; and it is these transgressions which lead to their condemnation (2:12, 25, 27). The "works of the law" which do not justify are the demands of the law that are not met, not those observed for the wrong reasons by Jews.

d. That Paul supports his rejection of the "works of the law" in Rom. 3:20, 28 by showing that Abraham was justified by faith, not works (4:1-5), is positively fatal to Dunn's proposal, as it was to that of Gaston. For the "works" by which Abraham could conceivably have been justified, and of which he might have boasted (4:2), were certainly not observances of the peculiarly Jewish parts of the Mosaic code. Paul is here demonstrating that the broad category of "works" cannot be a factor in salvation in order to exclude the subcategory, "works of law." Not particular works which set Jews apart, but works in general—anything "done" that might deserve a recompense (*misthos,* 4:4) or justify pride (*kauchēma,* v. 2)—are meant,[32] and that in contrast with the "faith" of one who does not work" but benefits by divine grace without any consideration of personal merit.[33] Since the issue ("works of law" *versus* "faith in Jesus Christ") permits restatement in terms of a general distinction between "works" and "faith," the point of the attack cannot be limited to statutes in the law which served as Jewish "identity markers."

3. Finally, a number of scholars, convinced that Paul could not have said that the law in any proper sense "rests on works," contend that the phrase "works of law" denotes deeds which spring from a Jewish distortion of the law into legalism. "Works of law" are then "deeds of obedience to formal statutes done in the legalistic spirit, with the expectation of thereby meriting and securing divine approval and award, such obedience, in other words, as the legalists rendered to the law of the O.T. as expanded and interpreted by them."[34] The phrase thus takes on a decidedly negative tone: "works of law" are themselves

32. Cf. Moo, "Law," 97.
33. We may compare Rom. 9:11-12; 11:6, where Paul also excludes "works," but where law observance is not in view.
34. Burton, *Galatians,* 120; cf. Moule, "Obligation," 393.

sinful. Fuller thinks they amount to "the sin of bribing God,"[35] and thus represent "a gross rebellion against the law, instead of compliance with it."[36]

But there is no need to be so negative.[37]

a. As we noted above, Paul uses "works of law" and "law" interchangeably. He would not have done so if "works of law" were tantamount to the law's perversion. And—to repeat again—*since Paul's thesis throughout Galatians is that the nature of the Mosaic law is such that it cannot justify, that the law's function is a more limited one, there is no reason to claim that the parallel statements about the "works of the law" in Gal. 2:16 (= Rom. 3:20, 28) concern a perversion of the law.*

b. The contrast between "works of law" and "faith in Jesus Christ" is developed in Rom. 4:1-6 in terms simply of "faith" and "works."[38] And there it is clear that the "works" are not themselves sinful; rather the distinction is drawn between one who believes but does not work and one who works and receives "his wages . . . as his due" (vv. 4-5). Similarly, in Romans 9:11-12, Paul insists that God's election depends on his call, not on human works, *whether those deeds are "good or bad."* Paul's point is that human works—good or bad—are not a factor in salvation, not that "works" in themselves are sinful.

c. Paul's usage of "work(s)" *(ergon/erga)* shows that the term for him is neutral, applicable to good as well as evil deeds (Rom. 2:6-7; 9:11-12; 13:3; 15:18; 1 Cor. 3:13-15; 15:58; etc.). Nothing in his normal usage prepares us for the claim that the connotations of "works of law" are pejorative.

d. Paul's declaration in Rom. 3:20 that "no human being will be justified in his sight by works of the law" concludes an argument which began at 1:18. But one searches the argument in vain for the notion that Jewish obedience to the law's statutes is marked by a "legalistic spirit." Paul contends rather that people will be judged *according to their "works"* (2:6; the term is neutral, cf. vv. 7-8), that Jews will need to be "doers" of the law, not simply hearers, if they are to be justified

35. Fuller, "Works," 33.

36. Fuller, *Gospel,* 95.

37. Cf. already Grafe, *Lehre,* 10, where the idea that "works of law" are themselves imperfect is rejected. In Grafe's day, however, the suggestion countered was that the phrase denoted a purely external, formal righteousness lacking a true (inner) morality. Cf. also Bläser, *Gesetz,* 96-97.

38. For the following, cf. Moo, "Law," 95-96.

(v. 13), that in fact they have transgressed the law (vv. 17-27) and thus, like Gentiles, find themselves "under the power of sin" (3:9). In the conclusion to this argument, "works of the law" can only be understood positively. That such works do not lead to justification follows simply from Paul's judgment that Jews do not do them.[39]

e. The point of Gal. 3:10 is no different. Those who are "of the works of the law" (so, literally, *ex ergōn nomou*) are the same as those "under the law" in 4:5. Of the former we are told that they are under a curse from which Christ redeems (3:10, 13); of the latter we are told that Christ came to redeem them (4:4-5). Since the redemption is for all those born under the law, the dilemma is equally universal. The Jew's personal understanding, interpretation, or distortion of the law does not enter the picture.[40] The point of Gal. 3:10 is not what happens to those who distort the law, but the effect of the law on all those within its sphere: it brings a curse, not life (cf. the similar point in Rom. 4:15). Thus to be "of the works of the law," as to be "under the law," means that one is subject both to the law's demands for works and to its sanctions.[41]

Why are all those subject to the demands of the law under its curse? In Gal. 3:10b Paul supplies an explanation: the curse strikes "every one who does not abide by all things written in the book of the law, and do them." In other words, transgression of the law draws upon the transgressor the law's condemnation—a point Paul makes abundantly clear elsewhere (Rom. 2:12, 27; 4:15; 5:13, etc.).[42] As in Rom. 3:20, it is failure to do the "works of the law" that is condemned, not the works themselves.

We are thus left with the view that the "works of law" are the deeds demanded by the Sinaitic law code, a "law" which "rests" on "works."

---

39. Rightly, Cranfield, *Romans,* 198. Cf. also Gutbrod, *"nomos,"* 1072: "Nevertheless, Paul says of the Law that it cannot give life, Gl. 3:21. This is because no one keeps it, not because Paul regards the works of the Law as sin. When Gentiles do by nature the works of the Law, these are acknowledged by Paul to be good works, R. 2:14."

40. The RSV rendering of 3:10 ("all who rely on works of the law") is thus misleading.

41. Similarly *tō ek tou nomou* in Rom. 4:16 means "the one who is subject to the law," "the Jew."

42. Cf. Räisänen, *Law,* 94-96, where the weaknesses of other readings of Gal. 3:10b are shown.

iii. The Law and Faith

As we noted in Chapter 1, Luther used "law" to refer to "whatever is not grace." All of scripture could then be divided between the categories of "law" and "gospel." Pauline usage, as we have defined it, does not generalize in this way: Paul's "law" does not, for example, include the demands of Jesus! Nonetheless, Luther has captured an essential aspect of Pauline thought. Though Paul's "law" refers specifically to the Mosaic code, he does view it as demand, and distinguish it from grace and the path of faith. To this extent, the contrast between "law" and "gospel," though never explicit in the epistles, does not distort Paul's point.

But such a contrast has come under increasing attack in recent literature. In part, the point of the attack is the simple reminder that the gospel, too, is accompanied by obligations[43]—a point which neither Paul nor Luther would have denied.[44] In part, the attack is theologically motivated by a concern for the unity of scripture,[45] or by a fear that the contrast between law and gospel implies "that the law was an unsuccessful first attempt on God's part at dealing with man's unhappy state, which had to be followed later by a second (more successful) attempt (a view which is theologically grotesque, for the God of the unsuccessful first attempt is hardly a God to be taken seriously)."[46] If, however, we confine our attention here to the basis of the attack in Pauline exegesis, two areas need consideration. Positively, it is claimed that in two crucial texts (Rom. 3:27 and 9:30-32)[47] Paul indicates that the law, properly understood, demands faith, and that the law's nature is distorted when it is seen as demanding "works." Negatively, it is claimed that *nomos* in a number of Pauline texts (particularly those

43. E.g. Barth, "Gospel," 3-27; Moule, "Obligation," 389-406.

44. We will discuss Pauline ethics in Chapter 10 below.

45. I.e., the unity of scripture is thought to be threatened when law and gospel are opposed. Here the distinction between "law" in the sense of the sacred (Old Testament) scriptures and "law" as the Sinaitic legislation is important: the claim that the Sinaitic code demands deeds does not (for Paul at least) compromise the witness of the scriptures to the righteousness of faith.

46. Cranfield, "Law," 68. Comments on this point will be offered at the end of section iv below.

47. From Rom. 3:31 we may deduce only that, according to Paul, the *true* nature and purpose of the law come to light when it is viewed from the perspective of justification by faith. A more specific definition of the law's nature and purpose can only be derived from other texts.

where it is linked with "works") means not "law," but "legalism." We will take up the positive challenge first.

1. After showing that God's "righteousness" is available "through faith in Jesus Christ" (Rom. 3:21-26), Paul continues: "Then what becomes of our boasting? It is excluded. On what principle? On the principle of works? No, but on the principle of faith." So, at least, the RSV renders Romans 3:27. But the Greek word translated "principle" is *nomos*, and, though "principle" is certainly a possible meaning for the term in other contexts, many recent scholars have argued that the term must refer here, as it does in the preceding verses, to the law of Moses. Paul is thought to be saying that the law of Moses, correctly understood, is a "law of faith," and as such it excludes the boasting which accompanies its perversion into a "law of works."

The current debate takes as its starting-point an article by Friedrich from 1954.[48] Scholars before that time who thought Paul's "law of faith" referred to the law of Moses were few and far between, while those who, since 1954, have espoused that view have appealed almost inevitably to Friedrich's argumentation. Friedrich pointed out that the phrase "law of faith" was not introduced by Paul in a casual, unreflective way. After all, it is preceded by the question: "By what sort of *law* (is boasting excluded)?" Paul has thus deliberately prepared for an answer using *law (nomos)*. And, though *nomos* may mean "rule," "principle," or "order" elsewhere (e.g., Rom. 7:21), it is unlikely to have that meaning in Rom. 3:27, since in the whole section from 3:19-31, the word consistently refers to the Mosaic law.

In Friedrich's view, Rom. 3:21 provides the key to the interpretation of 3:27. In the earlier verse, Paul speaks of the law in two ways: righteousness appears apart from the law, yet it is witnessed to by the law. "Apart from law" means, clearly, apart form the law's works (cf. v. 20), while the righteousness to which the law bears witness is that "through faith in Jesus Christ" (v. 22). Thus the law is seen from two perspectives: on the one hand, it demands deeds; on the other, it witnesses to faith. Similarly, in verse 27, Paul is speaking of the dual nature of the Mosaic law. Boasting is made impossible not by the Mosaic law in its role of demanding works, but by the Mosaic law as a witness to faith. Rom. 3:27-28 deliberately echoes verses 21-22: "apart from works of law" (v. 28) parallels "apart from law" (v. 21), the "law of faith" (v. 27) reminds us of the witness of the law (v. 21), and "by faith"

48. Friedrich, "Gesetz," 401-417.

(v. 28) parallels "through faith" (v. 22). It is this role of the law as a witness to faith which Paul claims to establish in verse 31 and which he elaborates in chapter 4. There, however, he drops the term "law of faith," using as its equivalent the word "promise."

In an article from 1973,[49] E. Lohse broadly accepted Friedrich's understanding of Rom. 3:27: the "law of faith" is the Old Testament law, which provides testimony to faith in a number of crucial texts. But whereas Friedrich finds in 3:27 a dual function of the law, and assumes the legitimacy of both aspects, for Lohse the law becomes a sum of demands ("law of works") only in its Jewish misinterpretation. God's law properly understood is a witness to the liberating promise which is experienced by those who show the faith of Abraham. This becomes, for Lohse's Paul, the valid and only true meaning of the Mosaic law.

The view that Paul here refers to the Mosaic law as a "law of faith" as opposed to works has become, almost "overnight,"[50] crucial to a number of presentations of Paul's understanding of the law.[51] But Räisänen has argued forcibly and, I believe, decisively against it.[52]

a. In a recent article,[53] Räisänen has amply demonstrated that Greek usage of *nomos* offers many parallels to a broader understanding of the term ("principle," "rule," "order"), so that such a rendering in Rom. 3:27 (and in 8:2) cannot be excluded on lexical grounds. In a sense, this task was unnecessary from the start, since few would contest that, at least in 7:21, *nomos* must mean something like "principle" ("a *nomos* that when I want to do right, evil lies close at hand"). Nonetheless, the collection of evidence is welcome and should lay to rest any suspicion that the use of *nomos* to mean "principle" in Rom. 3:27 is an unnatural rendering of the Greek.

b. Friedrich is correct in saying that Paul's usage of the phrase "law of faith" is deliberate. On the other hand, the deliberate use of *nomos* does not in itself prove that we are dealing with a statement about the Mosaic law, since the word could have been chosen deliberately but polemically as a contrast to the "law of works."

c. The fact that *nomos* in the immediate context does refer to the

49. Lohse, *"nomos,"* 279-287.
50. Räisänen, "Gesetz," 105.
51. This includes the presentation of Hübner, summarized above in section ii of Chapter 6. For further bibliography, see Räisänen, "Gesetz," 101-117.
52. Räisänen, "Gesetz," 101-117.
53. Idem., *"Nomos,"* 131-154.

Mosaic law is a serious consideration, but hardly decisive, since Paul uses the word with other meanings elsewhere, and even plays on different meanings in 7:21-25.

d. The most important argument raised by Friedrich is the parallel between 3:21-22 and 27-28. Both refer to justification which is by "faith" and "apart from (works of the) law." The parallel between the "witness" of "the law and the prophets" (v. 21) and the "law of faith" (v. 27) is, however, less clear, and certainly not compelling enough to determine the sense of the latter phrase.

e. If Rom. 3:27 is meant as a programmatic statement about the dual nature of the law, and "law of faith" has been deliberately chosen to establish the positive aspect of the law's function, then the sequel is hard to explain. The crucial phrase "law of faith" is not repeated, verse 31 speaks of the law as a unity, and chapter 4 in fact speaks of the law as something negative (4:13-15). Friedrich suggests that "promise" is introduced in Romans 4 as the equivalent of the "law of faith" from 3:27. But are we really to assume that Paul thought his readers would identify the two with the Mosaic law when he explicitly contrasts the "promise" with the "law" in 4:13-14?

The context provides an equally clear refutation of Lohse's interpretation of Rom. 3:27, namely, that the law, properly understood, is a "law of faith," and that it becomes a "law of works" only when it has been distorted by Jews. Throughout the passage (3:20-31) Paul uses "works of law" and "law" interchangeably. The climax of an argument which has occupied the better part of three chapters (1:18–3:20) is reached in the declaration that righteousness has been rewarded "apart from law"—by faith (3:21-22). Chapter 4 continues the contrast between law and faith, and rejects the claim that righteousness can come through the law by showing that Abraham was justified not by works, but by faith. In such a context, 3:27 can hardly be invoked to overthrow Paul's repeated emphasis that the law requires works—and is thus distinct from faith.

The context thus tells against the view that Rom. 3:27 is a programmatic statement about the nature of the Mosaic law. Indeed, the verse itself is introduced, not as a claim about the law, but as a statement about boasting. In what follows, too, it is clear that Paul's focus is on the "boasting" of the Jews. Nothing suggests that he is attempting to introduce—in the latter half of the verse—an important distinction about the nature of the law which then drops out of view in verse 28 and in the negative discussion of the law in chapter 4.

f. Still more decisive, however, is the fact that the "law of faith" in 3:27 is *the effective means by which boasting is once and for all excluded*. It will not do to paraphrase the verse as though it said that the law's true meaning is revealed by faith. The text tells us not what has happened to the law, but what the "law of faith" itself has accomplished. Since a single event is referred to, surely the new act of God's salvation in Christ, which Paul has just finished expounding in 3:21-26, is what is meant. This act of salvation, creating the new "order of faith," is what excludes boasting.

Understood thus, Rom. 3:28 follows 3:27 naturally, whereas if the earlier verse is speaking of the Mosaic law as a "law of faith," the claim is no sooner made than it is dropped. Certainly the *gar* ("for") of verse 28 leads us to expect a further reference to the two *nomoi* of verse 27—and that, in fact, is what we find. The "law of works" which is said not to exclude boasting in verse 27 is picked up in the reference to the "works of law" which are said not to justify in verse 28. The Mosaic code is intended. The "principle" or "order" of faith which is mentioned in verse 27 is spelled out in the thesis of verse 28, "a man is justified by faith." This latter righteousness is indeed witnessed to by "the law and the prophets" (i.e., the sacred scriptures, v. 21); but the "law" in the narrower sense, the Sinaitic legislation, is spoken of, here as elsewhere, as a "law of works."

2. And what of Rom. 9:30-32? Here Paul says that Gentiles have "attained" righteousness without even "pursuing" it, "that is, righteousness through faith." Israel, on the other hand, was actively engaged in pursuing the "law of righteousness" (so, literally, *nomon dikaiosynēs*) but did not "attain to the law" (so, literally, *eis nomon ouk ephthasen*). The reason given is that they did not carry on their pursuit (the verb *diōkein* must be understood in v. 32) "by faith, but as though (they could reach that goal, the law of righteousness) by works" (so we may fill out Paul's elliptical language). Does this not indicate that Israel had distorted the law's true nature in pursuing it by works rather than faith? Does it not imply that the law, properly understood, is based on faith?

a. It is important that we define the "law" of which Paul is speaking. Cranfield, here as elsewhere, does not distinguish between the Old Testament scriptures ("law" in a broad sense) and the Sinaitic legislation, but seems to think the former is intended. At any rate, Paul's reference to the "law of righteousness" is interpreted of the law's (= scripture's) witness to the righteousness of faith; Rom. 3:21-22 and 10:6-13 are cited as support.[54] For Badenas, too, *"nomos* in this context (9.31; 10.4, 5) . . . refers to the general concept of 'Torah' as it was understood in Paul's contemporary Judaism, and designates the OT, perhaps mainly in its revelatory aspects."[55]

But the Old Testament scriptures, and especially their "revelatory aspects," make a strange object for verbs of pursuing *(diōkein)* and attaining *(phthanein,* 9:31). The verse reads more naturally if the demands of the Mosaic legislation are meant. No doubt, with a little good will, a satisfactory sense for Paul's "law of righteousness" can be devised if the Old Testament scriptures are meant (e.g., "the Torah viewed from the perspective of the *dikaiosynē* it promises, aims at, or bears witness to"[56]). But since the "righteousness which is based on the law" in 10:5 is that which is required by the Mosaic code (note the quotation from Lev. 18:5), the "law of righteousness" in 9:31 is again more naturally understood as the Mosaic law code which demands righteousness. The appropriateness of the comparison with 10:5 is confirmed by the fact that Israel's pursuit of the "law of righteousness" in 9:31 is set against the "righteousness through faith" of verse 30, just as the "righteousness which is based on the law" in 10:5 is contrasted with the "righteousness based on faith" in verses 6-13 (see the discussion below). Finally, we should note the fact that Paul elsewhere speaks of Jewish zeal—indeed, his own former zeal—not for the Old Testament scriptures as such, but for meeting the standards of the Mosaic law code (Phil. 3:6, 9; Rom. 10:3, 5). The law pursued by Israel in Rom. 9:31, then, is the Mosaic legislation.

b. But to say that the Mosaic code is based on faith, not works, is simply incompatible with what Paul says elsewhere. In Phil. 3:6, 9 he contrasts the righteousness which is "by" or "of" the law *(en nomō; ek nomou)* with that of faith; there is no hint that the former designations refer to a *distortion* of the law. He could not be more explicit than he is in Gal. 3:12 in stating that the "law does not rest on faith"; he uses that claim as a crucial step in his argument that justification must be by faith, not by law, and supports it with a quotation from scripture. Nor does the evidence in Romans suggest that, at the time of its writing, Paul has changed his mind. Here, too, the righteousness of faith is emphatically set in contrast with the law (cf. Rom. 3:21-22: "But

54. Cranfield, *Romans,* 508.
55. Badenas, *End,* 143.
56. Ibid., 104.

now the righteousness of God has been manifested *apart from law,* . . . the righteousness of God through faith in Jesus Christ"; 4:13: "The promise to Abraham and his descendants . . . did not come through the law but through the righteousness of faith").

Most importantly, the righteousness of law and that of faith are contrasted in Rom. 10:5-6, in the immediate context of 9:30-32. It has, to be sure, been argued that Paul identifies rather than contrasts the two phrases here.[57] But this requires us to believe:

i. that, whereas he quotes Lev. 18:5, without elaborating on it, as a self-evident demonstration that "the law does *not* rest on faith" in Gal. 3:12, he quotes the same verse, without elaboration, as a self-evident demonstration that the law *does* rest on faith in Rom. 10:5;

ii. that, whereas Paul contrasts the righteousness of the law and that of faith in Phil. 3:9, he identifies them here;

iii. that, whereas in Phil. 3:9, Paul identifies his own righteousness with that which is based on law, here he distinguishes between Israel's own righteousness (Rom. 10:3) and the righteousness which is based on the law (v. 5); and

iv. that, whereas in Romans itself the righteousness of faith is emphatically set in contrast with law, Paul here equates it with the law's righteousness.

The faith which believes all these anomalies is certainly of the mountain-moving variety!

c. We return, then, to Rom. 9:30-32, aware that Paul in the immediate context, as well as elsewhere in his writings, contrasts the law's righteousness with that of faith. Are we to believe that he reverses himself here? Verses 31 and 32 make the following points:

i. Israel pursues a "law of righteousness."

ii. Israel did not attain to this law.

iii. The reason for the failure is that Israel pursued its goal, not by faith, but as though it could be attained by works.

Each of these three statements is consistent with Pauline arguments elsewhere. None of them implies that the law itself is based on faith rather than works.

i. That the Sinaitic law-code requires righteousness, and that Israel strives to attain that righteousness, is (as we have seen) self-evident to Paul.

ii. It is equally self-evident (from the perspective of Christian

57. Badenas, *End,* 118-125; Fuller, *Gospel,* 66-88; Howard, "End," 336-337.

faith) that Israel did not attain to the righteousness required by the law. Paul here simply restates the thesis of Rom. 3:20: "no human being will be justified in his sight by works of the law." In Romans 2–3, the argument was that, though the law promises righteousness and life to those who "do" its commands (2:13, 25), Jews have transgressed them, and so cannot be justified by the "works of the law"; they simply have not attained that goal. The point of 9:31 seems identical. Though the righteousness of the law is indeed a matter of works, and life is promised to those who perform the works (10:5 restates the principle of 2:13), those required to perform the works do not achieve that goal— they do not "attain to the law (of righteousness)."

iii. Jewish failure to "attain to the law (of righteousness)" can in fact be explained at two stages. In the first place, it is transgressions of the law which prevent those who are subject to the law from obtaining the life which the law promises. This is Paul's point in Romans 1–3; moreover, the transgressions and consequent judgment to which the law leads are touched upon in chapter 5 and developed at length in chapter 7. If Paul does not repeat in 9:32 what he has said in chapters 1–3; 5; and 7, and in 8:3, the reason, presumably, is that he feels no need "to say everything every time he opens his mouth,"[58] not that he has changed his mind about human transgressions. Since, however, life under the law inevitably leads (by way of transgressions) to death, the righteousness and life which the law promises are in fact only obtainable by faith apart from the law and its "works" (3:20-22); on a second level, then, the Jewish failure to arrive at the goal to which the law pointed can be ascribed to their persistence in the path of works rather than submitting to the righteousness based on faith; for, paradoxically, the *goal of the law* can only be attained *apart from the law,* by faith. The desired faith (Paul goes on to say) actually proves an offense to Israel (9:32b-33).

Paul's point here may be compared with his statements about the law's fulfillment (Rom. 8:4; 13:8-10; Gal. 5:14). In Paul's view, those "under the law" do not fulfill it. The law is even said to be too "weak" to bring about its own fulfillment (Rom. 8:3-4). Paradoxically, however, those who are "not under the law" but are "led by the Spirit" (Gal. 5:18) produce righteousness which the law cannot condemn (vv. 22-23), righteousness which in fact amounts to the law's "fulfillment" (Rom. 8:4; Gal. 5:14). Just as the law is "fulfilled" by those free from the law who live by the Spirit, so, in Rom. 9:30-32, the law can only

58. Deidun, Review, 48.

be "attained" by those who do not pursue the law, but live by faith. But this does not contradict Paul's claim that the law itself rests on works, not faith.

In the verses that follow, Paul faults the Jews with failing to submit to the righteousness of God as they seek to "establish their own" righteousness (Rom. 10:3). And, as we have seen, their "own" righteousness is equivalent to that of the law (10:5; cf. Phil. 3:9). The curious result, according to both Phil. 3:9 and Rom. 10:3-5, is that the righteousness of God's law is opposed to that of God. But Rom. 10:4 is intended to resolve the conundrum: "Christ is the end of the law, that every one who has faith may be justified." God's law promised righteousness to those who did its commands (10:5; cf. 2:13, 25), though righteousness was in fact never achieved that way.[59] With Christ, the righteousness of faith has "now" been "manifested" (Rom. 3:21), "faith" has "come" (Gal. 3:23), and the righteousness of the law has once for all been set aside.[60] Indeed, the Sinaitic economy, as Paul indicates elsewhere, was *temporary by design* (2 Cor. 3:7, 11; Gal. 3:23-25; 4:1-5). Its role was negative and preparatory: it "consigned all things to sin," acting as a "custodian until Christ came" (Gal. 3:23-24); it "increased" sin, so that grace might abound (Rom. 5:20); it was, for all its glory, a "dispensation of death" and of "condemnation" (2 Cor. 3:7, 9). But now that the "new covenant" has come (v. 6), the *"old covenant"* (v. 14) (in the nature of the case!) has come to its end. To pursue the righteousness of God's law after God has revealed its end in Christ (Rom. 10:4) is to defy the righteousness of God (v. 3).

iv. The Law and Legalism

Those who deny that Paul views the law as based on works frequently claim that he uses the term *nomos* at times for God's law itself but at

---

59. Of course Paul did not believe that God has condemned all those who lived "under law" before Christ; on the contrary, God had "passed over" sins committed before the revelation of his righteousness in Christ (Rom. 3:25). The point remains, however, that the law itself justifies no one.

60. Cf. Räisänen, *Law,* 54, on Rom. 10:4: "Bearing in mind that v. 5 is connected with an explanatory *gar* to the previous verse, the nomos in v. 4 must be associated with the righteousness from the law disqualified in v. 5. It must then belong together with the 'own' righteousness which the Jews try to establish (v. 3). With regard to such a law Christ can only be its end!" Cf. also Hahn, "Gesetzesverständnis," 50.

other times for its perversion into "legalism."[61] The attractiveness of the proposal is not hard to explain: it allows scholars to attribute to "legalism" any statement in Paul about the law which resists assimilation to a preferred reconstruction of his views. If, for example, one is convinced that the "law" has not been done away, one can always suggest that Rom. 10:4 refers to the "end" of the "misused" law,[62] or that 7:4 may mean that Christians have died to the "legalistic misunderstanding and misuse of the law."[63] That Christians are not "under law" (6:14) can be explained by saying that they have been freed from the illusions about the law held by Paul's Jewish contemporaries.[64] The "law" which is curiously linked with the "elemental spirits" in Gal. 4:1-10 can, again, be identified with "the legalistic misunderstanding and misuse" of God's law.[65] Obviously the possibilities opened by this hermeneutical device are endless.

Most significant for our purposes here is the claim that it is legalism, not God's law, which Paul depicts as incompatible with faith in texts like Gal. 3:12,[66] and with God's promise in verse 18.[67] Why would Paul use the same word *nomos* to mean both the God-given law and its distortion without giving any indication to his readers as to which he meant? Cranfield notes that

> the Greek language used by Paul had no word-group to denote 'legalism', 'legalist', and 'legalistic'. . . . This means, surely, that he was at a very considerable disadvantage. . . . We should, I think, be ready to reckon with the possibility that sometimes, when he appears to be disparaging the law, what he really has in mind may be not the law itself but the misunderstanding and misuse of it for which *we* have a convenient term.[68]

The argument, however, is specious.

61. Cf. the discussion of "works of the law" in section ii above.
62. Hübner, *Law*, 138; cf. Davies, *Studies*, 106; Moule, "Obligation," 402-403.
63. Cranfield, "Law," 56.
64. Cranfield, *Romans*, 320; Moule, "Obligation," 394-395, Hübner, *Law*, 135.
65. Cranfield, "Law," 63-64.
66. Cf. Fuller, "Works," 41, who suggests that the verse means that "legalism is an attitude of heart which cannot coexist with the attitude of faith."
67. Fuller, *Gospel*, 199-204. That theological convictions underlie such exegesis is noted by Moo, "Law," 87-88. They are spelled out by Cranfield, "Law," 67-68. Cf. also Fuller, "Works," 30; *Gospel*, 99, 103-105.
68. Cranfield, "Law," 55.

1. Whether or not the Greek language possessed a suitable single word for "legalism," it surely provided, and Paul's vocabulary included, sufficient resources for indicating whether he was speaking of the law as intended by God or in the (allegedly) perverted form in which it was regarded by Jews.[69]

2. A study of the passages in question shows that no such distinction is intended. How can the "law" in Gal. 3:18 (a text where its perversion is purportedly found) be any different from the law in verses 17 and 19, where the giving of the law (doubtless in its intended form) is spoken of? How can the law of 4:1-10 refer to a "misunderstanding" of what God meant when Christ himself is said to have been subject to it (v. 4)? How can the death of Christians *with Christ* have been to a misunderstanding of the law which Christ cannot have shared (Rom. 7:4)? How can Paul have intended Gal. 3:12 to state his opponents' view of the law when, rather than correcting it, he cites scripture in its support, and incorporates it into his argument that justification cannot come from the "law"? How can "under the law" mean "subject to an illusion about its nature" when Paul claims that he himself lives at times "as one under the law" (1 Cor. 9:20)?

3. As was shown above, the views that the law, in the sense of the Sinaitic legislation, rests on works (Gal. 3:12) and is distinct from God's promise (v. 18) are fully consistent with Paul's language elsewhere. We are dealing with fundamental Pauline theses, not Jewish misunderstandings.[70]

4. The term "legalism" itself needs definition.[71] Räisänen[72] has introduced a distinction which is absolutely critical to a clear discussion of the issue. He notes that, while legalism involves the view that "salvation consists of the observance of precepts," boasting and self-righteousness may, but do not always, accompany this notion. When they do not, we may speak of "a 'soft' or 'torah-centric' form of legalism";[73] when they do, we have a "hard" or "anthropocentric" legalism. To this we may add that "soft" legalists, who try to obey God's law be-

69. Cf. Räisänen, *Law,* 43; Moo, "Law," 86.
70. Cf. Ebeling, *Word,* 266.
71. Cf. Jackson, "Legalism," 2. Dr. Sanders (in conversation) questions the wisdom of attempts to define "legalism" as a neutral term, given its almost universally accepted pejorative connotations; hence his use of "nomism."
72. Räisänen, "Legalism," 63-83.
73. Ibid., 64. Cf. also Longenecker's distinction between "nomism" and "legalism," *Paul,* 78-83.

cause they believe God has commanded them to do so, may not believe that they are thereby "earning" their salvation, still less that they are "establishing a claim" on God based on their own "merit." Surely love for God, or even fear of his judgment, are adequate motives for obedience to his commands. No such explanation as hypocrisy, self-seeking, merit-mongering, and outright rebellion against God need be invoked to explain why religious people would attempt to do what they believe their God has commanded them. To think otherwise is to insist, for example, that Psalm 119 expresses the religion of a sham, and that Deut. 30:16 commands it.

Unfortunately, in most definitions of legalism by New Testament scholars, the possibility of "soft" legalism is not even considered. The "legalist," for Cranfield, is the one who tries to use the law "as a means to the establishment of a claim upon God, and so to the defence of his self-centredness and the assertion of a measure of independence over against God. He imagines that he can put God under an obligation to himself, that he will be able so adequately to fulfil the law's demands that he will earn for himself a righteous status before God."[74] For Moule, legalism is "the intention to claim God's favour by establishing one's own rightness."[75] For Hübner, those who see righteousness as based on works define their existence in terms of their own activities, leave God out of consideration, and, in effect, "see themselves as their own creator."[76] For Fuller, legalism "presumes that the Lord, who is not 'served by human hands, as though he needed anything' (Acts 17:25), can nevertheless be bribed and obligated to bestow blessing by the way men distinguish themselves."[77]

Such definitions would be innocent enough if they were accompanied by an awareness that "legalists" of this kind represent only some of those who interpreted Deut. 30:16 as saying that obedience to God's law was the way to life. But all too frequently there is no such awareness. The alternative to faith is not (as it is in Paul) simply "works," whether they are "good or bad"—a statement which embraces both "soft" and "hard" legalism—but rather the sinful, self-seeking, merit-claiming works of the (necessarily "hard") legalist. Whereas Paul can contrast faith in Christ with the "works of the law," and mean by the latter no more than the deeds demanded by the law, the very notion of

74. Cranfield, "Law," 47.
75. Moule, "Obligation," 393.
76. Hübner, *Law*, 120-121.
77. Fuller, "Works," 36-37.

"works" is so inextricably linked in the minds of some scholars with self-righteousness and pride that (as we have seen) the "works of the law" can only be conceived as sinful. It is not surprising that for such scholars, the "law" whose works are viewed as sinful cannot be seen as divine, but inevitably becomes the legalistically distorted form of God's law which prevailed (we are confidently told) among the Jews of Paul's day.[78] But—it must be emphasized—in Paul's argument it is human deeds of any kind which cannot justify, not simply deeds done "in a spirit of legalism." *Paul's very point is lost to view when his statements excluding the law and its works from justification are applied only to the law's perversion.*

5. Finally, a few comments on the theological problem posed by Cranfield are in order. Does the law represent an unsuccessful first attempt on God's part? Is the gospel God's remedy for an initial plan which has gone wrong?

a. While Paul does insist that the law demands deeds, and clearly says that the law promises life to those who carry out its commands (Rom. 2:13, 25; 7:10; 10:5; Gal. 3:12), in other texts he makes it clear that the law cannot justify (Gal. 2:16)—and was not even intended to do so (3:21)! The tension between these statements is real;[79] the whole argument of this chapter indicates that we cannot resolve the dilemma by eliminating the former statements from the epistles. On the other hand, the problem is hardly peculiar to Paul, and we do him an injustice if we regard his synthesis as less adequate than that of others who do not even face the issue.

The fact of the matter is that Paul could not conceive (as many moderns apparently can) of the "law" as simply a statement of God's eternal demands, valid regardless of time and place, and easily detached from the sanctions which accompany it. For Paul, the Mosaic legislation was God's gift to his people, Israel's peculiar "righteousness" and path to life, provided its commands were heeded. Such a view follows naturally, even inevitably, from a reading of Deuteronomy (4:1; 5:33; 6:24-25; 8:1; 11:26-28, etc.). As a Christian, however, Paul was convinced that the death of God's Son was essential to salvation; and this could only mean—whether or not Paul was alone in perceiving it—that the Mosaic law does not itself lead to the

78. Cf. Bultmann, "Anthropology," 148-149; Fuller, *Gospel,* 87, n. 33; Käsemann, *Perspectives,* 146-147.

79. Räisänen, *Law,* 150-154; cf. van Dülmen, *Theologie,* 212-213; Hahn, "Gesetzesverständnis," 56, n. 84.

life which it in fact promises,[80] and hence (if one chooses to use the term) that the covenant God made with Israel was "unsuccessful" (cf. Jer. 31:32!). Paul's solution to the dilemma—that an order based on "works" which could not save has been replaced by one based on faith—may not convince or satisfy many readers. Still, he cannot be accused of creating a problem where there was none.

b. But, of course, the replacement of the "old covenant" with the "new" (2 Cor. 3) is not the whole story, even for Paul. No doubt his solution would have been "neater" if he had simply presented the law as God's first, unsuccessful attempt at a remedy. But for Paul, God's word could not fail (Rom. 9:6). Paul's conception of God compelled him to believe that, if the law has proven inadequate, then God must have both foreseen and planned that it would do so. Similarly, God being who he is, he must have both foreseen and planned that justification would be by faith (cf. Gal. 3:8-9).[81] From this it follows that, while the law promises life, it was part of God's plan from the beginning that it would not lead to life, and Paul provides alternative explanations of God's purposes for the law (see Chapter 9 below). The result is that God's dealings can no longer be considered unsuccessful: everything has happened by design. The problem remains, however, that the law promises a life which in God's plan it would not and could not give.

c. Problems of this nature are inherent in any Christian theology and are not peculiar to Paul. Most Christian readers of Genesis 2–3 would believe that God gives there a command (2:17)—all the while knowing that it will be broken and having in mind the remedy to follow. Any Christian who believes that the death of Christ for sin was part of God's plan "before the foundation of the world" (1 Pet. 1:20) must believe that sin entered the world both contrary to God's will (God never "wills" sin!) and according to God's plan (which included, from the beginning, sin's remedy). Paul's view of God's designs with the law conforms to this pattern: God promises life to those who obey his commands, but has planned from the beginning his remedy for transgressors. In each case we may (if we like) speak of a God of "unsuccessful" first attempts and find such a view of the deity "theologically grotesque." It is a charge to which a faith in a God who is both Creator and Redeemer is inevitably susceptible.

80. Cf. Grafe, *Lehre,* 11; Kuss, "Nomos," 211-213.
81. Cf. Bultmann, *Theology,* I, 263.

v. The Law and Torah

To this point we have seen how Paul uses "law" *(nomos)* most frequently to mean the demands placed upon Israel at Mount Sinai, with the accompanying sanctions. The law demands deeds and is thus contrasted with faith, God's promise, and grace.

But such an understanding of Pauline usage exposes the apostle to attack on a different front: that Paul's *nomos* represents a gross distortion of the Hebrew word *torah,* which cannot be reduced to a "sum of prescriptions."[82] By way of response to this now common critique, the following considerations may be raised.[83]

1. The claim that Hebrew *torah* is incorrectly rendered *nomos* appears to have been introduced to the apologist's arsenal by Solomon Schechter.[84] In arguing that legalism has never "constituted the whole religion of the Jew, as declared by most modern critics," Schechter made the following claims:

> It must first be stated that the term *Law* or *Nomos* is not a correct rendering of the Hebrew word *Torah.* The legalistic element, which might rightly be called the Law, represents only one side of the Torah. To the Jew the word Torah means a teaching or an instruction of any kind. . . .

> It is true that in Rabbinic literature the term *Torah* is often applied to the Pentateuch to the exclusion of the Prophets and the Hagiographa. . . . But even the Pentateuch is no mere legal code, without edifying elements in it. The Book of Genesis, the greater part of Exodus, and even a part of Numbers are simple history. . . .

> Thus *Torah,* even as represented by the Pentateuch, is not mere Law, the Rabbis having discerned and appreciated in it other than merely legal elements. Moreover, the term *Torah* is not always confined to the Pentateuch. It also extends, as already indicated, to the whole of the Scriptures. . . . To the Jew, as already pointed out, the term *Torah* implied a teaching or instruction, and was therefore wide enough to embrace the whole of the Scriptures.

> It is the Torah as the sum total of the contents of revelation, without special regard to any particular element in it, the Torah as a faith, that is so dear to the Rabbi.[85]

---

82. Schoeps, *Paul,* 188.
83. The argument that follows represents a summary of my article "Meaning."
84. Schechter, *Aspects,* 116-126.
85. Ibid., 117, 118-119, 121, 125, 127.

Schechter's argument here shows an ambiguity which has dogged the debate ever since. He appears to be discussing the meaning of the word *torah* in general (note the first and third sentences of the first excerpt above); yet most of his attention focuses rather on the contents of "*the* Torah," now a technical term for the Pentateuch, or all of the sacred scriptures, or even the "sum total of the contents of revelation." But the issues need to be kept separate. The variety of traditional materials which have come to be called "the Torah" may justly form the basis for an argument that legalism is not "the whole religion of the Jew"; this does not, however, mean that the word *torah* itself cannot mean "law." After all, just as "Exodus" has come to be the title of a book of scripture because it contains (together with other materials) the story of the Exodus from Egypt, so "Torah" may have become the designation of a collection of materials because it contains (together with other materials) the laws known as the *torah* (in a narrower sense). But the ambiguity in the argument has largely gone unnoticed. It has become all too common to make categorical statements about what *torah* can and cannot mean on the basis of the contents of "the Torah":

> In Jewish usage these five books were and still are known by the collective name of the Torah. This alone shows that Torah is wrongly translated by "Law," because there is a great deal in the Pentateuch which is not law at all.[86]

> The word Torah is only very imperfectly translated by "Law". . . . It contained far more than mere "precept" or laws.[87]

> And when the Torah is called "the Law," the error is that only the Halachah is Law; the Haggadah is not Law.[88]

2. The widespread acceptance of the notion that *torah* does not mean *nomos* owes much to the fact that C. H. Dodd is believed to have substantiated it. He did not. On the contrary, Dodd noted that the Hebrew *torah* "could be used collectively both of the priestly code of ceremonial observance . . . and also, by an extension of meaning, of the code of commandments, statutes and judgments contained in Deuteronomy. . . . It is in this sense that *torah* can fairly be regarded

---

86. Herford, *Judaism*, 31.
87. Parkes, *Conflict*, 35-36.
88. Herford, *Judaism*, 58. Similarly misguided are claims that *torah* "properly" or "basically" has a given meaning which is derived from its (proposed) etymology. See Barr, *Semantics*, 107-160 for the fallacy involved.

as equivalent to *nomos*."[89] Dodd's complaint was rather that the Septuagint continued to use *nomos* where *torah* means something quite different than "law." His charge is justified, though it is occasioned rather by the Septuagint's propensity for stereotyped renderings[90] than by the excessive legalism of Hellenistic Judaism. But what Dodd actually said has become less important than what he has been perceived to have said. Since the publication of his study, it has become axiomatic for many that the Septuagint is to blame for the misunderstanding of *torah* as "law," and that the distortion introduced by the Septuagint is responsible for countless woes. For some authors, Paul is himself a victim of the distortion; for others, he is an accomplice in the crime.

> Nothing has contributed more to the misunderstanding between the two religions [Judaism and Christianity] than the fact that the Septuagint translated the word "Torah" by the narrower word *nomos* and the English still further reduced the meaning by rendering *nomos* as *law*.[91]

> In the LXX there takes place with the translation *torah—nomos—*a shift of emphasis towards legalism. . . . The source of many Pauline misunderstandings with regard to the evaluation of the law and covenant is to be sought in the legalistic distortion of the perspective for which Hellenistic Judaism was responsible.[92]

> Torah does not mean Law, and never did, and the example of Paul, who did most to perpetuate the mischievous error, does not justify either himself or those who have imitated him.[93]

> To debase divine *instruction* (a concept which linguistically as well as regarding content, corresponds to Torah) by equating it with the narrow-minded word *nomos* (the law)—all of this is an absurd caricature which finds its source in Paul.[94]

3. There are, however, any number of cases in the Old Testament where *torah* is (or where *toroth* are) said to be "commanded" to be "done" or "kept" and not "transgressed." In such cases, "law" (or "laws") would seem to be a more adequate rendering than "instruction" or "teaching" or "revelation."

89. Dodd, *Bible*, 30-31.
90. Cf. Tov, *Use*, 55.
91. Parkes, *Foundations*, xv.
92. Schoeps, *Paul*, 29.
93. Herford, *Judaism*, 30-31.
94. Lapide, *Paul*, 39.

> . . . because Abraham obeyed my voice and kept my charge, my commandments, my statutes, and my *laws*. (Gen. 26:5)

> And the Lord said to Moses, "How long do you refuse to keep my commandments and my *laws?*" (Exod. 16:28)

> These are the statutes and ordinances and *laws* which the Lord made between him and the people of Israel on Mount Sinai by Moses. (Lev. 26:46)

> They have transgressed the *laws*, violated the statutes. (Isa. 24:5)

> They did not obey thy voice or walk in thy *law;* they did nothing of all thou didst command them to do. (Jer. 32:23)

> . . . to the end that they should keep his statutes, and observe his *laws*. (Ps. 105:45)

Most importantly, in the Deuteronomistic literature "this *torah*" (or "the *torah* of Moses," or "this book of the *torah*," or "the book of the *torah* of Moses," etc.) is used of the substance of the Deuteronomic code, the sum of the commandments imposed upon Israel at Mount Sinai and accompanied by sanctions. Again, "law" is surely the most adequate rendering.

> And what great nation is there, that has statutes and ordinances so righteous as all this *law* which I set before you this day? (Deut. 4:8)

> Lay to heart all the words which I enjoin upon you this day, that you may command them to your children, that they may be careful to do all the words of this *law*. (Deut. 32:46)

> Only be strong and very courageous, being careful to do according to all the *law* which Moses my servant commanded you. (Josh. 1:7)

> And keep the charge of the Lord your God, walking in his ways and keeping his statutes, his commandments, his ordinances, and his testimonies, as it is written in the *law* of Moses. (1 Kings 2:3)

> Yet the Lord warned Israel and Judah by every prophet and every seer, saying, "Turn from your evil ways and keep my commandments and my statutes, in accordance with all the *law* which I commanded your fathers." (2 Kings 17:13)

This Deuteronomistic usage of *torah* to designate the requirements imposed upon Israel is taken up in the later literature of the Old Testament as well, though now extended to include, for example, the Priestly Code.[95]

---

95. Cf. Lindars, "Torah," 120-121.

All Israel has transgressed thy *law* and turned aside, refusing to obey thy voice. And the curse and oath which are written in the *law* of Moses the servant of God have been poured out upon us, because we have sinned against him. (Dan. 9:11)

And they found it written in the *law* that the Lord had commanded by Moses that the people of Israel should dwell in booths during the feast of the seventh month. (Neh. 8:14)

Our kings, our princes, our priests, and our fathers have not kept thy *law* or heeded thy commandments. (Neh. 9:34)[96]

4. By a natural development, the scope of "the *torah* of Moses" was later extended to include the whole of the Pentateuch;[97] and, naturally, the Greek followed suit and spoke of the Pentateuch as *ho nomos*. While a reminder of the scope of "the Torah" may well be in order, Hellenistic Judaism can scarcely be faulted for designating it "the law"; the title, in both Hebrew and Greek, has grown out of its Deuteronomistic usage, where it means "law."

5. It follows that, when Paul uses *nomos* to mean the sum of obligations imposed upon Israel at Mount Sinai, with the accompanying sanctions, such usage is a precise equivalent of what Deuteronomistic and later Old Testament literature meant by *torah*. That Paul's view of the role of the "law" in the divine scheme differs radically from that of the rabbis is only to be expected. It is not a consequence of his use of Greek *nomos*.

---

96. Perhaps the most interesting passage in this regard is Ezra 7:12-26. The passage, in Aramaic, refers to "the law of the God of heaven" (v. 12), "the law of your God" (vv. 14, 26); Ezra is referred to as "the scribe of the law of the God of heaven" (v. 21). The Aramaic word used *(dāth)* is well attested as meaning "decree," "law" (cf. Dan. 6:9, 13, 16 [vv. 8, 12, 15 in English versions]: "the *law* of the Medes and the Persians," etc.). In Ezra 7 it is clearly used as the equivalent of the Hebrew *torah:* in the immediate context, Ezra is called "a scribe skilled in the law *(torah)* of Moses which the Lord the God of Israel had given" (v. 6; cf. v. 21) and as one who "set his heart to study the law *(torah)* of the Lord, and to do it, and to teach his statutes and ordinances in Israel" (v. 10). Clearly the Septuagint was not original in translating *torah* with a word meaning "law"; those who condemn the Septuagint version and Hellenistic Jewry for rendering *torah* with *nomos* ought to apply the same judgment to the author and community of Ezra!

97. Cf. Clements, *Theology,* 110-120.

Chapter Eight

Justification by Faith

The central contentions emerging from the "new perspective" on Paul relate to Luther's "principal doctrine of Christianity": justification by faith, not by human "works." Traditionally, scholars have accepted the contrast as genuine to Paul and debated whether Paul saw the rejected "works" as good but inadequate (Wilckens) or as damnable sins (Bultmann). Today, however, a number of scholars deny that human "works" as such were even an issue for the apostle. Dunn, for example, thinks that Paul directed his opposition, not at "works" in general, but at Jewish exclusivism which required the peculiarly Jewish "works of the law" of those who would belong to God's people. Sanders finds no evidence that Paul thought human "works" wrong; texts which indicate that Paul found them inadequate are dismissed to the periphery of Paul's thought as representing mere arguments rather than his real reason for rejecting the law. For his part, Räisänen concedes that Paul does contrast faith and "works" and that he rejects the law in part because it is based on "works"; but he finds the contrast unjustifiable, Paul's understanding of Judaism erroneous, and his doctrine of *sola gratia* idiosyncratic and impractical. In short, either Paul did not really say what he has traditionally been thought to have said; or, though he may have spoken words to that effect, he did not really think that way; or, though he may have said and thought something like the traditional Lutheran view, he was really wrong. One way or another, the Lutheran understanding of Paul comes to grief.

All three scholars, Dunn, Sanders, and Räisänen, share the same starting-point: Judaism does not see salvation as a human achievement, earned by human "works." Räisänen, convinced that Paul nonetheless represents Judaism in these terms, concludes that the apostle is wrong. Sanders and Dunn argue that Paul neither opposes human "works" as such nor attributes a doctrine of salvation by "works" to Judaism. Clearly our review of the place of justification by faith in Paul's thinking about the law must begin with a discussion of the relation between salvation and "works" in Judaism.

The conclusions reached in the preceding chapter are crucial to the argument which follows. Here the following positions will be advanced.

1. Though it is misleading to represent Judaism as a religion of "works-salvation," observance of the law may be regarded as Israel's path to life; moreover, as a rule Judaism has not despaired of human capacity to render at least the token obedience which God requires of his people. Paul himself *agrees* that the law promises life to those who observe its commands.

2. On the other hand, Paul believes that human sin has rendered the righteousness of the law inoperable as a means to life. There is no doubt that this conclusion about the human plight was forced upon Paul by his Christian conviction that "Christ died for our sins" (1 Cor. 15:3); moreover, Paul has other arguments at hand to show that the law does not represent God's ultimate design. Still, when Paul explains why the law fails to provide the life it promises, human transgressions bear the blame.

3. Paul thus believes that humans do not and (apparently) cannot obey God's commandments in a way that satisfies divine requirements. Judaism is not (as a rule) so pessimistic. Conversely, Paul attributes salvation to divine grace to the exclusion of any role by human works in a way which is not typical of Judaism. And the tenet that justification is by faith *alone* is both necessary to Paul and pointless from the perspective of Judaism. We do not know at what point in his Christian career Paul first gave the doctrine the precise formulation found in Romans and Galatians; the underlying conviction of humanity's utter dependence on divine grace appears to be a constant factor in his writings.

4. Paul does not see the fundamental sin of Jews as "boasting" in their observance of the law, nor is the failing of the law that it leads to such misplaced arrogance. He does claim that salvation by divine grace, through faith in Christ, leaves no place for human boasting, whereas a salvation which depended on human observance of the law

would allow human boasting. That the emptiness of human pretensions should be exposed and God should be seen as "Source, Guide, and Goal of all that is" (Rom. 11:36 NEB) marks the fitting climax of the Pauline gospel.

i. Judaism and "Works"

Paul claims that the works of the law cannot "justify." But who, the question is now being asked, ever thought they could?

Perhaps the thesis most central to the "new perspective" on Paul is that, for Judaism at least, salvation was *not* based on works. To distinguish faith (or grace) from works (or the law) as alternative paths to salvation and suggest that Judaism advocated the latter is to misrepresent the faith of Paul's fathers. As we have noted, it is then disputed whether Paul himself or his interpreters bear primary responsibility for the misrepresentation. We may review three positions briefly.

Sanders's *Paul and Palestinian Judaism* marks the starting-point for the current debate. For Sanders, all branches of first-century Judaism shared the conviction that Israel's standing with God was initiated by God's gracious act in establishing a covenant with his people. Obedience to the law, far from constituting the basis of that relationship, represents Israel's proper *response* to God's grace. Thus salvation is not "earned" by human works, though Sanders certainly allows that obedience is necessary if the Israelite's relationship with God is to be maintained.[1] Paul himself understood the nature of Judaism.[2] His polemic against it was rooted, not in a rejection of "works," but in his exclusive soteriology and in his concern for the admission of Gentiles to the people of God.[3]

Sanders's picture of Judaism is enthusiastically endorsed by Dunn,[4] to whom we owe the provocative claim that "Paul is wholly at one with his fellow Jews in asserting that justification is *by faith*."[5] Dunn, like Sanders, attributes the view that Paul rejects Judaism because it is based on "works" to "the standard Protestant (mis)reading

1. Sanders, *Paul,* 420.
2. Ibid., 551.
3. Sanders, *Law,* 47.
4. Dunn, "Perspective," 97-100.
5. Ibid., 106. Note, however, the criticism of Räisänen, "Break," 546, of Dunn's exegesis of Gal. 2:15-16, on which this statement is more immediately based.

of Paul through Reformation spectacles."[6] The real point of Paul's attack is (again) not "works" as such, but, in Dunn's view, reliance on those particular "works of the law" which served as "identity and boundary markers"[7] for the Jewish people (circumcision, food laws, sabbath observance, and the like). "God's purposes and God's people have now expanded beyond Israel according to the flesh, and so God's righteousness can no longer be restricted in terms of works of the law which emphasize kinship at the level of the flesh."[8]

But this, according to Räisänen, is not the whole story. To be sure, Räisänen is convinced by Sanders's case that Judaism was not characterized by "legalism," that "*it did not even understand the law to be a means of salvation*. God's grace, expressed in the establishment of the covenant, held precedence over man's obedience."[9] But though this understanding of Tannaitic Judaism is taken to be all but irrefutable,[10] it differs, according to Räisänen, from Paul's own understanding. "For Paul, Judaism was legalism." In his view, "the Jews (including some Jewish Christians) ascribe saving value to the fulfilment of the precepts of the law."[11] Paul's view of the Jewish religion is a distorted one. "It should not have been possible to do away with the 'law as the way to salvation' for the simple reason that the law never was (or was conceived to be) that way. . . . Paul is wrong."[12]

Does Paul think Jews "ascribe saving value to the fulfilment of the precepts of the law"? Räisänen is, I believe, correct in saying that he does.[13] Gal. 5:4 speaks explicitly of those "who would be justified by the law"; with such people Paul contrasts those who, "by faith, . . .

6. Dunn, "Perspective," 119.

7. Dunn, "Works," 528.

8. Dunn, "Perspective," 117. Cf. also Wright, "Paul": "Judaism, so far from being a religion of works, is based on a clear understanding of grace, the grace that chose Israel in the first place to be a special people. Good works are simply gratitude" (80). "Works-righteousness" has been attributed to Judaism by the retrojection of the Protestant-Catholic debate (80). Paul finds Israel "guilty not of 'legalism' or 'works-righteousness' but of what I call 'national righteousness,' the belief that fleshly Jewish descent guarantees membership of God's true covenant people" (65). Seen in this way, "the categories with which we are to understand Paul, and for that matter the whole New Testament, are not the thin, tired and anachronistic ones of Lutheran polemic" (87).

9. Räisänen, "Legalism," 66.

10. Ibid., 66.

11. Ibid., 64.

12. Ibid., 72-73.

13. Räisänen, *Law,* 162-164.

wait for the hope of righteousness" (v. 5). Divine approval on the day of judgment is the goal of both groups; in Paul's terms, one group bases its hope on the law, the other on faith. Conceivably, of course, Paul would not have considered his Galatian opponents to be representative of first-century Judaism. But according to Rom. 9:30-31, *Israel* pursues "the righteousness which is based on law," a righteousness which is again contrasted with that "through faith." In the context, "righteousness" must refer to "righteous status in God's sight,"[14] for this is precisely what, according to Paul, Gentile believers have "attained . . . through faith" but Jews have not. The fundamental principle of the "righteousness which is based on the law," according to 10:5, is that life is given to those who obey the law's commands; yet, in its immediate context, the verse can only mean that the "righteousness" which finds life through the law is that sought by Jews (9:31; 10:1-3). Clearly Paul believes that the pursuit of life and approval with God by means of the law is typical of Judaism.

But to this recognition a crucial point must be added. It is not enough to say that Paul represents his *opponents* as believing that the law serves "a soteriological function";[15] in Paul's own view (as outlined in Chapter Seven above), the law was offered on precisely that basis. The claim that the law was given for "life" is Pauline (Rom. 7:10). Paul affirms (in principle at least) the thesis that the "doers of the law" will be "justified" (2:13; cf. v. 25). And Paul himself finds the essence of the law to rest in the assurance that those who "do" its commands will "live" (10:5; cf. Gal. 3:12). When he contrasts the righteousness of the law with that of faith, in neither case does he base his depiction on empirical observation of first-century communities; both principles he finds enunciated in scripture (Rom. 10:5-13). As spokesman for the view that the law promises life to its adherents, he cites, not Pharisaic theologians with whom he disagrees, but Moses himself (v. 5).[16]

14. Cranfield, *Romans,* 506.

15. Räisänen, *Law,* 178.

16. According to Sanders, Paul's point in Rom. 10:5-8 is that "Moses was incorrect," that "Scripture itself shows that real righteousness is by faith and leads to salvation for all who faith, without distinction" (*Law,* 41). But Moses could not be "incorrect" for Paul, and other texts show clearly that Paul affirms the basic Old Testament premise, here attributed to Moses, that obedience to God's commands brings life. Paul is bound to grant validity to a principle of life proclaimed by Moses—if only to deny that the law has been able to deliver on its promise. Cf. Gundry, "Grace," 18-19; Hübner, "Proprium," 462; and especially Dahl, *Paul,* 159-177.

The attribution to Moses makes Räisänen's explanation of the origin of Paul's notion highly unlikely. Räisänen suggests that Paul first came to view the law as Judaism's path to salvation in his battle with Jewish Christians who tried to exclude uncircumcised Gentile believers from table fellowship. Paul may then have concluded (wrongly) that such believers were thought to be excluded from salvation in Christ as well, and hence that the law was being made the means of salvation.[17] But such an explanation leaves out of account and unaccountable Paul's own affirmation that the law was given for life. Did he first encounter the idea as his own mistaken perception of his opponents' position, then search for scripture to support *their* case, and magnanimously concede that they had Moses on their side, before finally offering the alternative of faith? It does not seem likely of the Paul of the epistles.

That the law promises life is thus Paul's own conviction, though one which (he believes) he shares with the "Israel" of his day—indeed, one which he apparently held during his "former life" in Judaism (Gal. 1:13).[18] He cites scripture as supporting the notion; to search elsewhere for its derivation is to cross a brook looking for water. He quotes Lev. 18:5, and it suits his purpose well. But it is only one of dozens of texts from which Paul could conclude that keeping the law was Israel's path to life.

> You shall therefore keep my statutes and my ordinances, by doing which a man shall live: I am the Lord. (Lev. 18:5)
>
> And now, O Israel, give heed to the statutes and the ordinances which I teach you, and do them; that you may live. . . . (Deut. 4:1)
>
> You shall walk in all the way which the Lord your God has commanded you, that you may live. . . . (Deut. 5:33)
>
> And the Lord commanded us to do all these statutes, to fear the Lord our God, for our good always, that he might preserve us alive, as at this day. And it will be righteousness for us, if we are careful to do all this commandment before the Lord our God, as he has commanded us. (Deut. 6:24-25)
>
> All the commandment which I command you this day you shall be careful to do, that you may live. . . . (Deut. 8:1)
>
> See, I have set before you this day life and good, death and evil. If you obey the commandments of the Lord your God which I command

17. Räisänen, "Legalism," 78-82.
18. Cf. Kim, *Origin,* 349.

you this day, by loving the Lord your God, by walking in his ways, and by keeping his commandments and his statutes and his ordinances, then you shall live and multiply, and the Lord your God will bless you in the land which you are entering to take possession of it. But if your heart turns away and you will not hear, but are drawn away to worship other gods and serve them, I declare to you this day, that you shall perish. . . . (Deut. 30:15-18)

When the son has done what is lawful and right, and has been careful to observe all my statutes, he shall surely live. (Ezek. 18:19; cf. vv. 9, 21)

I gave them my statutes and showed them my ordinances, by whose observance man shall live. (Ezek. 20:11; cf. vv. 13, 21).

Yet they acted presumptuously and did not obey thy commandments, but sinned against thy ordinances, by the observance of which a man shall live. . . . (Neh. 9:29)

Texts such as these invite the following considerations:

1. A number of Old Testament passages clearly state that obedience to the commandments leads to the possession of life, a recognition of one's righteousness, and the enjoyment of God's blessing; conversely, it is taught that those who disobey the commandments are condemned as wicked and said to be subject to the divine curse and the sentence of "death." Now it is true that the notion of what "salvation" entails has developed considerably in Paul beyond its Old Testament implications. Furthermore, there are perils in speaking of "soteriology" in Judaism.[19] Nonetheless, if the term is to be used at all, then the law is surely attributed with "a soteriological function" in texts which make life, righteousness, and divine blessing dependent on its observation. If Paul is wrong in considering the law a path to salvation, it is an error he shares with Leviticus, Deuteronomy, and Ezekiel.

2. At the root of the denial that the law is a path to salvation in Judaism lies the identification of "gaining salvation" with "becoming a member of God's covenant people." Since, in Judaism, membership in God's people is the result of God's election of Israel, "salvation" can be said to result from an act of God's grace.[20] Hence it is claimed that for both Judaism and Paul, salvation is by grace, whereas the maintaining of one's status within God's covenant people depends on works. The basic "pattern" is perceived to be the same.[21]

19. Cf. Sanders, *Paul,* 17-18, 75.
20. Ibid., 220.
21. Sanders, *Paul,* 543; Räisänen, *Law,* 184-186.

The discussion has served to remind forgetful New Testament scholars that divine grace is not a category peculiar to Christian theology. Sanders has, I believe, decisively refuted the notion that keeping the law was regarded in Judaism as the sole and sufficient basis for salvation, that life was thought to be "earned" as a matter of human achievement. Judaism kept grace and works in balance.[22] Nonetheless, the claim that "grace" and "works" play an identical role in Judaism and in Paul remains, I believe, misleading. With eyes fixed on the death of Christ for the sins of humanity, Paul had every reason to make grace all-important, to see human endeavors as ineffectual at best. Generally speaking, Judaism has felt no such strictures and has viewed human capacities more optimistically. Divine grace is never ignored, but (in Montefiore's terms) it is "not supposed that human efforts count for nothing."[23] As a result, Judaism does not (as a rule) share Paul's perception of the need for *exclusive* reliance on God's grace.

a. Even if we accept the identification between "gaining salvation" and "becoming a member of God's covenant people," it is not true that Judaism dogmatically and consistently attributed the election of Israel to divine grace alone. As Sanders himself has shown, the election is sometimes explained with Israel's merit as a motivating factor, at other times with an emphasis on the gratuity of God's act.[24] The reason for the inconsistency, Sanders rightly notes, is that "the Rabbis did not have the Pauline/Lutheran problem of 'works-righteousness'. . . . Grace and merit did not seem to them to be in contradiction to each other."[25] Thus Paul, but not Judaism (as a rule), felt the need for a dogmatic insistence on salvation by grace which *excluded* human merit.

b. When Paul insists that "justification" is by faith, not by the works of the law, he means that the Christian hope for approval on the day of judgment rests on faith, not on observance of the law's demands (cf. Gal. 5:4-5). Those who are "justified by faith" are assured of being "saved . . . from the wrath of God" (Rom. 5:1-10); for them there is "no condemnation" (8:1). Indeed, already they enjoy the life of the new creation (6:4; 2 Cor. 5:17) and have experienced the Spirit as its "first fruits" and "guarantee" (Rom. 8:23; 2 Cor. 1:22). While the

22. Sanders, *Paul*, 426-427.
23. Montefiore, *Judaism*, 78.
24. Sanders, *Paul*, 87-101.
25. Ibid., 100.

moral behavior of believers may provide evidence of such life, and while grievous sins can forfeit that life (Rom. 11:22; 1 Cor. 10:1-13; Gal. 5:4; 1 Thess. 3:5, etc.), Christian "works" can hardly be regarded as a *condition* for acquiring what (in Paul's view) has already been granted. Indeed, any suggestion of a still outstanding requirement placed upon believers for the gaining of life would surely qualify as heresy for Paul.

But when "salvation" is defined in terms of approval on the day of judgment and enjoyment of the blessings of the age to come, then it is clear that "works" done in compliance with the law are given a role in Judaism which Pauline Christianity emphatically denies. The biblical texts quoted above suggest that Israel, though elect, encounters in the commandments a radical choice between life and death, blessing and curse.[26] Nothing really comparable to the Pauline assurance that what is decisive lies in the past, that Christians have *already* been "justified," is implied. The biblical condition of obedience to the law's demands remained in place when the "life" to which it led was later interpreted of the age to come. As Sanders has reminded us, Judaism never forgot that such obedience is "the *conditio sine qua non* of salvation."[27] God in his mercy may tip the scales in such a way that a single observance, or the slightest indication of an intention to obey, is sufficient for his approval; the issue remains one of obedience to the law. In this sense the law and human "works" are clearly given a soteriological function in Judaism which is denied them by Paul.

c. If the Sinaitic covenant requires obedience to the law as its condition for life, then, in *Paul's* terms, it "does not rest on faith." The point of Gal. 3:12, as we saw in Chapter Seven above, is precisely that a law which demands *deeds* is based on a different principle than that of *faith* (cf. Rom. 4:5 and the contrast between "works" and "faith" in Rom. 3:27; 9:32). Similarly, Paul's contrast between the law and "grace," and that between the law and God's promise, both hinge on the distinction, fundamental to Paul, that the law demands deeds as its condition for blessing whereas, *for Paul,* God's grace and promise must depend on the exercise of his sovereign will alone (Rom. 4:14, 16; Gal. 3:18; cf. Rom. 4:4; 9:11, 16; 11:6). Paul thus posits a basic difference in nature, not simply between his view of the gospel and that of the "Judaizers," but between God's revelation of righteousness

26. Cf. Zimmerli, *Law,* 47-60.
27. Sanders, *Paul,* 141.

in Jesus Christ and the righteousness proclaimed by Moses: the former is an expression of God's grace to the exclusion of a requirement for deeds, whereas the law demands deeds.

Paul's opponents, of course, did not see it that way. The methodological error has often been committed in the past of concluding that, since Paul contrasts grace and works and argues for salvation by grace, his opponents (and, ultimately, Judaism) must have worked with the same distinction but argued for salvation by works. Clearly this distorts Judaism, which never thought that divine grace was incompatible with divine requirements. But we become guilty of a similar methodological error if we conclude that, since Paul's opponents did not distinguish between grace and requirements, Paul himself could not have done so either: the evidence shows that he did, giving "grace" an exclusive sense (eliminating any role by "works"; cf. Rom. 4:4; 11:6) and "faith" a narrower definition (it "does not work"; Rom. 4:5; cf. Gal. 3:12) than was normal in Jewish writings. Hence the contrast that Paul introduces between the law and its "works" on the one side and divine grace and human faith on the other does not imply that Judaism is innocent of the latter notions, but simply (as we have seen) that it does not share Paul's perception of the need for *exclusive* reliance upon them. Such a judgment, it seems to me, is no caricature of Judaism, though, to be sure, the Jewish position could hardly be reconstructed on the basis of Paul's writings alone.

The methodological point is crucial. Paul must not be allowed to be our main witness for Judaism, nor must Judaism, or the position of Paul's opponents, determine the limits within which Paul is to be interpreted. The basis for Paul's rejection of the law must not be determined solely by asking what his foes were proposing any more than we may see Judaism's own perspective of the law in Paul's rejected version of it. Paul moves the whole discussion onto a different level. While *agreeing* that the law demands obedience, Paul perceives (as his opponents did not) that the truth of the gospel implies the inadequacy of the law to convey life; since, however, divine purposes cannot fail, God's design from the very beginning must have been to grant life by means of faith in Christ, not the law. Forced to explain (as his opponents were not) both the law's inadequacy and the distinction between the path of faith and that of the law, Paul characterized the law and the gospel in terms crucial to his case, but foreign to the understanding of his opponents.

We turn, then, to Paul's explanation of the law's inadequacy.

ii. The "Weakness" of the Law

At this point two distinctions need to be introduced. The first, drawn by Sanders, will not be used in the subsequent argument. The second, proposed here, is critical to the case.

Fundamental to Sanders's discussion is his distinction between "the reason for which [Paul] held a view and the arguments which he adduces in favor of it."[28] In reviewing Paul's reasons for rejecting obedience to the law as an "entrance requirement,"[29] Sanders dismisses some of the explanations proposed because they lack any support in the text, others because, though cited by Paul himself, they prove to be mere arguments conceived to defend a position of which Paul was already convinced on other grounds. From such arguments Sanders distinguishes what he considers Paul's real reasons for rejecting the law: his exclusivist soteriology (salvation is only by faith in Christ, and therefore, by a process of elimination, it cannot be by the law) and his concern that the Gentiles are to be saved on the same basis as the Jews (hence not by the *Jewish* law).

The distinction between Paul's (real) reasons and his (mere) arguments appears to underlie Sanders's now famous claims about what, for Paul, is wrong with Judaism: "In short, *this is what Paul finds wrong in Judaism: it is not Christianity.*"[30] Convinced by his Damascus experience that salvation is available only in Christ, Paul was forced to concede that "the following of *any* other path is wrong. . . . Doing the law, in short, is wrong only because it is not faith."[31] Such statements are patently untrue if we allow Paul's *arguments* a place in a description of what he finds wrong with the law. Sanders agrees, for example, that Paul appeals to "universal transgression" in explaining why the law cannot make one righteous; but since "the various statements of human transgression are arguments in favor of a position to which Paul came on some other ground,"[32] they do not figure in Sanders's account of what Paul found wrong with the law.

Such a distinction is both useful and potentially misleading. Its usefulness lies in the reminder that, so far as we can tell, Paul harbored no serious misgivings about the "righteousness based on law" before

28. Sanders, *Law,* 4.
29. Ibid., 17-64.
30. Sanders, *Paul,* 552.
31. Ibid., 550.
32. Sanders, *Law,* 36.

he encountered the risen Christ.[33] This in turn means that the various criticisms Paul brings to bear against the law, and his explanations as to its purpose, must all come under the category of Christian theology (the term, needless to say, is not meant to be pejorative!) and cannot be used in any direct way as evidence of how a faithful Jew perceived life "under the law." Paul, the Christian apostle, was forced to reassess the nature, function, and efficacy of the law. The problems he faced are crucial to Christian theology, and remain of interest in that sphere; but clearly they become problems only when the inadequacy of the law is assumed. Thus, if we are to be fair in our portrayal of Judaism, we need to distinguish between Paul's initial reason for abandoning his "former life" (cf. Gal. 1:13) and the later explanations he supplies as to its shortcomings.

On the other hand, if our concern is to delineate the achievement of the apostle, it will no longer do to focus our attention primarily on the starting-point of his thought, the conviction that occasioned his re-assessment of the law.[34] To exclude from an account of "what Paul finds wrong in Judaism" any argument which was not itself the initial cause of his reevaluation is to exclude from the discussion any thinking Paul may have done on the topic. To be sure, a consideration of his thought inevitably means crossing the frontier from a historical description of first-century religion into a description of (one variety of)

33. To this extent the arguments of Kümmel and Stendahl, summarized in Chapter Four above, are correct. Note, however, Kim's warning against denying that Paul shared something of the human experiences portrayed in Romans 7 (i.e., the arousal of desire for what is forbidden in response to its prohibition, and the conflict between the desire to do good and the act of evil): "To deny to Paul these human, all too human, experiences is to make him twice divine. For it would imply that Paul was a super-human being who was exempted from such experiences as are common to man, and yet that without having suffered them, he could still describe them as vividly as he does in Rom 7. Furthermore, it is to rob Paul's statements about the freedom in Christ from the law of their empirical reality. For he who has had no experience of the bondage of the law (of sin) cannot know freedom from it, either" (*Origin,* 53). Cf. also Davies, *Studies,* 94; Beker, *Paul,* 240-243; and the balanced comments of Sanders, *Paul,* 443-444, n. 5; *Law,* 152-153. Kim goes on to say, however, that other passages in Paul (Gal. 1:14; Phil. 3:4-6) make it clear that such common experiences were not regarded by Paul before his conversion as problematic, and that he was "rather satisfied with his achievement in Judaism" (*Origin,* 54).

34. Note that Dahl, Review, 157, finds justification for treating the "human plight" as "the logical starting point for an analysis of Paul's *theology,* even though faith in Christ made Paul reach his assessment of human plight."

first-century Christian theology, even if the goal is an accurate historical rather than normative description of the latter. If Paul's view of the
law is our subject, such a venture simply has to be made. We may find
Paul's theology foreign and difficult to grasp; Paul without his theology is hardly worth the effort.

The basic orientation of the following discussion of the inadequacy of the law is thus different from that in Sanders's works. What
Sanders labels Paul's "real reason" after secondary argumentation has
been dismissed is here regarded simply as the starting-point of his
thought; primary attention will be focused precisely on Paul's developed views, as expressed in the extant and acknowledged epistles, as
to why the law is unable to save.

A quite different, but, I believe, useful distinction is here proposed for the discussion of what Paul finds wrong with the law. As we
have seen, Paul was faced with the task of explaining the relation between three convictions apparently in tension with each other:
1. According to Old Testament texts which Paul is bound to take seriously, Jews are promised life if they obey God's commands.
2. Since God sent his Son to redeem humanity, salvation is possible
   only through him.
3. God, being God, must have intended salvation through faith in
   Christ from the beginning.

Thus, on the one hand, Paul is concerned to show that faith in
Christ, not obedience to the law, represents—and has always represented—God's intended plan for salvation. On the other hand, he needs
to explain why the law does not provide the life which (as Paul himself both allows and affirms) it in fact promises. In both cases, of
course, Paul's reasoning runs (in Sanders's terms) "from solution to
plight": it is because Paul, the Christian, is convinced of the truth of
the second proposition that the first becomes problematic and the third
requires proving. But two separate issues are at stake, and it seems to
me useful to keep them apart.[35]

---

35. In general, Galatians is more concerned with showing that salvation
by faith in Christ was God's eternal plan, and that the law was merely a parenthesis between the giving of the promise to Abraham and its fulfillment in Christ. In
Romans, on the other hand, "Paul does not face an apostasy of Judaizers but is
engaged in a dialogue with Jews and Jewish Christians about his stance toward
the Torah as consistent with the faithfulness of God toward Israel in the gospel"
(Beker, *Paul*, 104). Here of necessity Paul considers in detail the problem of why
the law does not lead to the life it promises.

Paul argues, for example, that the scripture "foresaw" that the Gentiles would be justified by faith (Gal. 3:8) when it promised that the nations would be "blessed" in Abraham, who himself was declared righteous because of his faith (vv. 6-9). He finds in Hab. 2:4 a proof that God intended justification to be by faith; the law is excluded since it is based on a different principle (Gal. 3:11-12). Moreover, the promise to Abraham preceded the giving of the law: God's ultimate purposes, Paul argues, are thus apparent in the former institution, and cannot be set aside by the latter (vv. 15-18). In fact, the law serves functions quite different from that of imparting life (vv. 19-25). In each case, Paul attempts to show that God "knew all along," and intended, that faith, not the law, would lead to life. But none of these arguments accounts for the claim of God's law to provide life for its adherents and the failure of the law (evident once it is realized that salvation is to be found only in Christ) to deliver on its promises.

Above all, the problem of Gentile admission to the people of God does not answer the question why the law cannot lead its adherents to life. There is no need, in the current state of the debate, to emphasize the centrality of the Gentile mission to Paul's thinking. For Paul, it was obvious that God intended from the beginning that Gentiles would belong to his people and equally obvious that faith in Christ, not the Jewish law, was the intended means of the Gentiles' inclusion. God is *not* the God of Jews only (Rom. 3:29). Abraham was to be the father of all who believe, whether they are circumcised or uncircumcised (4:11-12). If the promise was to be effective for *all* of Abraham's "seed," then faith, not the Jewish law, had to be the means of appropriating it (v. 16). All who are in Christ—Jew or Greek, slave or free, male and female—are "Abraham's offspring, heirs according to promise" (Gal. 3:28-29). That Gentiles have a place in God's plan is for Paul the ultimate demonstration that faith in Christ, not the Jewish law, lies at its center.

But the problem remains.[36] God's promise that those who obey his commands will live cannot be set aside simply because Gentiles were not present when the law was given. When God's Son came on the scene, God's law was already in place—Christ himself was born "under" the law (Gal. 4:4). An old and divine covenant was in force before the new was established (2 Cor. 3; cf. Gal. 4:24); a righteousness based on law was proclaimed by Moses (Rom. 10:5) before the righ-

36. Cf. Bläser, *Gesetz,* 46.

teousness apart from the law was "manifested" through faith in Jesus Christ (3:21-22; cf. Gal. 3:23). It is thus not enough to say that faith in Christ leads to life whereas the law does not. The law cannot be dismissed simply as a false path to life adopted by Judaizers. On the contrary, so seriously does Paul take the institution of the law, and such validity does he attribute to its sanctions, that he believes humanity must be redeemed from its curse, that believers must actually *die to the law,* if they are to be saved.[37] But why does the law bring a curse, condemnation and death, rather than life to its adherents?

Paul's exclusivist soteriology provokes, but does not answer, the question of the law's inadequacy. Certainly his conviction that salvation is available only in Christ—who, after all, did not die in vain (Gal. 2:21)—was a sufficient reason for believing that salvation is not found in the law.[38] But exclusivist soteriology does not explain how the law has failed.[39] Nor is it sufficient to say that Paul thought in black-and-white terms, so that, if life is available in Christ, the law, by way of contrast, must be linked with condemnation and death.[40] What reason did Paul have for making the law part of the dilemma? Does the fact that the law cannot impart life lead of itself to the conclusion that it curses, condemns, and *kills* (Gal. 3:10; 2 Cor. 3:6, 7, 9; Rom. 7:10; 8:2)?

When the question of the law's *failure* is posed, the debate necessarily returns to the issues raised by Bultmann and Wilckens: Does the law fail to provide life because its conditions are not met and its commandments are transgressed? Or is the problem that the Jews' very compliance with its commands leads them into the more fundamental sins of self-righteousness and boasting? The latter alternative will be considered below (iv. The Exclusion of Boasting). Here we will consider the role of human transgressions in Paul's view of the law's "weakness."

The critical passage is Rom. 1:18–3:20. In the course of the argument Paul himself affirms the basic principles of the righteousness

37. Cf. Beker, *Paul,* 187: "Unlike Marcion, [Paul] does not conclude that the law is an inferior dispensation that does not conform to God's will and plan of salvation. To the contrary, Christ died 'for our sins,' that is, for the sins incurred under the law. Christ's death is a sacrificial death that acknowledges our just condemnation by the law. . . ."

38. Cf. Kuss, "Nomos," 211-213.

39. Cf. Byrne, "Sons," 231; van Dülmen, *Theologie,* 178.

40. As Sanders, *Law,* 137-141, thinks.

based on law (cf. 10:5): God "will render to every man according to his works" (2:6). He will reward with eternal life "those who by patience in well-doing seek for glory and honor and immortality," while "wrath and fury" await the wicked (vv. 7-8). God requires more than the possession of the law of those who would be justified: "It is not the hearers of the law who are righteous before God, but the doers of the law who will be justified" (v. 13). On the other hand, the passage reaches its conclusion in the claim that "no human being will be justified in [God's] sight by works of the law," and that "now the righteousness of God has been manifested apart from law . . . through faith in Jesus Christ" (3:20-22). Here, then, we find Paul expressing, and presumably explaining the relation between, the propositions with which we began: the Old Testament promises life to those who obey God's commands, yet salvation is possible only through Christ, not through observance of the law.

There is, it seems to me, no reason to deny Paul's sincerity in affirming the first proposition. Nothing in the passage suggests that he is merely adopting his opponents' understanding for the sake of an argument. Paul clearly believes that the law does not lead to life, that God was achieving quite different purposes through its promulgation; nonetheless, the sanctions of life as well as death, blessing as well as curse, are part of the divine record, and Paul was not one who could ignore them. What he needs to show is why only the law's curse has become operative.

His answer, in a sense, is straightforward enough. The law promises life to those who adhere to its commands, but threatens with death those who disobey; clearly, then, since the law does not lead to life, all must have transgressed its demands. "All have sinned and fall short of the glory of God" (3:23). Though the law promises life, what it brings is "knowledge of sin" (v. 20). In the words of scripture, "All have turned aside, together they have gone wrong; no one does good, not even one" (v. 12). Human transgression is Paul's explanation of why the law does not provide the life it promises.

Paul's conclusion is clear, but the path by which he reaches his goal contains a number of surprises, and the question may well be asked whether Paul's argument supports the conclusion he desires. The passage requires a closer look.

1. The relation between Jews and Gentiles is never far from Paul's mind; here it provides the structure for Paul's presentation of the human dilemma. Rom. 3:9 suggests that the argument which

precedes it was meant to demonstrate the guilt of "both Jews and Greeks," and in fact 1:18-32 does seem to catalogue characteristic Gentile vices, whereas in 2:17-29, Jews are explicitly addressed. Paul's point, in part, must be that Jews and Greeks share the same dilemma— hence the same divine solution applies to both.

But Paul consistently treats the pressing issues of the moment within the framework of broader theological concerns, and Romans 1–3 is no exception. The immediate problem facing Paul in Galatians was the terms on which Gentiles are to be admitted to the people of God; but Paul responds to the matter with a wide-ranging discussion of the nature and function of the divine law. Similarly, while Paul's pressing concern in the opening chapters of Romans may be to support a gospel of salvation for Gentiles as well as Jews through faith in Christ apart from the law, we underestimate his theological achievement if we fail to see that he has raised the level of the discussion above the practical concerns of the first-century Church in depicting in general terms the plight of humanity before its Creator and Judge. Thus, whereas Rom. 1:18-32 details sins for which pagans were notorious in Jewish polemics, Paul himself does not use the word "heathen" *(ethnē)* in the portrayal. Instead he addresses "all ungodliness and wickedness of men" (1:18) perpetrated in the face of the Creator's goodness (v. 25), and drawing upon humanity "the wrath of God" (v. 18). Again, though Jews are perhaps primarily in mind already in the beginning of chapter 2, the address is not limited to them:[41] "You have no excuse, O man" (2:1; cf. vv. 3, 6). Paul's concern is to show all humanity under divine sentence, accountable to God, yet defenseless before his judgment: "that every mouth may be stopped, and the whole world may be held accountable to God" (3:19).[42]

41. Cf. Zeller, *Mission,* 149; and, even more emphatically, Stowers, *Diatribe,* 112.

42. Cf. Bornkamm, *Experience,* 59. We may compare the opening of 1 Corinthians. The problem at hand is Corinthian claims to wisdom. Paul deals with the matter by contrasting the futility of human wisdom in general with the power and wisdom of God (1:25; cf. 3:19). Faith must therefore rest in the power of God, not in the "wisdom of men" (2:5). The wisdom, righteousness, sanctification, and redemption in which believers share are theirs through Jesus Christ (1:30); only in him may they boast (1:31). Paul treats separate issues in Romans and 1 Corinthians; in both cases, however, immediate concerns are illuminated by basic convictions about the bankruptcy of human endeavors and the sufficiency of God's redemption in Christ.

2. But does Paul's argument bear the weight of his conclusions?[43] In 1:18-32, Paul declares (he can hardly be said to demonstrate) that humanity is guilty of wicked behavior, idolatrous worship, and suppression of the truth. No exceptions seem to be allowed. Yet in chapter 2, Paul appears to reckon with Gentiles who fulfill the requirements of God's law. His accusations are now directed at Jews, whom he finds guilty of egregious sins; yet here too Paul appears to allow for the possibility that they may "obey the law" (2:25) and thus prove to be "real" Jews whom God will praise (vv. 28-29). In 3:10-18 his "demonstration" amounts to no more than a collection of scripture texts denouncing human sins; and some of the passages quoted (Ps. 5:9 [MT 10]; 140:3 [MT 4]; 10:7; 36:1 [MT 2]) are from contexts in which the righteous denounce the wrongs of the wicked with no implication that the evils are universal; yet universality is necessarily Paul's point. It is not surprising, then, that many readers feel that Paul has not proven his case.

a. In fairness to Paul, it might be asked how universal transgression could ever be proven to the satisfaction of a neutral observer. Such a conviction, by its very nature, is not susceptible to empirical demonstration.[44] Paul's argument, of necessity, is homiletic and traditional in nature,[45] directed to readers familiar with the motifs and liable to be impressed by their recollection. The prophetic literature is filled with denunciations of the nations, and especially of Israel, in which particularly lurid wrongs are cited and yet guilt is held to be universal, and divine judgment is expected for all. Such literature is simply not to be judged by the probative force of the argumentation. If Paul's denunciations are faulted as too sweeping, what are we to say of passages like the following, taken from Jeremiah but abundantly paralleled in the other prophets?

> They are all stubbornly rebellious, going about with slanders; they are bronze and iron, all of them act corruptly. (Jer. 6:28)

> No man repents of his wickedness, saying, "What have I done?" Every one turns to his own course. (8:6)

43. Cf. Räisänen, *Law,* 97-109; Sanders, *Law,* 123-132.
44. Cf. Pfleiderer, *Paulinism,* I, 35-36.
45. Cf. Wilson, "Religion," 340-341: "It would be a mistake to read 1.19f. as a neutral or comprehensive assessment of Jewish and Gentile piety; it is rather an impassioned, selective, even tendentious critique from the perspective of the gospel. . . . It is a prophetic judgement which is different from, and cannot be used as evidence for, the scientific study of religion."

They are all adulterers, a company of treacherous men. They bend their tongue like a bow; falsehood and not truth has grown strong in the land; for they proceed from evil to evil, and they do not know me, says the Lord. Let every one beware of his neighbor, and put no trust in any brother; for every brother is a supplanter, and every neighbor goes about as a slanderer. Every one deceives his neighbor, and no one speaks the truth; they have taught their tongue to speak lies; they commit iniquity and are too weary to repent. Heaping oppression upon oppression, and deceit upon deceit, they refuse to know me, says the Lord. (9:2-6 [MT 1-5])

b. What, then, are we to make of the contradiction between the claim in Romans 3 that "all men, both Jews and Greeks, are under the power of sin" (v. 9) and the allowance in chapter 2 of the possibility that Jews and Gentiles may gain life by obeying God's commands? Three considerations may lessen (but not resolve) the tension between these claims.

First, as we have seen, Paul finds in scripture, and here repeats as valid, the principle that obedience to God's law leads to life. The sequel will show why, in Paul's mind, that principle has failed. Nevertheless, in depicting the dilemma which led to the cross, Paul restates the principle of righteousness which operated under the Sinaitic economy before the righteousness of faith in Christ was revealed. In the light of what follows, his statements have necessarily a provisional nature.[46]

Second, though Paul includes Jews in his denunciation of human sins, and finds them guilty of the same wrongs they condemn in others (2:1-3, 21-23), the thrust of his argument in Romans 2 lies in meeting an objection, not to the truth, but to the relevance of the point. His primary concern is not to prove that Jews are guilty of transgressions to those who think them innocent, but to insist that Jews, for all their privileges, are as responsible as Gentile sinners for the transgressions they commit (2:3, 9-11, 12, 25-27). Once Paul has shown that Jewish privileges do not exempt them from judgment, Paul can draw the conclusion that the "whole world" lies guilty and defenseless before God (3:19). In this way, the thrust of the argument of Romans 2 does support the conclusion Paul reaches in chapter 3.

Third, it is in the course of this argument against Jewish privileges, not in his assessment of the Gentile plight, that Paul compares righteous Gentiles to sinful Jews and claims that the former will con-

46. Cf. Hahn, "Gesetzesverständnis," 32.

demn the latter at the judgment.[47] In suggesting that some Gentiles will be approved by God on the basis of their works, Paul appears to allow in Romans 2 what chapters 1 and 3 categorically deny.[48] Perhaps the traditional motif which compared (relatively) righteous Gentiles with sinful Jews, to the latter's shame and condemnation, has influenced Paul here (cf. Ezek. 3:6-7; 5:6-7; 16:27, 32-34, 44-52; Matt. 12:41-42).

c. Paul does quote in Romans 3 (as elsewhere!) Old Testament texts in a sense foreign to their original context. On the other hand, at least Eccl. 7:20 and Ps. 14:2-3 support a case for universal transgression, and Isa. 59:7-8 is taken from a general condemnation of God's people. Moreover, as we have seen, many other texts from the prophets, equally sweeping in their denunciation, could have been quoted. Universal transgression was not a notion foreign to Judaism, though Paul radicalizes its implications.

3. Though Sanders and Räisänen both concede that Paul argues for universal sinfulness in Romans 1–3, the tenet is dismissed to the periphery of Paul's thought.[49] Paul's argument is perceived as inconsistent and illogical. Other passages show, it is said, that Paul was not particularly troubled by the problem of sin. What we find in Romans 1–3 is a mere argument for rejecting the law, whereas Paul's real reasons for doing so were quite different.

It is certainly true that Paul did not start with a conviction about the hopelessness of the human predicament under sin, then grasp at Christ as the answer to the dilemma.[50] On the other hand, Paul inherited—he did not first posit—the notion that Christ's death was "for our sins" (the traditional phrase in 1 Cor. 15:3; cf. Rom. 3:25; 4:24-25, etc.); hence, broadly speaking, the solution imposed its own view of the human plight on Paul, and the plight thus defined was no more an option to Paul than was the solution itself. That a conviction of universal sin cannot be independently proven is no reason for thinking it less than fundamental to Paul. Moreover, the conviction itself dictates neither a particular view of the origin of sin nor a precise definition of the nature of its power. Paul's wrestlings with these latter issues (to which we return in Chapter Nine) confirms rather than undermines the

47. Cf. Wilson, "Religion," 341; Räisänen, *Law,* 106; Watson, "Faith," 215.

48. That Gentile *Christians* are meant in Romans 2 is unlikely; cf. Räisänen, *Law,* 104-105.

49. Sanders, *Law,* 35-36; Räisänen, *Law,* 107-109.

50. Sanders, *Paul,* 443, 499.

central place occupied by sin in Paul's thinking about the human plight. Surely a belief that God's Son died for the sins of humanity would lead Paul to take human sin with an awesome earnest![51]

Other passages show that he did just that. In Romans 4, we encounter the startling—and undoubtedly Pauline—formulation, the justification of the "ungodly" (v. 5). Not less startling is the way Paul includes himself among the "weak," the "ungodly," the "sinners," and the "enemies" of God for whom Christ died (5:6-10).[52] In Romans 6–7, Paul describes the desperateness of the human plight as involving actual bondage to sin requiring deliverance rather than simply transgressions and guilt needing atonement.[53] Here the claim is repeated that the law's failure is due to human sin. Though given for "life" (7:10), its coming served only to revive sin and thus lead to death.

> I was once alive apart from the law, but when the commandment came, sin revived and I died; the very commandment which promised life proved to be death to me. For sin, finding opportunity in the commandment, deceived me and by it killed me. (7:9-11)

The law's commandments are good (v. 12), but the "weakness" of the

51. In attributing Paul's pessimism about the human condition to his preconversion (Hellenistic Jewish) religion, Montefiore fails to realize the amount of rethinking required by Paul's new faith in a crucified Messiah. See above, section i of Chapter Three.

52. For Paul's own sense of sin, see also 1 Cor. 15:9; Gal. 1:13; Phil. 3:6, 12. It is true that Paul sees his persecuting activity as an expression of his fervor for Judaism; but there is no question that he could have regarded as anything but a heinous sin the "violent" persecution of the "church of God" and the attempt "to destroy it" (Gal. 1:13). Note also how Paul personalizes the death of Christ in Gal. 2:20. For the view that Paul should not be made an exception to the human plight as portrayed in Romans 7, see note 33 above. His description of his life under the law as "blameless" (Phil. 3:6) perhaps reflects his preconversion assessment, though the polemical context in which the claim is made—a comparison with Paul's detractors, self-proclaimed devotees of the law—should be kept in mind as well. There is no warrant for detaching Phil. 3:6 from its context, then elevating the isolated claim to Paul's "real" assessment of human capacities, setting aside Romans 1–3, 5, 7, etc. in the process. Cf. Espy, "Conscience," 161-188.

53. The two explanations should not be played off against each other; transgression leads to bondage, and bondage is expressed in transgression (cf. Rom. 6:16, 19-21; 7:15-23). Note how Rom. 3:9 (all are under the power of sin, *huph' hamartian*) follows from Paul's claim in the preceding chapters that Gentiles and Jews commit sins. Cf. Räisänen, *Law,* 99-100, n. 29. For the importance of "juristic thinking" to Paul's theology, cf. Hübner, "Proprium," 467-471; Gundry, "Grace," 28-34.

law is shown by the inability of "sinful flesh" to meet its demands (8:3-4).

As we have seen, Rom. 9:31-32 presupposes the same argument. Only faith in Christ, not "works," can lead to righteousness. Not that "works" are themselves wrong; the righteousness based on the law demanded them (10:5). But those who pursue such righteousness do not attain their goal (9:31)—and, in the context of the argument in Romans, transgressions are certainly the underlying reason. To pursue righteousness by works, not faith, is wrong since the former path has failed and has been replaced by the latter (3:20, 22; 10:4). Yet Israel, in its unenlightened zeal for what has now passed away, stumbles at God's righteousness offered in Christ (9:32–10:3).

Gal. 3:10 is based on the same premise. What the law brings to its adherents, Paul says, is a curse, not a blessing. To prove his point, he cites Deut. 27:26: "Cursed be every one who does not abide by all things written in the book of the law, and do them." Here, as elsewhere, it is the failure to "abide" by the law, the failure to "do" its commands, that draws upon men and women "the curse of the law" (Gal. 3:13).[54]

Finally, Paul's comparison of the old and new covenants in 2 Corinthians 3 assumes the same conviction. Both covenants—the old as well as the new—are divine and glorious. But the old covenant "kills" whereas the new gives life (v. 6). The old is a "dispensation of death" and "condemnation" (vv. 7, 9), whereas the new leads to righteousness. In the context, Paul is explaining the splendors of his own "ministry," and he does not pause to explain the dilemma to which the ministry of Moses led. But to suggest that the law "condemns" something other than its transgression is to depart from what common sense says about any law as well as from what Paul, in harmony with a host of Old Testament texts, says elsewhere about the Mosaic code (cf. especially Rom. 4:15).

All of this—let me repeat—is Paul's Christian theology; Sand-

---

54. Against Sanders's view (*Law*, 20-22) that Paul quotes the text in Deuteronomy simply because it links the law and the divine curse, see Räisänen, *Law*, 95-96, n. 13: even a Paul is not likely to have derived from a verse condemning *transgressions* of the law a proof that the law's *acceptance* brings a curse! Similarly, Paul's point cannot be that trying to "do" the law brings a curse, since the curse is explicitly said to be pronounced over those who *fail* to do what the law commands. Since Paul's own statements elsewhere (cf. Rom. 2:12; 4:15; 7:10-11) connect the ill effects of the law with its transgression, and this is the obvious sense of the verse he quotes here, there is no need to distinguish between what Paul wants the words of his quotation to say and what they actually say.

ers rightly pillories historians of religion who portray Judaism and its law in terms borrowed from Paul's account of their shortcomings.[55] As far as we can tell, Paul before his conversion did not believe that the law had failed, nor did he long for a savior to deliver him from its bondage. Only faith in a crucified Messiah forced Paul to explain why the law had not led to life. Still, in an account of the views of Paul the apostle, we cannot rest with the claim that the law was wrong only because it was not faith. The law, for Paul, failed because of human transgressions.

By now it should be evident why Paul gave the human dimension of the law (its demand for compliance) an emphasis foreign to Judaism as a whole and to the understanding of his opponents. What for others seemed inconceivable Paul was forced to explain: the law had failed to bring life. Since the divine part in the giving of the law cannot be faulted with its shortcomings, the demand for human works becomes the center of Paul's attention: the law must "rest" on works. Conversely, since the gospel succeeds where the law has failed, Paul must exclude from his definition of "grace" and "faith" the human activity which doomed the law to failure: "faith" does not work, nor can "grace" be the reward of the one who does. It is because Paul believes the coming of the new covenant implies the inadequacy of the old that he characterizes the one as resting on divine grace, the other on human works.

Perhaps we should add a postscript at this point. Paul was not the first to deduce the incorrigible sin of God's people from what he perceived as an act of divine judgment; nor was he the first to conclude that, as a result of such sin, the Sinaitic covenant had proved inadequate.[56]

55. Sanders, *Paul,* 4.
56. Note also Jer. 11:1-13; Hos. 1:9; 2:2 (MT 2:4). The point is stressed in von Rad's *Theology.* Whereas Deuteronomy regards the commandments as easy to obey, such confidence was shattered by the prophets. The earlier prophets spoke of "Israel's utter and complete failure *vis-à-vis* Jahweh"; Jeremiah and Ezekiel go further, reaching "the insight that she is inherently utterly unable to obey him" (II, 398). It is characteristic of the prophets that they see the "security" given Israel by her "election traditions" as "cancelled out because of her guilt" (II, 117). "They consigned their audience, and all their contemporaries, to a kingdom of death where they could no longer be reached by the salvation coming from the old saving events" (II, 272). As a result, the only thing Israel could "hold on to" was "a new historical act on the part of Jahweh. . . . The prophetic message differs from all previous Israelite theology, which was based on the past saving history,

> Behold, the days are coming, says the Lord, when I will make a new
> covenant with the house of Israel and the house of Judah, not like the
> covenant which I made with their fathers when I took them by the
> hand to bring them out of the land of Egypt, my covenant which they
> broke, though I was their husband. (Jer. 31:31-32)

Indeed, Paul was not the first to think (though he was the first to sys-
tematize the conviction) that since the Sinaitic covenant had failed
through human transgressions, any further dealings of God with his
people must be based on God's character and grace alone.[57]

> Therefore the Lord has kept ready the calamity and has brought it
> upon us; for the Lord our God is righteous in all the works which he
> has done, and we have not obeyed his voice. . . . We have sinned, we
> have done wickedly. . . . O my God, incline thy ear and hear; open
> thy eyes and behold our desolations, and the city which is called by
> thy name; for we do not present our supplications before thee on the
> ground of our righteousness, but on the ground of thy great mercy. O
> Lord, hear; O Lord, forgive; O Lord, give heed and act; delay not, for
> thy own sake, O my God, because thy city and thy people are called
> by thy name. (Dan. 9:14-15, 18-19)[58]

---

in that the prophets looked for the decisive factor in Israel's whole existence—
her life or her death—in some future event" (II, 117). Thus, whereas for Deuteronomy God's commands are given "for life," their fulfillment is not a problem,
and what is required is simply a reaffirmation of the old covenant, for Jeremiah
and Ezekiel "Jahweh's commandments have turned into a law that judges and de-
stroys" (II, 269). Israel is incapable of observing them, yet the future holds out
the hope of a new covenant brought about by a new saving act on the part of
Israel's God. Cf. also Zimmerli, *Law,* 76; Ridderbos, *Paul,* 157; Stuhlmacher,
Reconciliation, 114.

I am not sure on what basis Räisänen concludes that "if something is truly
divine, it is hardly capable of being abrogated" (*Law,* 265), and that, as a result,
Paul's view of the law is necessarily untenable. Jewish and Christian thinkers
through the ages have not placed that kind of restriction on the Almighty's dealings with his world. As Jeremiah 31 and Hos. 1:9 indicate, Paul was not the first
to think that the Sinaitic covenant had been annulled by human sin. Divine institutions like prophecy, human government, marriage, ritual laws, etc. have
frequently been thought to be tied to "this age," or even a part of it. And was
Judaism invalidated when the temple worship it believed was divinely appointed
was nonetheless brought to an end?

57. Cf. Meyer, *Christians,* 129-131.
58. Cf. also Ezek. 36:22-32; Deut. 9:4-29; Hos. 11:8-9.

iii. The Centrality of Grace

If Paul regards the mark of the old covenant as its demand for obedience and sees the reason for its failure in human transgressions, then the mark of the new covenant, and the basis for his confidence in its success, is its exclusive dependence on God's grace.[59] Believers in Christ have been called into (a status of) grace (Gal. 1:6).[60] They stand in grace (Rom. 5:2). To return to the law is to "nullify the grace of God," to risk "[falling] away from grace" (Gal. 2:21; 5:4; cf. 1:6). Once believers lived "under law," but, by dying with Christ, they "died to the law" and left its sphere (Rom. 7:4-6); now they "are not under law but under grace" (6:14).

The (specifically Pauline)[61] emphasis on grace and the contrast between grace and law is not difficult to explain once the character and failure of the law are defined in Pauline terms. Grace is the obvious antidote to the plight which resulted from life "under law."

> But the free gift is not like the trespass. For if many died through one man's trespass, much more have the grace of God and the free gift in the grace of that one man Jesus Christ abounded for many. . . . If, because of one man's trespass, death reigned through that one man, much more will those who receive the abundance of grace and the free gift of righteousness reign in life through the one man Jesus Christ. . . . Law came in, to increase the trespass; but where sin increased, grace abounded all the more, so that, as sin reigned in death, grace also might reign through righteousness to eternal life through Jesus Christ our Lord. (Rom. 5:15, 17, 20-21; cf. 3:24; 6:23; 2 Cor. 6:1)

In these verses, "grace" clearly involves forgiveness from transgressions and deliverance from the "reign" of sin; it thus reverses the dilemma created under the law's hegemony. But the term also implies the complete freedom with which God bestows those favors; this, too, involves a contrast with the order based on the law and its "works," where divine blessing, Paul insists, is linked to human obedience (Rom. 4:4; 10:5).[62] Repeatedly Paul parallels the grace *(charis)* of God with his "free gift" *(dōrea,* Rom. 5:15, 17; cf. 3:24; 6:23). Grace is a gift lavished on sinners, on the ungodly, solely at the discretion and by

59. Cf. Bläser, *Gesetz,* 194.
60. Cf. Burton, *Galatians,* 21.
61. Cf. Beker, *Paul,* 265-266.
62. Ibid., 266.

the goodness of God. It is God's to bestow, and he bestows it "upon whomever he wills" (9:18). Were human "works" a factor, "grace would no longer be grace" (11:6).

Thus human "works" and the law which demands them are necessarily excluded from a justification based on grace.[63] It does not follow that Jews are wrong in attempting to obey God's law; on the contrary, Paul commends them for their zeal (10:2). But, since they fail to attain their goal, only divine grace can convey life. A "faith" which involves no "pursuit" of righteousness must be substituted for the "works" of those who strive but fall short (9:30-32). Such faith implies the abandonment of one's "own," inadequate righteousness, with submission to "the righteousness that comes from God" (10:3; cf. Phil. 3:9).

This understanding of the relationship between faith and works emerges most clearly in Romans 3 and 4. The "works of the law" do not justify because "all have sinned and fall short of the glory of God" (3:20, 23). Hence God has manifested a "righteousness . . . apart from law . . . through faith in Jesus Christ" (vv. 21-22), a justification bestowed *"by his grace as a gift (dōrean tē autou chariti)"* (v. 24). When Paul claims that "a man is justified by faith apart from works of law" (v. 28), he can only mean, in the conclusion to this argument, that human attempts to keep God's law have failed, that acceptance of God's grace revealed in Christ is the only path to life.

The opening verses of Romans 4 confirm the view that "justification by faith" implies the exclusion of human "works" from any role in salvation.[64] Grace would not be grace if given in response to the activity of "one who works" (4:4); justification by faith is the mark of the "one who does not work but trusts him who justifies the ungodly" (v. 5).

The essentials of Paul's position in Romans—though not the logical arrangement—are all found in Galatians as well: the contrast between the law and faith, based on the demand of the law for deeds (3:11-12); the contrast between a gospel of God's grace and a message (hardly to be called a "gospel") which requires submission to the law (1:6-7; 2:21; 5:4); the insistence that the law pronounces a curse on

63. See the discussion above, section ii of Chapter Seven.
64. The emphasis is, of course, clear beyond dispute in the disputed epistles: Eph. 2:8-9; Tit. 3:4-7. Such texts ought at least to warn us that "Reformation spectacles" are not required to read Paul as denying that human "works" are a factor in salvation.

those who do "not abide by all things written in the book of the law, and do them" (3:10); the claim that God's inheritance must be bestowed by his sovereign act alone (the promise) rather than by means of law, where human compliance is indispensable (vv. 15-18). Paul's argumentation is clearer in Romans; nothing suggests a substantial shift in his thinking on the subject.

But even when the point of justification by faith is recognized as the exclusion of human "works" from salvation, the centrality of the conviction is often questioned. In both Romans and Galatians, the formulation "justified by faith" occurs in the context of the first-century dispute concerning Gentile admission to the early Church (Rom. 3:28; cf. 4:1-17; Gal. 2:14-16). Was the doctrine, as Wrede argued,[65] merely a polemical tool devised to counter the demand that Gentile believers submit to the Jewish law?

That the doctrine in an explicit form occurs only in contexts where the Gentile problem is discussed (cf. however Phil. 3:9) is not in itself decisive.[66] Pagan converts would not normally have been tempted to think that deeds done in the days of their idolatry could commend them to the living God. Apart from the question whether observance of the Jewish law was necessary, then, Paul could ignore the problem of "works"; the silence of particular epistles on the issue is no indication that Paul had not yet given it thought.

When, however, Paul did deal with the problem posed by the Mosaic law, he explained its failure by insisting that the law's demand for "works" had not been met, that divine grace was the only remedy. Thus the fundamental principle affirmed by Paul's thesis of justification by faith, not works of the law, is that of humanity's dependence on divine grace; and that conviction, it may safely be said, underlies everything Paul wrote.

The Thessalonians may have "turned to God from idols" (1 Thess. 1:9), but Paul stresses that this was in response to God's calling (1:4; 2:12; 5:24), that God was the one who "destined" them "to obtain salvation" (5:9).[67] The Corinthians were emphatically reminded that God's call is directed to the "foolish," the "weak," "what is low and despised in the world, even things that are not, to bring to nothing things that are, so that no human being might boast in the presence of

65. See the review of Wrede above, section i of Chapter Two.

66. Cf. Hübner, "Proprium," 454-455; Pfleiderer, *Paulinism,* I, 30.

67. Hübner ("Proprium," 454-458) develops in detail the correspondence between justification by faith and Paul's thinking as reflected in 1 Thessalonians.

God" (1 Cor. 1:27-29).[68] The new creation of which Christians are a part is entirely "from God" (2 Cor. 5:17-18). The Galatian believers at one point came "to know God"—but the matter is better expressed by saying that they came "to be known by God" (Gal. 4:9). In the letter to the Romans, the contrast between grace and works figures not only in Paul's discussion of justification by faith, but also in his account of the election of God's people through the ages (9:10-13, 16; 11:5-6).

Nor does human dependence on divine grace end with conversion.[69] Paul's understanding of Christian behavior will be the subject of a later chapter; here we may simply note his insistence that the God who "began a good work" when believers first received the gospel is the one who "will bring it to completion at the day of Jesus Christ" (Phil. 1:6; cf. 1 Thess. 5:24). He is "at work" in believers, "both to will and to work for his good pleasure" (Phil. 2:13). He is the one who will "make [them] stand" (Rom. 14:4). Believers are not to imagine that they know anything (1 Cor. 8:2), that they are anything (Gal. 6:3), or that they have anything apart from what they have received from God (1 Cor. 4:7). They are enabled to function in the Church only because gifts of grace *(charismata)* have been granted to them (Rom. 12:6; cf. 1 Cor. 1:4-7; 12:6; even 2 Cor. 8:1, 7!). They do not even know how to pray as they ought (Rom. 8:26). They owe their standing to God's kindness and will maintain it only as they "continue in his kindness" (11:22).[70]

It is typical of Paul to qualify statements of his own accomplishments with a telling "Yet not I":

> But by the grace of God I am what I am, and his grace toward me was not in vain. On the contrary, I worked harder than any of them, though it was not I, but the grace of God which is with me. (1 Cor. 15:10)
>
> In Christ Jesus, then, I have reason to be proud of my work for God. For I will not venture to speak of anything except what Christ has wrought through me to win obedience from the Gentiles, by word and deed. (Rom. 15:17-18; cf. 2 Cor. 12:11)

His appointment to apostleship was made by divine grace (Rom. 1:5; 15:15-16; Gal. 1:15-16; 2:9), and grace made his work effective (1 Cor. 3:5, 10; 2 Cor. 1:12; cf. Gal. 2:8). His competence was from God, not

68. Cf. Hooker, *Pieces,* 27-28.

69. Cf. Gundry, "Grace," 8-10.

70. None of these texts implies passivity or indolence on the part of Christians; the point is simply Paul's insistence that God is "at work" in whatever a believer does. Cf. Lyonnet, "Gratuité," 107-110; Deidun, *Morality,* 51-84.

himself (2 Cor. 3:5); he dared not rely on himself, but only on God (1:9). He was an earthen vessel; power came from God, not himself (4:7). His very weakness gave God the opportunity to display the power of Christ within him (12:9-10).

Modesty, true or false, will not explain the almost wearisome way in which Paul protests his impotence; nor does it account for his insistence on the impotence of others. We are dealing with specifically Pauline dogma. If the above texts mean anything, they prove that an emphasis on divine grace as opposed to human achievement is a genuine Pauline concern, not one foisted upon him by Reformation interpreters. Judaism knows much of divine grace; its view of humanity's plight, however, is less drastic than Paul's and, as a result, it does not speak in Paul's exclusive language of the need for divine grace. Paul's convictions on both scores were formulated in the light of the cross of Christ. Held throughout his ministry, these convictions found their most memorable expression when Paul, responding to the controversy surrounding the admission of Gentiles to the Church, declared his doctrine of justification for Jews and Gentiles alike by faith in Jesus Christ, apart from the works of the law.

iv. The Exclusion of Boasting

In the opening chapters of Romans, Paul has shown that the law promises life to those who do its commands, but that sin has left the world guilty before God; justification, however, is available by God's grace as a gift to those who believe in Jesus Christ. Paul continues: "Then what becomes of our boasting? It is excluded. On what principle *(dia poiou nomou)*? On the principle of works? No, but on the principle of faith" (3:27).

Paul's use of *nomos* in this controversial verse was discussed in the preceding chapter. The *nomos* of works here excluded is best seen as the law of Moses which demands works; note how, in the summary of Paul's argument in verse 28, the "works" of the Mosaic law are indeed said to be excluded from the process of justification. *Nomos pisteōs* is perhaps best rendered "principle of faith," though Paul uses the ambiguity of Greek *nomos* to form a pointed, polemical contrast with the Mosaic order.

But what "boasting" is excluded? What "boasting" would be legitimate if righteousness were indeed achieved under a law demanding works, but is ruled out since righteousness can only be gained under the "principle of faith"? The answer seems clear. "Boasting" may be appropriate if something has been done to warrant it; if, however, "works" are excluded and divine grace is the sole basis for justification, then no place is left for human "boasting."

That "boasting" in one's achievements is uppermost in Paul's mind is apparent from the opening verses of Romans 4. Abraham would have had "something to boast about" if he had been "justified by works" (v. 2); obviously the exclusion of "boasting" in 3:27 is being picked up and developed. But Abraham has nothing to boast about, for he was counted righteous because of his faith (4:3), and faith is the mark of the "one who does not work but trusts him who justifies the ungodly" (v. 5). God would have to respond to "works" by rewarding the worker, not according to divine grace *(kata charin)*, but according to the worker's own "due" *(kata opheilēma,* v. 4); such a righteousness leaves the "one who works" with grounds for boasting. But these are eliminated when justification is by faith.

To this brief review of a crucial passage, three comments must be added:

1. The only "boasting" mentioned in Romans before 3:27 is that of Jews in their possession, not their observance, of the divine law (2:17, 23). Hence a number of scholars believe that this is the boasting Paul excludes in 3:27.[71] Confirmation of the view is found in 3:29: if justification were by the Jewish law, Jews could boast of its possession while Gentiles would be without hope; since, however, God is the God of Gentiles as well as Jews, justification must be available on the same terms (i.e., faith) for both, and Jews can no longer boast of their possession of the law. That Paul's argument in chapter 2 precludes such boasting is clear enough, and it is possible that its exclusion is part of what he has in mind in 3:27 as well. But the progression of his argument as outlined above, and especially the way in which he develops the exclusion of boasting in 4:1-5, show that the primary emphasis is on boasting of one's achievements.[72]

2. Rom. 4:2 ends in an ambiguous phrase: "For if Abraham was justified by works, he has something to boast about, but not before God *(ou pros theon).*" The words are sometimes taken[73] as implying that

---

71. Cf. Räisänen, *Law,* 170-171; Sanders, *Law,* 33.

72. Eph. 2:9 can at least be said to support this interpretation. For the connection between Rom. 3:28 and 29, see Käsemann, *Romans,* 104; Beker, *Paul,* 82.

73. E.g., Sanday and Headlam, *Romans,* 99-100.

Abraham's boasting of his achievements would be legitimate before people but illegitimate before God. But this seems unlikely.[74] How is Paul's argument served by the implication that boasting before people is legitimate? Moreover, such a reading leaves the possibility posed in the opening of verse 2 ("For if Abraham was justified by works . . .") unchallenged before the beginning of verse 3; but verse 3, while intended to support the claim that Abraham was not so justified, does not state the claim that he was not. Logically, then, the final words of verse 2 must be Paul's emphatic way of denying the truth of the supposition just proposed: "It is not so in God's eyes *(pros theon)*," "God does not see the matter so, for what does the scripture say? . . ." Underlying the emphatic denial is Paul's revulsion at the very suggestion that humans might have any ground for boasting before God.

3. Paul's doctrine of justification by faith thus results in the exclusion of boasting in human achievement. That Paul finds the exclusion appropriate is obvious, given his tenacious insistence on the centrality of divine grace and his explicit condemnation elsewhere of boasting in anything but the "Lord" and his cross (1 Cor. 1:29, 31; 2 Cor. 10:17; Gal. 6:14). But Sanders seems to be correct in finding in the passage in Romans "no indication that Paul thought that the law had failed *because* it leads to the wrong attitude or that his opposition to boasting *accounts* for his saying that righteousness is not by law."[75] On the contrary, the implication that boasting would be legitimate if "works" had been performed shows that the failure of the law is due to transgressions and not to any self-righteousness and boasting which might have followed on its observance. And this, of course, is precisely the point of Romans 2 and 3.

The story elsewhere in Paul is the same: the failure of the law is attributed to transgressions, not to attitudes which attended its observance. According to Rom. 4:15, the effect of the law is to bring wrath to bear on transgressors (cf. 5:13). According to Rom. 5:20, the introduction of the law multiplied the evil of transgressions. Romans 6 depicts life "under law" as marked, not by self-righteous observance, but by bondage to uncleanness and lawlessness (6:19) and the doing of shameful deeds (v. 21). In Romans 7:5 "sinful passions" are said to be aroused by the law—and the smugness of the "righteous" is not what Paul has in mind! Paul portrays those subject to the law in Ro-

---

74. Cf. Cranfield, *Romans,* 228; Räisänen, *Law,* 171, n. 56.
75. Sanders, *Law,* 35.

mans 7 as knowing the good but unable to do it,[76] and in 8:3 refers to this inability as a mark of the law's "weakness."

In short, Paul nowhere suggests that the law fails because its careful observance leads to self-righteousness and boasting; nor are the latter sins portrayed as characteristic flaws of Jews. Twice Paul refers to the righteousness based on the law which Jews pursue as their "own" righteousness (Rom. 10:3; Phil. 3:9); but this expression reflects the conviction that the law requires of its subjects personal obedience to its commands, whereas the righteousness of faith comes from God (*ek theou,* Phil. 3:9) as a gift of his grace. One's "own" righteousness thus need not imply self-righteousness; nor can such righteousness, commanded by God's law, be inherently wrong. What is wrong, of course, is the pursuit of the law's righteousness now that Christ has come and revealed God's righteousness through faith, thus bringing to an end the role of the law as a possible path to life (Rom. 10:4).

Paul does not fault the law with leading to self-righteousness and boasting. Yet the same message of the cross which demonstrates the folly of human wisdom (1 Cor. 1:20) also declares the bankruptcy of human righteousness (1 Cor. 1:30; Rom. 1:18–3:20); consequently, boasting of human wisdom and righteousness are alike excluded by Paul's gospel (Rom. 3:27; 4:1-5; 1 Cor. 1:30-31). Naturally, the exclusion itself, in Paul's mind, was part of the divine plan. When all humanity has been "consigned" to sin, divine mercy becomes the only basis for life (Rom. 11:32); and this, Paul assures us, was the eternal plan of God, "from" whom, "through" whom, and "to" whom "are all things" (v. 36). God's intention from the beginning was that his unilateral promise, rather than a law which required human compliance, should be the basis of his blessing (Gal. 3:15-18; Rom. 4:13-16). Not human "will" or "exertion," but divine "mercy" is, and has always been, the principle by which men and women stand before God (Rom. 9:16). Thus, though on one level the law "failed" because of human transgressions, on another level that very failure formed a part of God's design with the law. To a fuller consideration of Paul's view of that plan we turn in Chapter Nine.

But here we must conclude with an acknowledgment of Paul's achievement. It is to the apostle that we owe the characterization of

---

76. For Bultmann's interpretation of Romans 7 (Bultmann, "Anthropology," 147-157), see my "Letter," 232-233, 237-239.

salvation as the sheer gift of God's grace in Christ. Christian faith, for Paul, is merely a response to that grace; Paul distinguishes it from human "works." It is Paul's view that the law demands "works" as its condition for life, and Paul's explanation that the law failed as a path to human life because of universal human sin. That justification by grace through faith demonstrates the inadequacy of human righteousness and excludes human boasting are conclusions drawn by the apostle Paul.

Christians of different ages and traditions have varied in the weight they have assigned to these convictions. Where they are prominent—as they are, above all, in Martin Luther—the reading of Paul is inevitably the reason. There is more of Paul in Luther than many twentieth-century scholars are inclined to allow.

But the insights of the "new perspective" must not be lost to view. Paul's convictions need to be identified; they must also be recognized as Christian theology. When Paul's conclusion that the path of the law is dependent on human works is used to posit a rabbinic doctrine of salvation by works, and when his claim that God's grace in Christ excludes human boasting is used to portray rabbinic Jews as self-righteous boasters, the results (in Johnsonian terms) are "pernicious as well as false." When, moreover, the doctrine of merit perceived by Luther in the Catholicism of his day is read into the Judaism of the first Christian centuries, the results are worthless for historical study. Students who want to know how a rabbinic Jew perceived humanity's place in God's world will read Paul with caution and Luther not at all. On the other hand, students who want to understand Paul but feel they have nothing to learn from a Martin Luther should consider a career in metallurgy. Exegesis is learned from the masters.

Chapter Nine

The Law in God's Scheme

Nathaniel Hawthorne is best known for his absorbing account of the psychology of guilt in *The Scarlet Letter.* In a later, little-read novel, *The Marble Faun,* he allows one of his characters the following provocative speculation:

> Is Sin, then—which we deem such a dreadful blackness in the Universe—is it, like Sorrow, merely an element of human education, through which we struggle to a higher and purer state than we could otherwise have attained? Did Adam fall, that we might ultimately rise to a far loftier Paradise than his?

The very thought strikes a pious listener of the opposite sex as "terrible":

> Do not you perceive what a mockery your creed makes, not only of all religious sentiment, but of moral law, and how it annuls and obliterates whatever precepts of Heaven are written deepest within us?[1]

The initial question is abandoned as the incredible musings of a wandering mind. Attention shifts to the more pressing business of a blossoming romance.

An analogous question to that from which the pious Hilda recoils is considered by the apostle Paul, and he answers it in the affirmative. Briefly, we may sketch the background once again. The law of God was given with sanctions of life and death, blessing and curse. From the death of God's Son for humanity's sins, Paul concludes that the law has been broken, that only its sanction of death has become

1. Hawthorne, *Faun,* 460.

operative. Yet God would not be God if he were surprised by the latter development, or if it found no place in his plan. Was, then, the sin to which the law led itself a part of God's design? Paul believes that it was.

God's design included sin—yet Hilda's dismay is rooted in convictions which Paul of course shared. Sin remains a violation of God's will; neither God nor the law he instituted is responsible for the law's transgression. The relation between these statements—each of which is fundamental to Christian faith—poses one of the classic problems of Christian theology, and Paul's wrestlings with its various aspects must be seen in that light. The problems are scarcely of Paul's making, nor do they mark an incoherence peculiar to him. And while we do not expect of Paul a systematic treatment of the relation between God's foreknowledge and plan on the one side and human responsibility on the other, we do him an injustice if we fail to see that he deliberately and persistently affirms both principles. In accordance with God's design, the law led to sin for which, however, neither God nor his law can be held responsible; the consignment by the law of all humanity to sin is—again by God's design—merely the prelude to the demonstration of divine mercy in Christ.

The following discussion of God's purpose with the law is conducted primarily in dialogue with the recent works of Sanders and Räisänen. Both writers believe Paul was compelled by dogmatic considerations to attribute a negative function to the law. Both find his attempts to do so tentative, arbitrary, and inconsistent. In Räisänen's case, the interpretation in these terms offers further support for a general thesis of Pauline inconsistency. They may be right. It may well be that many of us are too influenced by the authority accorded Paul's writings for two thousand years to see the contradictions at their core.[2] Here it will be argued, however, that more attention to the context of Paul's statements will at least reduce the number of inconsistencies we find in his writings. Furthermore, the tasks which Paul attributes to the law represent, not arbitrary inventions, but restatements of principles long maintained within his inherited religion. Finally, though the application of these principles leads to logical problems, these problems are staple elements in Jewish and Christian thought everywhere.

2. Cf. Räisänen, *Law,* 1-15, and the pointed remark of Sanders, *Law,* 124: "We have become too accustomed to thinking of Paul as stating not only the truth of the gospel, but also the gospel truth."

The argument will be developed under the following points:

1. In Galatians as well as elsewhere in Paul's epistles, the divine origin of the law is not in question.
2. The coming of the law had the effect of transforming already existing sin into acts of demonstrable defiance against God's commands, subject to the sanctions duly prescribed for transgressions. Moreover, the law "increased" the number as well as the sinfulness of sins committed, since temptations to disobey first present themselves when a law is enacted. Finally, an awareness of their sin is brought to sinners by the law.
3. Though sin is always seen as a violation of God's will, Paul believes that the deepening bondage of humanity to sin which resulted from the giving of the law was itself a part of God's plan, a necessary prelude to the revelation of his grace in Christ.
4. Strictly speaking, only Jews are subject to the (Mosaic) law. But the plight of Gentiles as defined by Paul is at least analogous to that of Jews "under the law," and Paul at times disregards the distinction.
5. The epoch in which the law performed its role marked, for Paul, a stage in salvation history. For those who are a part of God's "new creation," the law, in a sense, is a thing of the past. Its hegemony remains a reality, however, among unbelievers, and believers themselves run the risk of returning to its bondage.

i. Is the Law the Creation of Angels?

That Paul normally thought the law was divine is not in serious doubt;[3] still the question has been raised whether, in the heat of the Galatian debate, he departs from that position. Schweitzer interpreted Galatians as indicating that "the Law was given by Angels who desired thereby to make men subservient to themselves."[4] Schoeps understood Gal. 3:19 in a similar way: "In the last analysis this means that the law springs not from God but from the angels."[5] Drane and Hübner agree, and find in this one of the ways in which Paul's position in the earlier epistle differs from his stance in Romans.[6] For Räisänen, Paul at least "toys" with the idea of angels as the source of the law in Galatians,

---

3. Cf. Räisänen, *Law,* 128.
4. Schweitzer, *Mysticism,* 69.
5. Schoeps, *Paul,* 183.
6. See above, Chapter 6, sections i and ii.

and his entertaining of the notion is a further reflection of the inconsistency of his thought.[7]

What can be known about the background to Gal. 3:19 has been assembled in many places;[8] our summary here may be brief. The Old Testament narrative itself excludes the notion that Moses received the law from anyone but God:

> Who is there of all flesh, that has heard the voice of the living God speaking out of the midst of fire, as we have, and has still lived? (Deut. 5:26; cf. 4:33, 36; 5:22, 24)

Tradition did allow, however, that angels were present when God gave the law, and the notion that an angel actually delivered God's law to Moses (perhaps based on Moses' conversation with the "angel of the Lord" in Exod. 3) was not uncommon in Paul's day (cf. Acts 7:38, 53; Heb. 2:2; Jub. 1:29–2:1, etc.). The tradition, then, is a common one. But Paul's use of the tradition, on any reading, is radical.

For Paul, the giving of the law through angels is a dramatic indication of the law's inferiority to God's promise. To be sure, even Hebrews compares "the message declared by angels" (2:2) with that "declared . . . by the Lord" (v. 3), and concludes that the latter must be treated with greater solemnity. Still, no denigration of the law is intended. But in Galatians 3 Paul seems bent on showing the law's limitations on all counts: chronologically later than the divine promise (3:15-17), valid only "till the offspring should come to whom the promise had been made" (v. 19), unable to impart life (v. 21), but given "because of transgressions" (v. 19), the law, moreover, was "ordained by angels through an intermediary" whose presence excludes the possibility of a direct revelation by God (vv. 19-20). For the moment, at least, Paul has nothing good to say about the law.

But does he intend to say more than that God allowed angels to pass on his law to Moses? Is he suggesting that angels created the Mosaic code? The participle (*diatageis*, rendered "ordained" by RSV, "promulgated" by NEB) certainly indicates that the Israelites received their orders from angels, but does not in itself determine whether the angels were the source or, alternatively, the mediators of the commands. The preposition *dia* is ambiguous in the same way.[9] Only context can determine which is meant—hardly an unusual situation in the

---

7. Räisänen, *Law,* 133.
8. E.g. Callan, "Midrash," 549-657.
9. Cf. Bauer, Arndt, Gingrich, Danker, *Lexicon, s.v. dia* III.2.a-b (p. 180).

interpretation of texts! Yet the context shows clearly enough that Paul is speaking of the communication by angels of a law divine in its origin.

1. Admittedly, Paul speaks of the Abrahamic covenant as "ratified by God" in 3:17, but says of the law quite baldly that it "came." Still, the failure to stress divine origin should occasion no surprise in a passage not concerned to balance the law's credits with its debits but concentrating exclusively on the latter. In such a context, an argument from silence means little.

2. Admittedly again, Paul's analogy of a person's will which an outsider cannot alter perhaps suggests that Paul is thinking of the law as coming from outsiders (angels) who are unable (though they would like) to alter the conditions of God's promise. But analogies are never perfect, and Paul's, as a rule, less so than most. A detail which Paul himself does not press in an illustration which shares the limitations of the species is a dubious base for a challenge to the fundamental conviction that God gave the law.[10]

3. Without stating the divine origin of the law, Paul assumes the traditional view throughout Galatians.[11] The law contains God's will which believers fulfill (5:14). Transgression of the law involves sin and draws upon sinners the divine curse (3:10; cf. 2:17-18). God's purposes for the law are a subject for discussion (3:19-24). That a law which states the divine will, invokes the divine curse, and was designed to serve divine purposes had its origin in the independent—even hostile—activity of angels is scarcely conceivable.[12]

4. It is the purpose, not of hostile angels, but of God himself that the law should promote transgressions. The point of the enigmatic phrase of 3:19 ("because of transgressions") is developed in verse 22 and especially in Romans, always with God's intentions in view. In Gal. 3:19 itself, the adjacent phrase ("till the offspring should come to whom the promise had been made") refers to God's design with the law, thus precluding the possibility that the preceding words reflect demonic purposes. The thought that God should give the law to make sin worse is indeed striking; it is undeniably Pauline.

5. Gal. 3:20 derives from the role of a mediator the conclusion that God himself was not a party at the giving of the law. The point, perhaps, is that the presence of a plurality of angels necessitated that a spokesman deliver their message, whereas God—being one—would

10. Cf. Bläser, *Gesetz,* 53.
11. Cf. Sanders, *Law,* 67-68.
12. Cf. Bläser, *Gesetz,* 51-53.

have handled the matter himself.[13] The verse requires angelic mediation, but not an angelic origin, for the law.

6. If the argument throughout Galatians, including 3:19a, implies the normal view that the Mosaic law is divine, then the ambiguous expression of 3:19b ("ordained by angels") should be interpreted in a way consistent with this implication.

God instituted the law. But why did he do so? Since Paul is convinced that the Mosaic code cannot lead to life, the question becomes for him one of special moment.

ii. The Law's Relationship to Sin

Whenever Paul explains God's purposes for the law, a link with sin is posited. The complex relationship can, I think, be summarized in the following series of statements, each to be developed below.

1. Sin precedes the law and exists where there is no law. Even apart from law, sin is culpable and incurs divine judgment.
2. The coming of the law transforms sin into violations of God's commands, subject to stated sanctions.
3. Moreover, the coming of the law creates a situation in which "sin" can tempt the law's subjects to disobey its commands. In this way, the actual number of sins is increased.
4. The law also serves to bring sinners some awareness of their dilemma.

1. That, in the checkered history of humanity, wrongdoing preceded the formulation of law codes is a proposition which few would challenge though none, perhaps, could prove. For Paul the matter was decided by comparing the relative positions of Adam and Moses in scripture's genealogical tree: "Sin came into the world through one man [Adam]. . . . Sin indeed was in the world before the law was given. . . . Law came in, to increase the trespass" (Rom. 5:12, 13, 20). It follows, then, that the definition of sin as "the transgression of the law"[14] is not quite adequate—if we can speak legitimately of "sin" before the law was given.

Paul at least does so, with good biblical precedent. He also presupposes—again, with ample justification—the existence of sin among Gentiles who do not have the law: "All who have sinned

13. Cf. Vanhoye, "Médiateur," 403-411.
14. That the KJV misreads 1 John 3:4 is generally agreed; cf. Marshall, *Epistles,* 176-177.

without the law will also perish without the law" (Rom. 2:12). Throughout Romans 1–3, Paul argues not only that Gentiles sin but also that they are responsible for their wrongdoing and liable to judgment: Paul knows no guiltless sinners! Gentiles are "without excuse" (1:20); God's wrath is on them as well as on Jews (v. 18), though the law will play a role only in the assessment of the latter (2:12).

Räisänen is among those who find Rom. 5:12-14 inconsistent with the earlier passage.[15] Romans 2 declares judgment for those who sin without the law, whereas in Romans 5 we are told that "sin is not counted where there is no law." The critical words, of course, are *ouk ellogeitai,* "is not counted" (v. 13). The words perhaps suggest that sin is somehow not treated as sin nor held against the sinner in the absence of law, a conclusion which does not mesh with 2:12. One might, of course, argue that Paul can hardly have forgotten in Romans 5 what he wrote in Romans 2, and hence that the context within which Romans 5 is to be interpreted must include the earlier chapter; a weakening of the force of *ouk ellogeitai* would naturally follow. But such a procedure, though normal enough in the interpretation of texts, will hardly do when Paul's consistency of thought is the point in question. If, however, the immediate context of Rom. 5:12-14 shows that Paul is still bent on maintaining the position he argued in chapter 2, then we can hardly deny the appropriateness of a weaker reading of 5:13b.

According to Rom. 5:12 sin and death entered the world through Adam's transgression of a specific commandment *(parabasis);* death then became the lot of all, inasmuch as "all men sinned." However we define the relation between Adam's sin and that of his offspring, *pantes hēmarton* most naturally means that all committed concrete sins,[16] and the preceding prepositional phrase (*eph' hō,* "inasmuch as" [RSV "because"])[17] affirms that their sins led to their death. The same point is made in verse 14: Paul stresses both the guilt and the punishment of all, though noting, significantly enough, that the later sins were not of the same character as Adam's ("death reigned from Adam to Moses, even over those whose sins were not like the transgression of Adam"). The law, by implication, effects a change from sin to transgression, but hardly one from innocence to guilt. Between these two verses, we find yet another statement that sin was "in the world" (i.e., sins were committed) even before the law was given. Since the closing words of verse

15. Räisänen, *Law,* 145-147.
16. Cf. Cranfield, *Romans,* 279.
17. Meyer, *Christians,* 122, n. 3; Lyonnet, "Sens," 436-456.

12, the first half of verse 13, and the opening of verse 14 are devoted
to an insistence that those living before Moses did sin, and that death
resulted from their sin, there appears to be little warrant for reading
13b as though it meant that sins committed in the absence of law were
not quite worthy of the name or held against the sinners. To repeat,
Paul knows no innocent sinners.[18] Whatever his precise point in verse
13b may be, the culpability of sins committed prior to the giving of the
law is not in question. *Ouk ellogeitai* must refer, not to an absence of
guilt or punishment, but to a difference in the way sins are prosecuted.

Before we examine more closely Paul's view of the change introduced by the law, we must look at another passage in Romans in
connection with which the priority of sin over the law has been questioned. Paul's thesis in Rom. 7:7-13 is that the law itself is holy and
must not be held responsible for sin. The passage is one of the most
controversial in all of Paul's writings, but much of the discussion need
not be entered here. Kümmel's arguments regarding the subject ("I")
of the passage have already been summarized at length above.[19] He
concludes—rightly, I believe—that Paul is not speaking of a particular occurrence in his own past, in the life of Adam,[20] or in the history
of Israel.[21] Rather, in acquitting the law of responsibility for sin, Paul
provides a rhetorical illustration of what happens when humanity encounters the law of God. No specific instance in history corresponds

18. Cranfield, *Romans,* 282.

19. See Chapter 4, section i above.

20. Of course, Paul may have had the story of Adam in mind, adapting it
for his portrayal of the human encounter with God's commandments. But the law
whose effects are under discussion is the Sinaitic code, and Paul is emphatic in
placing its introduction in the time of Moses (Rom. 5:12-14, 20; Gal. 3:17). Thus
echoes from the story of Adam are present only because Adam's experience is
typical of that of humanity as a whole.

21. Moo, "Israel," 122-135, argues that Israel must be the subject (the "I")
on whom the law works in Rom. 7:7-13, since it was to Israel that the law was
given through Moses (cf. 5:13-14). Crucial to his thesis is the claim that Paul
"generally confines the purview of *nomos* to Jews" (124); but, as we shall see, he
does not always do so, and Rom. 7:4-6 appears to be an instance where the limi-
tation is not in view. Above all, however, the interpretation goes against the fundamental principle that, since Paul intended to communicate with his readers, a
meaning should not be attributed to a passage which no reader could be expected
to derive from its terms. Neither parallels from Lamentations nor the dubious proposal that another Pauline text (Gal. 2:18-21) "may involve a similar 'corporate'
relationship between Paul and Israel" (129) is reason sufficient to think that, when
Paul said "I," he could expect his readers to think "Israel."

with each detail of the illustration. Paul has abstracted from scripture and, no doubt, from his own observation, the *essence* of an experience common to humankind.

Now for Räisänen, Paul's point here is that "the intervention of the law is necessary to induce man to sin."[22] "It is only the law with its commandments that *brings about* actual sinning."[23] Such a position is then contrasted with Paul's position elsewhere that "transgressions and sin are concrete realities already *before* the intervention of the law."[24] But in fact, all of Romans 7—including verses 7-11—presupposes the existence of sin before the coming of the command. Sin was "dead" but it could be "revived" (vv. 8, 9); it needed only the "opportunity" presented by the coming of the law to show its character and bring about deception and death. The language is highly metaphorical, and, in pressing its details either to confirm or contradict what Paul says in other passages, we may well give them more weight than they were designed to bear. But if we must press the picture, then surely the presence of sin before the law was given is essential both to the illustration and to Paul's argument that the law is not responsible for sin. And if the "reign" of sin elsewhere in Paul is a figurative way of speaking of a reality in which people commit sins,[25] then the presence of sin before the coming of the law can only mean that concrete sins were actually being committed. That "sin" was "dead" but later "revived" when the law came thus does not imply a state of innocence before the coming of the commandments. If the metaphor must be reduced to dogmatic prose, then surely Paul himself should be allowed to interpret his intentions: sin did not first arise, but it was "shown to be sin" and became "sinful beyond measure" through the operation of the law (v. 13). Paul's point—whether or not we find his illustration successful—is that the law somehow both brings sin's true nature to light and increases its gravity. Such a point seems fully compatible with 5:12-14; nor does it conflict with the sequence presupposed in 7:14-25 (humanity, already "sold under sin," proves incapable of doing the good which the law commands).

The conviction is, then, everywhere the same: sin precedes the law, though the law makes humanity's plight more desperate.

2. If, then, humanity was already "sold under sin" before the law

22. Räisänen, *Law,* 142.
23. Ibid., 144.
24. Ibid., 144.
25. Ibid., 99-100, n. 29; 144, 150.

appeared, and was even subject to God's judgment, what effect can be attributed to the coming of the law?

Räisänen agrees that Paul "tries to show that, as regards man and sin, the coming of the law makes a difference." But Paul fails: "what he actually shows is that there is none."[26] At best he can point to "a technical trifle": "until the law sin had been punished because it was sin; since the law, the very same punishments are imposed because of 'transgression.'" The technicality of the change thus "would seem to be a matter of no consequence whatsoever."[27] Paul's dilemma, according to Räisänen, is that, having rejected the law by an "aprioristic theological thesis (Christ has superseded the law)," he is now forced to "undergird his thesis" by showing "that the effects of the law are negative, and only negative"; such a thesis can only be "carried through . . . with violence."[28]

But is Paul's procedure as arbitrary as Räisänen suggests? According to Rom. 4:15, "the law brings wrath, but where there is no law there is no transgression." We must not, of course, deduce from the claim that the "law brings wrath" the conclusion that God does not punish sins committed in the absence of law; Paul everywhere assumes that he does. In a sense, then, what the law introduces is a new category of sin: wrongdoing there may be, but violation of a command is impossible where no command is in place. "Sin indeed was in the world before the law was given" (5:13)—but not transgression (cf. v. 14). The coming of the law thus transformed the evil deeds of those who became its subjects into transgressions of God's revealed commands. But such a change is more than a technicality of terms: clearly the breaking of God's concrete demand implies a greater challenge to his authority, a more flagrant act of insubordination, than the same deed done in defiance of no law. And though a sovereign God is always free to punish sin, there is both an appropriateness and an inexorability about God's wrath when it becomes operative as the stated sanction attached to a given law.

The same transformation of sin into a more clearly defined act of rebellion, subject to the defined sanctions of the law, is implied in Rom. 5:13. The term used—*ellogein*—"has here to do with heavenly book-keeping."[29] That sin is "not counted" in the absence of law does

26. Ibid., 146, n. 91.
27. Ibid., 146.
28. Ibid., 149-150.
29. Ibid., 145.

not mean that it goes unpunished—the immediate context affirms the opposite—but simply that God cannot judge "according to the book." Ample power to punish sin is ever at his disposal—forty days of uninterrupted rain are more than adequate for the task—but God's grievance against humanity is not one which a court of law would recognize: no statute has been transgressed. For the due registration of wrongs committed, and the consequent demonstration of human culpability and divine justice in punishing, the institution of the law proves necessary. Does its coming make a difference? Not, perhaps, one which the objects of divine wrath have the inclination or the leisure to appreciate; but it cannot be said that a display of human guilt and a vindication of God's justice are matters of "no consequence" to Paul, nor should the means by which those ends are achieved be considered "a technical trifle."

A parallel from Amos is, I think, illuminating. In Amos 1:3–2:3, the prophet denounces wrongs perpetrated by the people of Damascus, the Philistine cities, Tyre, Edom, the Ammonites, and the Moabites. For their foul and damnable sins, God will not revoke his punishment; sundry judgments are luridly portrayed. Amos then turns to his own people:

> Hear this word that the Lord has spoken against you, O people of Israel, against the whole family which I brought up out of the land of Egypt: "You only have I known of all the families of the earth: therefore I will punish you for all your iniquities." (Amos 3:1-2)

Why is God justified in punishing Israel? Because, of all the nations of the earth, he has "known" Israel alone.[30] Does this mean, then, that the nations whom God has not "known" are exempt from his punishment—in flagrant contradiction of Amos 1–2? Detached from their context, the words appear to permit no other reading; but no one reads them so. Israel has been given special privileges. These are accompanied by special responsibilities and a unique liability to judgment: the principle is biblical to the core. Other nations, though not subject to the same standards of judgment, are nevertheless held responsible for their sins. The distinction implied by Amos between God's dealings with Israel and the nations on the basis of election nicely parallels Paul's distinction on the basis of the law.

30. The claim that God "knows" only Israel is, of course, in turn "contradicted" in Amos 9:7, where it is insisted that God deals with Ethiopians, Philistines, and Syrians in the same way. A thesis of self-contradiction, once ventured upon, allows itself to be proved with beguiling ease.

The effect which Paul attributes to the law in Rom. 4:15; 5:13 is thus consistent with convictions fundamental to Jewish as well as Christian faith. Though God's giving of the law was undoubtedly a great privilege for those entrusted with it (9:4), and though the law indeed promised life to those who obeyed its commands (10:5, etc.), those who received the law became at the same time liable to God's judgment in a unique way. The law transgressed became a fearful curse (Exod. 20:5; Lev. 26:14-39; Deut. 28:15-68, etc.). That (as in the prophets!)[31] the negative side of the law's sanctions has become its sole practical effect was, to be sure, a conclusion determined for Paul by his conviction (in Christ) that the law had not led to life. The point to be made here, however, is that Paul did not create for his convenience the notion that the "law brings wrath," nor did he affirm a fundamental biblical principle merely as an arbitrary attempt to discover a negative role for the law. What the Old Testament scriptures declare to have been the law's effect Paul affirms as its purpose.

3. But Paul goes further still. Not only does the law transform sin into acts of defiance against God's commands; in a sense, it actually *provokes* transgressions. This is Paul's point in Rom. 7:7-13. By itself verse 7 is ambiguous: "If it had not been for the law, I should not have known sin. I should not have known what it is to covet if the law had not said, 'You shall not covet.'" Paul's words here are certainly susceptible of interpretation along lines suggested by 4:15 and 5:13: though no doubt "I" might have longed for what belonged to someone else living before the commandment came, "I" would not have recognized "my" longing as the sin of "coveting" apart from the law's prohibition. The stress here not found in chapters 4 and 5 would be that sinners themselves gain a "knowledge" of sin—a recognition that they are acting in defiance of God's law—through the coming of the command.

But Paul goes on to say that "sin, finding opportunity in the commandment, wrought in me all kinds of covetousness."[32] It was first at

---

31. It is difficult to find anywhere in the prophetic literature an indication that good resulted from God's giving of the law to Israel. Everywhere the response is depicted as one of rebellion and sin, leading to judgment. Cf. Jer. 5:4, 5; 6:19-21; 7:21-29; 8:7; 9:12-16; 11:6-11; 17:21-23; 32:23; 34:13-14; 44:10, 23; Ezek. 20:10-31; Hos. 4:6; 8:1, 12-13; Amos 2:4-5; Zech. 7:12.

32. Bultmann, anxious to find confirmation for his thesis that the fundamental sin of Jews is their attempt to establish their own righteousness by fulfilling the law, suggested that the "desire" to do so is at least included in the *pasan epithumian* of 7:8 ("Anthropology," 154). But the desires aroused according to verse 8 are clearly understood as violations of the law's command cited in verse

the appearance of the law that the temptation to disobey arose; the very prohibition creates, not sin itself, but possibilities of sin which do not exist without it. It provides a focus on which a slumbering, inchoate rebelliousness can fasten, spring to life and expression.[33] The law thus served to worsen the human dilemma not only by adding definition to human culpability, but also by increasing the number of sins committed. There are "sinful passions" which are themselves "aroused by the law" (Rom. 7:5). The coming of the law led to an "increase" in (an already present) sin (5:20). The cryptic claim of Galatians 3:19—the law "was added because of transgressions"—is presumably an abbreviated way of making the same point that we find in Romans: through the law human bondage to sin is defined and increased, in order that deliverance may be found exclusively by faith in Christ (Gal. 3:22).

That Paul has taken an everyday experience—that the giving of commands creates temptations to disobey them—and applied it to God's law need not be questioned; and Räisänen seems to be correct in his claim that the Old Testament provides no parallel to Paul's "attributing to the law a negative, sin-provoking and sin-engendering function."[34] But it does not follow that Paul's thinking represents a purely arbitrary, idiosyncratic attempt to assign a negative role to the law. After all, biblical faith in an omnipotent God makes the progression from a notion that the law had a given effect to the notion that God intended it to do so an easy one to make. And that the giving of the law to Israel had the effect of bringing to expression the rebelliousness of a "stubborn and stiff-necked people" is a view abundantly attested in the Old Testament scriptures. Paul's contribution, again, is to see in the response which tradition affirmed that the law had received the working out of a divine purpose.

4. And what, finally, are we to make of Rom. 3:20? Here Paul

7, and that command prohibits covetousness. Hence *pasan epithumian* means "covetousness for all manner of things," in defiance of the command; a "desire" to fulfill the command is hardly in view. See my "Letter," 237-238.

33. In Paul's picture, the "I" who was "alive" before the law came is deceived by sin at the coming of the command and "dies." An imperfect illustration should not be used as the basis for claiming that Paul *here* believes that sin does not exist, or goes unpunished, in the absence of law. If we remove the metaphor, Paul appears to mean no more than that the transgression of the law inevitably invokes the law's sanction of death; hence, in a mental abstraction with no exact parallel in history (though the story of Adam may have served as its model), he pictures a time of "life" before the law came with its sentence of death.

34. Räisänen, *Law,* 161.

concludes his lengthy indictment of humanity (1:18–3:20) with these words: "For no human being will be justified in his sight by works of the law, since through the law comes knowledge of sin." The second half of the verse is apparently offered as support for the thesis stated in the opening clause, but its precise force is unclear. If the opening words are taken by themselves as the conclusion to the preceding argument, then the final phrase ("through the law comes knowledge of sin") may introduce a new (though supporting) point to be developed in a later context.[35] In this case, and in the light of 4:15 and 5:13, the "knowledge of sin" might refer to the recognition brought to sinners that the wrongs they commit are violations of God's stated will for which they are liable for punishment. Less likely, perhaps, is the suggestion that "knowledge of sin" means a practical experience of sin as developed in 7:7-11: without the law, one would not "know" (i.e., experience) the sin of disobeying God's concrete demands. Paul's words are certainly ambiguous enough to allow either interpretation.

On the other hand, we may well feel that the bringing of a "knowledge of sin" corresponds very nicely with the concerns of the first three chapters of Romans, and that 3:20b, as well as 3:20a, should be seen as a summary of the preceding argument. How does the argument of 1:18–3:20 relate the law to the "knowledge of sin"?

Certainly the law brings no such knowledge to Gentiles. They "have not the law" (2:14), sin "without the law," and perish "without the law" (v. 12). Paul's indictment in chapter 1 is directed generally to all humanity (1:18), but it is stated in terms which leave Gentiles "without excuse" (v. 20) even though they do not have God's law: "What can be known about God is plain to them. . . . Although they knew God they did not honor him as God. . . . They exchanged the truth about God for a lie" (1:19, 21, 25). Paul seems deliberately to avoid using the law of Moses to convict Gentiles of sin.

On the other hand, "all who have sinned under the law will be judged by the law" (2:12). Paul insists that Jews are required to obey the law's commands and that they will be condemned for their transgressions. Thus the law effects the conviction of Jews before the divine tribunal.

But is a demonstration of guilt at the divine tribunal what Paul means by the "knowledge of sin" in 3:20? Surely human, not divine, knowledge is intended; and if the knowledge of sin which the law

35. Cf. Rom. 6:14, where Paul introduces the notion "not under law" which, however, he does not develop until 7:1-6.

brings to men and women becomes theirs first on the day of judgment, its appearance is too tardy to be of much use. It is possible, then, to read Rom. 3:20 as saying that the law in some way brings to Jews an awareness that they, too, are sinners and will be judged as such. Two possibilities from the preceding argument suggest themselves.

a. In 3:19, Paul concludes on the basis of a number of quotations from "the law" (i.e., the scriptures) that those "under the law" are guilty before God. This may be Paul's point in verse 20: Jews should learn from scripture's testimony that "no one does good" (v. 12) and, hence, that they too are sinners. Note, however, that the "law" which brings this knowledge is the scripture as a whole, not specifically the Mosaic law code. Since the "works of the law" which do not justify, according to verse 20a, are the deeds demanded by the Mosaic code, one would expect Paul's explanation of what the "law" does accomplish, in verse 20b, to refer to the same body of commands.

b. In 2:17-24, Paul probes his imagined Jewish interlocutor on the subject of personal obedience to the specific commands of the law: "Do you steal? . . . Do you commit adultery? . . . Do you rob temples? . . . Do you dishonor God by breaking the law?" Perhaps, then, Paul means that reflection on the commands of the law should arouse in Jews an awareness of transgressions, thus leading to a "knowledge of sin."[36]

Such a reading roughly corresponds with Luther's understanding of the "principal use" of the law: confronted with the law's demands, sinners are convinced of their guilt, tremble at the thought of God's judgment, and grasp at God's mercy offered in Christ. Luther, to be sure, does not restrict "law" to the Mosaic code,[37] nor are the sinners whose pangs of conscience the law awakens limited to Jews. The question remains: Does Paul believe the Mosaic code functions among Jews in a way comparable to Luther's "principal use" of the law?

The suggestion is routinely rejected by many scholars. We may recall Stendahl's argument.[38] Paul was not himself given to introspection, nor does he give any indication of suffering from a troubled conscience. That the law served as a "custodian *eis Christon*" (Gal. 3:24) means that it performed its task among Jews "until Christ came," not that it leads sinners through remorse for transgressions to a merciful Savior. The opening chapters in Romans are designed to show that,

36. Cf. Beker, *Paul,* 107; Wilckens, *Römer,* I, 180.
37. Cf. Ebeling, *Word,* 262.
38. See above, Chapter 4, section ii.

since Jews and Gentiles share the same predicament, the same solution is open to both. Paul is not attempting to arouse a "sense of sin" in his (Christian!) readers.

The case is a forceful one, but it may have been overstated. Certainly Gal. 3:24 does not speak of the way the law prepares sinners psychologically for the reception of the gospel, but rather of the temporal limitations placed on the law's validity (see section v below). Yet Paul's message of salvation in Christ demands a negative complement, a dilemma from which Christ delivers.[39] Paul's missionary preaching certainly included warnings to Gentiles of the "wrath to come" (1 Thess. 1:10; 5:1-9), even if the Mosaic law was not proclaimed as the basis of their condemnation. Is it unlikely, then, that Jews were threatened with the same wrath, told that election was no substitute for obedience, and that transgressions of the law would lead to their condemnation? In the present context the argument of Romans 2 is addressed to Christian readers; but may it not reflect at least the general pattern of Paul's message in the synagogues? Such a proclamation would, after all, be entirely in line with the message of the prophets, of John the Baptist, and, indeed, of Jesus himself.[40]

Nor are we entirely dependent on conjectures. Rom. 3:20 and 7:7[41] both speak of a "knowledge of sin" conveyed to sinners through the law. Naturally, for Paul, such "knowledge of sin" could not be an end in itself, but must be meant to induce a cry like that of 7:24 ("Who will deliver . . . ?"), to be answered with the redemption for which verse 25 gives thanks. Luther's "principal function" of the law gives its pedagogical role an emphasis which towers out of all proportion to the few allusive references in the Pauline texts; but Paul at least provides the foundation.

iii. A Conflict of Interests?

In discussing the purpose of the law,[42] Sanders introduces a novel and suggestive proposal for the progression of Paul's thought. Different

---

39. Sanders (*Paul,* 444) finds indications in Paul's letters that, in his missionary preaching, "he did not *start* from man's need, but from God's deed." The distinction is neat on paper, but impossible, I suspect, to maintain in synagogue or market-place addresses. One without the other can hardly be *preached.*

40. Cf. Räisänen, *Law,* 161.

41. Even if the "knowledge" of Rom. 7:7 is primarily experiential, an awareness of the experience on the part of the subject can scarcely be excluded.

42. Sanders, *Law,* 65-81.

passages assess differently the relationship between God's will and the law's effects. Sanders believes that Paul kept trying, but never quite managed, to provide a satisfactory explanation of the relationship. His argument, in brief, is as follows.

According to Gal. 3:22, 24 and Rom. 5:20-21, "the law was given in order to increase the trespass";[43] thus both sin and the law are assigned a role—albeit a negative one—in God's plan of salvation. The problem here, of course, is that a God whose plan includes sin can hardly be cleared of responsibility when it appears. In an attempt to escape the consequences of his first proposal, Paul treats sin in Rom. 6:1–7:6 not as an "instrument of God," but as a power "not subject to God's control" and "outside God's will."[44] It follows that now "the law could no longer be said to produce sin or to multiply transgression as part of God's overall plan, since the realm of sin is now considered entirely outside that plan."[45] Instead Paul suggests now that God gave the law to save (7:10), but that sin frustrated God's plan. "Sin grasps the law away from God. It uses it to promote transgression (7:8, 11, 13), and the result is that the law kills (7:10f.). In 7:7-13 the law is still connected to sin, but sin is not attributed to God's will."[46] This solution, too, is unsatisfactory, since it leaves God's "law on the side of death, sin, and the flesh."[47]

Paul "recoils" from the implication of his own argument and proposes yet another line of thought (7:14–8:8): here the law itself does not provoke transgressions, but merely states God's righteous demands; the only "fault" of the law now is "that it does not bear within itself the power to enable people to observe it."[48] This solution allows the law to remain entirely on God's side—it is no longer a tool of sin; furthermore, both God and his law are now exonerated from responsibility for sin. But even this solution is far from satisfactory, for now God's design with the law appears to have gone awry; God is forced "to launch a second effort"[49] by sending his Son to succeed where the law had failed. In short, Paul never really manages to combine his convictions "that God gave the law but that salvation is only through faith in Christ."[50]

43. Ibid., 70.
44. Ibid., 73.
45. Ibid., 73 (emphasis removed).
46. Ibid., 74.
47. Ibid., 79.
48. Ibid., 74-75.
49. Ibid., 80.
50. Ibid., 80.

Considered by itself, Sanders's reconstruction of the meanderings of Paul's mind seems plausible enough; and certainly the problems to which he has drawn attention are real. What it fails to convey adequately, I believe, is the *traditional* nature of the problem posed[51]—and the *traditional* character of Paul's response. The impression given is that of an apostle forced to wrestle with problems which no one else had ever considered, with nary a resource at his disposal but the tentative hypotheses which his own wit could devise. Yet some of the hesitant suggestions which Sanders attributes to Paul were fundamental convictions shared by faithful Jews and Christians alike; others are all but inconceivable to either. For centuries Jews had *combined* a firm conviction that sin was a violation of God's will with an equally firm assurance that God used sin to his own good purpose, accomplishing his goals through its means. The sin of Joseph's brothers was God's tool to preserve Israel from famine (Gen. 50:20). The dread violence of the Chaldeans proved the instrument as well as the object of God's judgment (Jer. 51; Hab. 1–2). God turns the very "wrath of men" to his praise (Ps. 76:10 [MT 11]).[52] Paul can claim no copyright for the notion that God uses sin to achieve his own ends—nor does he need to recoil from its implications. When, on the other hand, Paul stresses the opposition of sin to God's will, he no more implies the inconceivable proposition that sin is outside God's control[53] than do the prophets who denounce in God's name the crimes of his people.

In one context, Paul chooses to emphasize God's overriding purpose; in another, the opposition of sin. Yet Paul's convictions on both counts remain constant for the simple reason that they were axiomatic for most first-century Jews. Galatians stresses that God uses sin for his own ends; but sin remains God's foe (cf. 2:17), the object of his curse (3:10, 13), the manifestation of a "flesh" opposed to his Spirit (5:19-21), and the root of a dilemma from which his Son must provide deliverance (1:4). Thus the opposition between sin and God posited in Romans 7 hardly represents a different view of the relation. Moreover, God's overriding purpose is a theme of Romans 7 as well, for it is surely God's design that sin, through the law, is "shown to be sin" and

51. Sanders does, however, allude briefly (ibid., 79) to a similar problem in Job and 4 Ezra.

52. Note Paul's further usage of the traditional motif in Romans 9–11: Israel's very rejection of the gospel, an apparent frustration of God's plans (10:21), proves to be the means by which God brings reconciliation to the world (11:11-32).

53. Cf. van Dülmen, *Theologie,* 199-201.

thus becomes "sinful beyond measure" (v. 13; cf. v. 7).[54] In neither text does Paul provide a systematic treatment of the relation between the sinfulness of sin and the sovereignty of God; but both texts manifest the firmness with which he maintained the traditional convictions.

Paul's argument, again, involves the restatement of views fundamental to the faith of his fathers: sin violates God's will; God uses sin for his purposes; the giving of the law led to sin. What is new in Paul, as we have already seen, is the insistence that God must have *intended* the law to lead to sin. This insistence leads to the curious result that the law sometimes seems a tool in sin's employ, while at other times it remains firmly in God's hand. Sanders rightly points out the anomaly but fails to stress its traditional character. Here too the picture of a Paul pursuing arbitrary solutions to problems of his own making needs to be replaced with that of an apostle creatively applying basic principles of his inherited religion to the human situation as revealed by Christ's cross.

iv. Gentiles and the Jewish Law

Through the law, human culpability was demonstrated and increased, this being a prelude to the revelation of God's grace in Christ. But on whom did the law work its effects? Who are the subjects of the law?

The answer should be straightforward. If, as we have seen, Paul normally uses *nomos* of the Mosaic code given to Israel on Mount Sinai, then Jews are its subjects. God "declares his word to Jacob, his statutes and ordinances to Israel. He has not dealt thus with any other nation; they do not know his ordinances. Praise the Lord!" (Ps. 147:19-20). The distinction is at times just as clear in Paul: Jews who "are instructed in the law" (Rom. 2:18; cf. 9:4) are contrasted with Gentiles "who have not the law" (2:14); Paul behaves differently in the presence of Jews, who are "under the law," than he does when among Gentiles, who are "outside the law" (1 Cor. 9:20-21). But Räisänen is among the many scholars who have pointed out that when Paul depicts the human dilemma outside of Christ, he sometimes appears to treat Jew and Gentile alike as subjects of the law.[55]

---

54. Cf. Deidun, Review, 48. Rom. 7:14-25 is not yet another attempt to explain the relationship between sin, the law, and God's will, but rather Paul's account of why the coming of the law has the effect on the individual outlined in verses 7-13.

55. Räisänen, *Law,* 18-23, with ample bibliography.

Here again there is no scholarly consensus, and the counter-position has recently been argued with some force by Donaldson.[56] We may begin with the relevant texts in Romans.

In Rom. 6:14-15, Paul declares that the Roman believers are "not under law but under grace"; the implication would seem to be that, prior to their experience of "grace," they were in bondage to the law. Still clearer is 7:4-6: those to whom Paul writes have "died to the law"; in the process they were "discharged" from it. Donaldson suggests that "on the basis of such verses as 2.12, 14; 7.1 and 9.4 an argument could be constructed that in Rom 5–8 Paul is speaking of the law from an exclusively Jewish Christian perspective."[57] If, on the other hand, we assume that Gentiles *are* included among those "under the law," then "it is not because Paul takes this for granted, but rather because he has already laid the groundwork in chapters 1 and 2."[58] There Paul argued that Gentiles may be led by conscience to conform to the law's requirements, thus becoming a "law to themselves" (2:14). As a result, Gentiles, like Jews, can be spoken of as "under the law."

Neither of these proposals can be excluded as impossible; neither commends itself as likely. Much of Romans does deal with problems of special concern to Jewish Christians; furthermore, the constituency of the Roman church included Jews as well as Gentiles,[59] and Paul at times directs his remarks exclusively to one of these groups (e.g., 11:13-32). But to read Paul's statements of bondage and deliverance in Romans 5 through 8 as limited to *Jewish* Christian experience requires such prodigious concentration that one may doubt whether Paul's intentions were so narrow. Rom. 7:1 ("I am speaking to those who know the law") is sometimes taken as an indication that Jews are addressed; but Paul's detailed usage of the Old Testament in his letter to the Galatians shows that he did not think Jews alone were competent to understand an argument based on the law.[60] And there simply are no other hints in these chapters that the encouragement, admonitions, and arguments offered are intended for but a segment of the Roman church.

Does Paul, then, deliberately speak of all nations as "under law" on the basis of his argument that Gentiles may be "a law to themselves"?

56. Donaldson, "Curse," 94-112.
57. Ibid., 95-96.
58. Ibid., 96.
59. Cf. Cranfield, *Romans,* 16-22.
60. Whether the Galatians themselves shared his optimism remains one of history's great unanswered questions.

It seems unlikely. The point of the argument in Romans 1 and 2 is that Gentiles are responsible before God in spite of the fact that *they do not have the law;* what knowledge they have is a sufficient basis for judgment. Their sins are said to be committed "without the law." Their judgment will take place "without the law" (2:12). And the argument which follows continues to assume that possession of the law is a prerogative of the Jews (2:17-24; 3:28-29; 4:14, 16). Those who are "under the law" according to 3:19 are undoubtedly Jews.[61] Thus the argument of Romans 1 and 2 can hardly have been intended to pave the way for a description of Jews and Gentiles alike as "under the law."

The most likely explanation remains that of Sanders:[62] Paul's own presuppositions are Jewish. He speaks in a natural, probably unreflected way of Abraham as "our forefather according to the flesh" (Rom. 4:1), or of the wilderness generation as "our fathers" (1 Cor. 10:1), even when he is writing to churches predominantly Gentile. Similarly, he at times depicts the plight of all humanity in terms borrowed from, and (strictly speaking) appropriate only to, the Jewish situation ("under the law"). Quite likely the generalization took place unconsciously. Paul *could,* no doubt, have defended his usage with a simple reminder that Gentile awareness of God's demands, or Gentile incurring of God's wrath, creates at least an analogous situation to that of Jews. But he does not do so, and his argument in Rom. 7:7-13 shows that the bondage of which he is thinking in verses 4-6 results from an encounter between the individual and the explicit demands of the Mosaic code. The Jewish situation is in mind, but Paul treats it as though it was universal.

The references in Galatians are more difficult, but may be dealt with briefly here, since a precedent for imprecise usage has already been established. Donaldson finds an interesting pattern in Gal. 3:13-14, 23-29; and 4:3-7: in each case (a) a plight is described of which the law is a part, and to which a group referred to with first person plural pronouns is subject; (b) Christ is then said to identify himself with the plight and (c) to provide redemption for those under it, so that (d) saving blessings might be made available to all believers. Donaldson believes that Jews are the subject of the plight (a) and the objects of Christ's redemption (c); the progression from the redemption of Jews to blessing for all believers is thought to follow a pattern well-attested

61. Cf. Cranfield, *Romans,* 195-196.
62. Sanders, *Law,* 82.

in Jewish eschatological expectation, where Israel's redemption paves the way for salvation to be extended to the Gentiles.

But the passages in Galatians give us little reason to believe that Paul had such a progression in mind here. On the contrary, both 3:26 and 4:6 seem simply to apply to the Galatian Christians the blessings referred to in the preceding verses—they, too, have been set free and adopted as sons—without a hint that Gentiles participated on terms different from those of Jews (cf. 1:4; 5:1, 13). Gal. 3:13-14, too, can be read as saying that Christ's death for all brings blessings to all.

It seems safest to conclude that Paul does picture Gentiles as sharing the Jewish dilemma; he has not systematically maintained the distinction between Jews who are "under the law" and Gentiles who are not. His primary concern in the passages in question is to show that God's law fulfilled a divine function, though it did not lead to life. In outlining that function for Gentile readers, he sometimes speaks as though they too have felt its effects. That their situation, in Paul's mind, was analogous to that of Jews is clear enough (cf. Rom. 1:18–3:20; Gal. 4:1-11). Still, since Paul raises no argument in its defense, his usage of the phrase "under the law" to include Gentiles was likely an unconscious generalization.

v. The Epoch of the Law

No doubt Paul's best known picture of the office of the law is found in Gal. 3:24-25: it was "our custodian (KJV "schoolmaster"; Gk. *paidagōgos*) until Christ came."

> The term "pedagogue" does not refer to the "teacher" *(didaskalos)*, but to the slave who accompanied the school boy to the school and back, and carried his books and writing utensils. The task of this slave was to protect the child against molesters and accidents, and also to make sure he learned good manners. . . . The school boy remained under the supervision of this pedagogue until the time of puberty.[63]

It is probably pointless to ask which part of the "pedagogue's" task Paul has in mind in applying the figure to the law. It is true that the pedagogue, though distinct from the child's teacher, did play a role in his education: the child's manners were his special concern, and he is said to review with his charge the school lessons of the day.[64] But

63. Betz, *Galatians*, 177.
64. Bruce, *Galatians*, 182.

the context in Galatians makes no mention of an educational role played by the law; and, since any teaching which a pedagogue may have done was a lesser part of his task, Paul can hardly have chosen the term specifically to attribute a propaedeutic function to the law. More likely the figure was thought appropriate simply because it suggested a period of unpleasant restraint; this, indeed, corresponds to Paul's account of the law in 3:23.

One thing is clear: the significance of the "pedagogue" in Galatians 3 is less the function he performed than the limited time during which he performed it. The child would one day outgrow his need of the slave's restraint; in the same way, the epoch of the law was to last only "until Christ came." This temporal reading of *eis Christon* is demanded by the whole context: according to Gal. 3:19, the law was "added . . . till the offspring should come"; the confinement of the law, according to verse 23, was to last "until faith should be revealed"; verse 25 assures us that, with the coming of faith, "we are no longer under a custodian." In the opening verses of chapter 4 as well, the temporal limits of the law's validity are stressed, though with slightly different pictures.

The deliverance of believers from the rule of the law will be discussed more fully in our next chapter. Two points are in order here.

1. Since Paul limits the period of the law to an already concluded stage in salvation history, he cannot here be thinking of the law's function as primarily related to the psychology of the individual. If the law performed its role in the period from Moses to Christ (cf. 3:19), that task was not one of creating in individuals a perceived need for the Christian gospel. For Paul, the essential role of the law is to demonstrate and deepen the bondage of humanity to sin (cf. v. 22).

2. The language of Gal. 3:23-25 perhaps invites an oversimplification of Paul's thought. Humanity as a whole has not been redeemed from the law immediately, automatically, and permanently by the very appearance of "faith." The law is the mark of the old age, faith characterizes the new; but for a time at least, the two ages coexist. Christ's enemies are still in the process of being subjected to his rule (1 Cor. 15:25). Not all who hear the gospel "put on Christ," become God's sons, and so escape the law's hegemony (Gal. 3:23-29). Even for those who do, the danger remains that they will revert to the slavery they experienced before they were "known by God" (4:8-11). Believers alone have "died to the law through the body of Christ" (Rom. 7:4), and even they must "stand fast" in their newly gained freedom (Gal. 5:1; cf.

4:21). "God is not dead nor doth he sleep" (Longfellow); but neither, yet, do his foes.

For Paul, a first-century Jew conscripted into the service of Jesus Christ, it was axiomatic that God has a scheme for the ages. For a faith like Paul's, the spread of sin, the rule of evil, and the rejection of God's salvation by his people can all be explained with a simple reference to the "depth" of God's wisdom, the "unsearchable" nature of his judgments, the inscrutability of his ways (Rom. 11:33). It is hardly surprising that such a solution proves unsatisfying to many, or that the bold way in which Paul affirms both the sinfulness of humanity and the sovereignty of God leads to tensions for which moderns beg a resolution. The problems are real—but they are not of Paul's making, nor does he deal with them in ways of his own invention. What has happened has a place in God's plan; the giving of the law met with rebellion, not obedience, and led to judgment, not life: these notions were not the creations of Paul. But Paul shows a unique interest among New Testament writers in accounting for God's gift of the law in the light of his salvation in Christ. Traditional notions were at his disposal, but he transformed them into a scheme by which the sinfulness to which the law led and which it inevitably condemned was but the necessary preparation for the display of God's grace. All were consigned to disobedience, that God might have mercy on all (Rom. 11:32).

Chapter Ten

The Law and Christian Behavior

Exegetes cannot agree whether or not Paul thought Christians are subject to the law; perhaps, then, Paul's own mind was divided on the issue. So, at least, Räisänen proposes:[1] Paul's letters contain both "radical statements" of the law's abolition and "conservative" ones which imply its continuing validity.[2] "Depending on the situation, he asserts, as it were, now the *katalusai* now the *plērōsai* of Mt 5.17."[3] The result, as throughout Räisänen's study, is "that Paul's theology of the law can only be understood if the tensions and self-contradictions in it are taken seriously."[4]

The question is, of course, ever open whether scholarly disagreement on Paul's understanding of the law is itself primarily indicative of the state of New Testament scholarship or (as Räisänen suggests) of unresolved tensions in Paul's own thinking. The latter claim would be strengthened considerably if the missing scholarly likemindedness could be discerned in other areas of comparable significance; I remain skeptical. But the argument from scholarly disagreement is particularly hazardous in this case, where reasons for insisting that Paul cannot have meant what he seems to be saying are bound to occur to those who share his concern for moral living but lack his optimism about the sufficient power of the Spirit to produce it: if the foundations of the law be destroyed, what won't the righteous do? In Paul's own day, his

1. Räisänen, *Law*, 3-15, 42-93.
2. Ibid., 63, emphasis removed; cf. 199.
3. Ibid., 82.
4. Ibid., 83.

position was thought to encourage sin (cf. Rom. 3:8; 6:1, 15; Gal. 2:17; 5:13). Exemption from criticism has since been granted his views, but immunity from tampering is harder to come by: those who cannot conceive of the apostle's thought as provocative of sin are wont to read his letters in ways that eliminate the offense. Still, the tempered apostle of many proposals proves too innocuous to convince. A Paul who meant that the law's curse has been removed, though its precepts must be followed, or that the moral law stands, though the ritual law has been done away with, would hardly be pressed to refute the charge of promoting iniquity. But the Paul of the epistles was faced with just such a charge.[5]

Paul's statements on the abolition of the law show a basic coherence, though the subject is never treated systematically. This claim is supported in the five sections of this chapter by the following considerations:

1. That the ethical behavior which Paul expects of believers corresponds in content to the moral demands of the Mosaic code cannot be used to argue the abiding validity of the law.
2. Paul's statements that Christians "fulfill" the law are, again, an inadequate base for arguing that Christians are obligated to adhere to its precepts.
3. Paul consistently argues and assumes that Christians are no longer bound by the Mosaic code.
4. The mark of Christian ethics is life in the Spirit, an ethic which Paul explicitly contrasts with obligation to the law.
5. Paul's refusal to allow the Mosaic law a place in Christian ethics follows inevitably from his understanding of the nature of the law. Torah is, for him, not a statement of God's will for people of every age and place, but the covenantal obligations imposed on Israel with sanctions of life and death, blessing and curse. Since the Sinaitic covenant proved unable to convey life, Christians had to be delivered from both its demands and its sanctions to serve God under a new covenant.

i. The Overlap in Content

Those who move from one country to another may no longer be bound by the laws of the land they leave; still, freedom to do whatever was

5. Ibid., 47.

forbidden in the old country is assumed at their peril. Murder and theft will likely be prosecuted, not—to be sure—as violations of statutes which no longer apply, but as transgressions of the new laws to which the immigrants have become subject. The overlapping of laws between lands is considerable.

The analogy is imperfect, for Paul replaces the Mosaic code, not with another system of law, but with life in the Spirit. The point remains, however, that freedom from the law does not mean for Paul liberty to do all that Moses prohibited, since falsehood and adultery, idolatry and theft are sins against the Spirit just as they once transgressed the Mosaic code. That Paul inveighs against immorality proves only that immorality has no place in his understanding of Christian behavior; it does not follow that the Mosaic code which condemns it is the foundation of Pauline ethics.

Yet arguments to the latter effect are common in the literature. No one believes Paul viewed the whole Mosaic code as binding for believers; the principle, for many, is to preserve as much as possible. Circumcision must perforce be jettisoned; the dismissal of laws prescribing foods and festivals brings neither hesitation nor regret. Upon reflection we may want to dispense with the regulations governing sacrifice as well, for though, to our knowledge, Paul never pronounced explicitly on the subject,[6] his views of the death of Christ leave little for that of sheep and goats to accomplish. But beyond these concessions many dare not go. The alternative to obligation to the remainder of the Mosaic code is portrayed as an ethic in which theft and adultery are open possibilities for Christians to consider, with Paul at best expressing a hope that they would find better things to do. Against the straw figure of a permissive Paul it is pointed out that Paul would not truck with adulterers or thieves; hence, it is concluded, the moral law of God stands firm.

But that Paul, like most preachers, opposed sin is not in question. At issue is rather the basis on which Paul defines sin for believers and insists that they not commit it. Does Paul denounce immorality because it is prohibited in the Mosaic code, to which believers are *ex hypothesi* obligated? Or does he claim that immorality somehow violates fundamental principles of *Christian* living? We return to the basis of Pauline ethics below. The point here to be made is simply that

6. Cf., however, Rom. 3:25, and the discussion by Stuhlmacher, *Reconciliation*, 94-109.

the partial overlap between the demands of Moses and those of Paul is in itself no argument for the (partial!) validity of the Mosaic code.[7]

ii. The Law's Fulfillment

In three texts, Paul speaks of the "fulfillment" of the Mosaic law by Christians (Rom. 8:4; 13:8-10; Gal. 5:14).[8] Such statements should not be transformed into declarations that Christian duty is prescribed by the Mosaic code.[9]

For Paul it is important to say that the death and resurrection of God's Son and the gift of God's Spirit have made a difference in the way God's people live.[10] Since Paul's charge against Jews is that they have transgressed the law, Paul's counterclaim for Christians is that they fulfill it. Three comments are in order here.

1. In each case, Paul is describing, not prescribing, Christian behavior. When Paul *prescribes* what Christians are to do, the language used is not that of fulfilling the Mosaic law:[11] "Walk by the Spirit, and do not gratify the desires of the flesh" (Gal. 5:16; cf. Rom. 8:12-13). Naturally, it is from Paul's *prescriptions* that we must derive his view of the basis for Christian obligation. Nonetheless, when Paul *describes the results* of a life lived in conformity with Christian principles, it is, for polemical reasons,[12] important for him to say that Christian behavior is condemned by no law (Gal. 5:23), that the love which is the hallmark of Christian conduct in fact fulfills the law (Gal. 5:14; Rom.

7. Rightly, Deidun, *Morality,* 160.

8. The following discussion represents a summary of my article "Fulfilling."

9. Cf. Grafe, *Lehre,* 18-19.

10. Cf. Räisänen, *Law,* 144.

11. 1 Cor. 7:19 might be cited to the contrary; the Mosaic law is not, however, in view in this chapter (the only "commandments" mentioned are Pauline and dominical; cf. vv. 10, 17, 25, and the frequent Pauline imperatives), and the statement need mean no more than that submitting to God's will is essential.

On two (!) occasions Paul apparently draws from a *precept* in Torah additional support for his position on a matter of behavior: Deut. 25:4 is cited and interpreted allegorically (its literal force is rejected!) in the midst of a lengthy justification of Paul's right to be supported by his churches (1 Cor. 9:8-10); and in 1 Cor. 14:34 (the authenticity of which has been questioned), the command that women are to be silent in church is said to be "also" found in Torah (no one knows quite where). In neither case is Torah treated as the direct source of Christian duty. Cf. Deidun, *Morality,* 157-160.

12. Cf. Feine, *Evangelium,* 215.

13:8-10). The Galatians needed to be assured that the conduct produced by the Spirit *apart* from the law (cf. Gal. 5:18) was better, not worse, than that produced by those living in subjection to its demands (cf. 5:13; 6:13).

After Paul's dramatic portrayal in Romans 7 of the impotence of those living under the law to obey it, he clinches his argument by claiming that God's Son succeeds where the law proved weak; the possibility has been opened "that the just requirement of the law might be fulfilled in us, who walk not according to the flesh but according to the Spirit" (8:4). When, in Rom. 13:9, Paul repeats several demands of the Decalogue, he is again, not commanding their observance, but arguing that Christian love inevitably meets the standards set by the law. When Christian ethics is related to the Mosaic law in the fulfillment passages, the view is retrospective.[13] Paul's purpose is to provide assurance of the quality of Christian conduct, not to define its several duties.

2. The law which believers are said to fulfill in these passages is the Mosaic code.[14] Yet Paul does not expect Christian behavior to conform with Torah's demands of circumcision, purity, or festival occasions. How can Christians be said to "fulfill" the law when a significant number of its commands are disregarded?[15]

Again, we need to recall Paul's point in making the claim. Paul is concerned to show that the ethical behavior of Christians is better, not worse, than that of those living "under the law." Truthfulness, sexual purity, and devotion to the well-being of others are relevant issues, whereas the food one eats is not. Paul never faults Jews with laxity in ritual observance, but neither does he regard attention to such matters as a mark of one's conformity to the law (cf. Rom. 2:25). The crucial tests are moral: Do you steal? do you commit adultery? and the like (vv. 21-23). Here Jewish observance of the law, Paul contends, falls short; and it is here that the love which Christians are to show stands the test.[16]

13. Cf. Betz, *Galatians*, 275; Gerhardsson, *Ethos*, 66-67; van Dülmen, *Theologie*, 229-230.

14. Hübner (*Law*, 37) denies that the Mosaic law is meant in Gal. 5:14. For a decisive refutation, see Sanders, *Law*, 96-97.

15. Cf. Sanders, *Law*, 99; Räisänen, *Law*, 62-73.

16. Räisänen (*Law*, 118) rightly points out that Paul's claims about Christian "fulfillment" of the law have a "doctrinaire" character and that they are at best supported by a highly selective use of the empirical data. Cf. also van Dülmen, *Theologie*, 151. The point here is simply that such claims are a necessary consequence of his thought, not a reversal of his proclamation of Christian liberty.

3. This leads us to another distinction, undoubtedly intended by Paul. The instructor of an undergraduate music course in which a concert pianist enrolls may quickly—perhaps with some embarrassment—grant that the "student" has more than adequately "fulfilled" a number of requirements for the course even though the specific work normally demanded has not been "done." Indeed, the accomplished musician views the exercises and norms imposed on beginners with a knowing detachment, recognizing their limitations as well as their pedagogic importance and feeling free to ignore what now hinders rather than promotes the making of music. Such a failure to follow the norms while nonetheless achieving their intended purpose should be distinguished from the stubborn refusal of a novice to be subject to a necessary discipline. The consummate musician "fulfills" the intention of the rules without always observing them; but the recalcitrant novice neither "does" nor "fulfills" the "law" of the musical trade.

In a similar way, Paul can only believe that a life directed by God's Holy Spirit more than adequately "fulfills" the requirements of the law, even though specific demands have not been "done" and commands that are perceived to serve a purpose no longer have been ignored. What is crucial to note is that Paul consistently distinguishes between the "doing" of the law's commands required of those subject to it and the "fulfilling" of the law by Christians.[17]

The verb *poiein* is of course very general and may occur in any context, including where the Christian practice of righteousness is the topic (cf. Rom. 13:3; 1 Cor. 9:23; 10:31; Gal. 6:9). It must be noted, however, that for Paul, while Christians are never said to "do" *(poiein)* the law,[18] those "under the law" are seen as obligated to "do" its commands (Rom. 10:5; Gal. 3:10, 12; 5:3); indeed, as we have seen, the law itself, in Paul's mind, rests on the principle of "doing" as opposed to "believing" (Gal. 3:12; Rom. 10:5-6). If, then, the essence of life

17. Cf. Betz, *Galatians,* 275; Bläser, *Gesetz,* 242.

18. I am assuming that Christians are not in view in Rom. 2:13-14. Räisänen (*Law,* 63-64, n. 104) uses this passage as evidence against the view that Paul distinguished between "doing" and "fulfilling" the law, since "the Gentiles Paul had in mind could not 'do' the law (or its *ergon*) in any other sense than the Christians 'fulfilled' it, i.e. by living according to its central principle(s)." For practical purposes this may be so, but Paul is bent on scoring a theological point in the passages in which he insists that Christians "fulfill" the law; since that theological point (the more-than-adequate character of Christian conduct) is not in view in the reference to Gentiles in Romans 2, a verb of "doing" suffices. The pattern of Paul's usage of "do" and "fulfill" is too striking to be downplayed.

"under the law" is the requirement to "do" its commands, it is not strange that Paul avoids the term in contexts where he relates Christian behavior to the law. On the other hand, where specifically Christian behavior is related positively to the Mosaic law, the verb *plēroun* or a cognate inevitably occurs (Rom. 8:4; 13:8, 10; Gal. 5:14); yet these terms are *never* used where the requirements or achievements of those living "under the law" are in view. Given the occasional nature of Paul's correspondence, such a consistent distinction in usage is striking indeed and demands some explanation.

What Paul means by "doing" the law is clear enough: those "under the law" are obligated to carry out, to perform, its individual and specific requirements (Gal. 5:3). Certainly the verb *plēroun* can also mean "to perform" (cf. Col. 4:17), but there are nuances to its usage which should not be overlooked. The verb "is used . . . with an impersonal object, originally at least pictured to the mind as a receptacle to be filled, an empty form to be filled with reality; thus of a promise, prophecy, or statement of fact, 'to satisfy the purport of,' 'to fit the terms of' . . . ; of commands and laws, 'to satisfy the requirements of,' 'to obey fully.'"[19] To "fulfill" the law thus implies that the obedience offered *completely satisfies* what is required. But this in turn means that *plēroun* is specially suited, whereas *poiein* is not, for use by an author who claims to have superior insight into what is required to satisfy the "true" intention of the lawgiver or the "real" demand of the law. Matt. 5:17 is a perfect illustration: *plērōsai* says something different, something more, than what *poiēsai* would say in the context.[20] The meaning must not be reduced to the bald claim that Jesus "does" the law (and the prophets!) by carrying out each of the specific requirements it contains; rather in some not clearly defined way (the verb *plēroun* has the advantage of positive connotations but not the liability of excessive specificity)[21] the "true" meaning of the Old Testament scriptures is satisfied, and they reach their intended goal, in Jesus' ministry.

Paul's usage seems similar. He would scarcely have been content with the bald claim that the one who loves his neighbor has "done" *(pepoiēken)* the law (contrast Rom. 13:8). On the one hand, so prosaic an assertion would be too blatantly open to the objection that circumcision and food laws need to be "done" as well; on the other hand,

19. Burton, *Galatians*, 295.
20. Cf. Luz, "Erfüllung," 416.
21. Luz, "Erfüllung," 413; Räisänen, *Law*, 87-88; Trilling, *Israel*, 178-179.

the term would give no expression to Paul's implicit claim to know what God "really" requires. For Paul it is important to say that Christians "fulfill" the whole law, and thus to claim that their conduct (and theirs alone) fully satisfies the "real" purport of the law in its entirety while allowing the ambiguity of the term to blunt the force of the objection that certain individual requirements (with which, Paul would maintain, Christian behavior was never meant to conform) have not been "done."

Thus statements of the law's "fulfillment" should not be seen as compromising Paul's claim that the law does not bind believers. Christians serve God, Paul maintains, not in the old way where conduct is prescribed by the law's "letter," but in the new way of the Spirit (Rom. 7:6). Paradoxically, the results (not the requirements!) of the "old way" are said to be sinful passions, transgressions of the law, and death (Rom. 7:5; 2 Cor. 3:6; Gal. 3:19). Paradoxically again, the "fruit" (but not the requirement!) of the "new way" is the "fulfillment" of the law (Rom. 8:4). The paradox is deliberate; it is hardly the expression of unresolved tensions in Paul's thought.

iii. Christian Freedom from the Law

Arguments based on the correspondence between approved Christian behavior and the demands of the Mosaic law, or on Paul's statements that Christians "fulfill" the law, fall short of proving that he (sometimes?) thought Christians are bound by the Mosaic code. On the other hand, the evidence that he believed Christians are free from the law is both explicit and abundant.

1. The Jew,[22] according to Paul, is *"under the law"* (1 Cor. 9:20); the Christian is not (Rom. 6:14-15; 1 Cor. 9:20). What does Paul mean by the phrase? Those who insist that the demands of the law are still binding on the Christian are compelled to understand it as meaning "under the law's curse," or "attempting to observe the law *in order to be justified*,"[23] or the like. Yet a look at the passages in which it is used indicates that Paul is referring to an obligation to observe the commands of the law. It is true that such an obligation inevitably leads humanity "in the flesh" into bondage to sin and liability to the divine curse, and that, at times, the phrase may carry with it connotations of

22. And sometimes, by extension, the Gentiles *outside* of Christ; cf. the discussion above, Chapter 9, section iv.

23. E.g., Moule, "Obligation," 394-395.

this whole desperate situation (cf. Gal. 4:5). But the primary meaning is clear enough in 1 Cor. 9:20: "to those under the law (i.e., obligated to observe its commands) I became as one under the law—though not being myself under the law—that I might win those under the law." In saying that he acted as though he were "under the law," Paul of course does not mean that he behaved as though he were in bondage to sin, or under a divine curse, or under the illusion that he had to keep the law in order to be justified; he simply means that, in order not to offend those obligated to observe the statutes of the law of God, he himself acted as though he were bound by the same duty, though in fact, he insists, he is not. As a Christian, he has been freed from an obligation which applied to Jews under the old dispensation, that of observing the demands of the law.

2. Christians have "died to the law" (Rom. 7:4; cf. Gal. 2:19). Again, the meaning cannot be simply that they have died to the law's curse, to the law as a means of justification, or to a misunderstanding of the law. The phrase clearly includes release from the law's demands as well.

Gal. 2:17 appears to voice a complaint with which Paul was forced to contend: if, as a Christian, he feels free to disregard (and thus transgress) the law's commands, then faith in Christ has been made a pretext for sin and Christ has become sin's agent. Paul emphatically denies that this is the case, arguing that *he cannot be said to transgress a law to which he is no longer subject;* only if the law which has been done away with is reinstituted can he become its transgressor: "But if I build up again those things which I tore down, *then* I prove myself a transgressor" (v. 18). At this point, and in support of the claim that he cannot transgress commands which no longer bind him, Paul introduces the cryptic phrase: "For I through the law died to the law . . ." (v. 19). However we understand death "through the law . . . to the law" to have taken place, the result, as the context requires, is a deliverance from the *demands* of the law which makes their "transgression" impossible.

The same point is made in Rom. 7:1-6. A married woman who has sexual relations with a man other than her husband transgresses the law which forbids such an encounter. She is, however, freed from that law if her husband dies. The analogy is not the most perspicuous in the literature; but Paul's essential point is that, just as the woman is freed by her husband's death, not only from the *punishment* for adultery, but also from the need to comply with a command or be guilty of (the transgression of) adultery, so Christians, who have died to the Mosaic law, are freed from its demands.

3. Paul's statements in Galatians about the temporal limitations on the law's validity (3:19–4:5) cannot be restricted to the law's curse, to the law as a means of salvation, or to a misunderstanding of the law. Paul's very point in stressing that the epoch of the law has passed is that Christians do not need to submit to its *demand* for circumcision. Neither obligation to the law's precepts nor subjection to its curse now burdens believers. Only if, by submitting to the requirement of circumcision, they return to the yoke of the law will they be "bound to keep the whole law" (5:1, 3); the obvious implication of 5:3 is that, as Christians, the Galatians are not obliged to keep the law.

4. In 1 Cor. 9:20, Paul points out that he is not obligated to observe the law's demands. That he felt no such obligation is apparent at a number of points.[24] Anyone obligated to observe the law's demands must recognize that some food is clean, other food unclean (Lev. 11; Deut. 14:3-21). Paul does not: "I know and am persuaded in the Lord Jesus that nothing is unclean in itself" (Rom. 14:14). The law demands that the seventh day be kept holy, and that other festival days be observed as well. For Paul, such observance is entirely optional: "One man esteems one day as better than another, while another man esteems all days alike. Let every one be fully convinced in his own mind" (v. 5). It is not clear what "days, and months, and seasons, and years" the Galatians were observing (Gal. 4:10). But it is certain that observances of that kind are prescribed by the Mosaic law and equally certain that Paul regards such observance as belonging to the period of human bondage to which the Christian is not to revert (vv. 9-11).

At this point, the objection is frequently raised that, while Paul does not believe the Christian is obligated to observe the Old Testament ceremonial law, he does believe the Christian is obligated to observe its moral commands.[25] Such distinctions are the inevitable result of the view that the law still states the binding requirements of God for the Christian, since no one imagines that Paul thought Christians were

24. Since 1 Cor. 9:21 can only mean that, in the presence of Gentiles, Paul did not observe the ritual demands of Torah, the frequent assertion in the scholarly literature that he himself kept the law is false. Among other clear indications to the same effect, see Gal. 2:11-14 (which surely implies that Paul himself ate with Gentiles), 18; 4:12. See further the discussion by Räisänen, *Law,* 73-77.

25. E.g. Cranfield, "Law," 67; Wendland, *Ethik,* 57; for the contrary position, see Lyonnet, "Freedom," 149.

obligated to observe its statutes of circumcision or ritual purity. Were it true, however, that Paul considered the law or any part of it still binding for the Christian, he would have had to provide his churches with detailed instructions as to which commands they were obligated to observe and which they were not: this would obviously be a very important matter! But there is no evidence that he made any such distinctions. On the contrary, it is clear that, for Paul, Torah was a unit.[26] On this point he did not differ from the standard Jewish view: the person who is obligated to observe the law is obligated to observe its every precept.[27] That, for Paul, is true of the person who is under the law (cf. Gal. 5:3); it is not true of the Christian.

5. Paul concedes the truth of the slogan "All things are lawful for me" (1 Cor. 6:12; 10:23), even though he is quick to point out its inadequacies as a guideline for Christian behavior: not everything is profitable or edifying, and some practices would lead to a new bondage. Both the slogan itself and Paul's non-legal way of qualifying it clearly indicate that the Christian is not thought to be obligated to observe the demands of the law.[28] The law, after all, forbids as well as commands; of no one subject to its demands can it be said that everything is "lawful."

What makes Paul's refusal to reject the slogan "All things are lawful" even more astonishing is the contexts in which it is raised: discussions of fornication with prostitutes (1 Cor. 6:12-20), and of the propriety of eating food offered to idols (chs. 8, 10). Surely, if Paul was ever to "lay down the law," if Torah was to be invoked in any sphere as the standard for Christian behavior, then the subjects of sexual morality and commerce with idolatry presented him with opportunities without equal. But Paul declined the temptation. His argument from Christian principles is both more complicated and less decisive than a simple reference to the prohibitions of God's law would have been. Clearly Paul's proclamation of freedom from the law left him with no other choice.

6. Though Christians are free from obligation to the law, they are obviously not free to engage in any and every kind of possible activ-

---

26. Cf. Bläser, *Gesetz,* 41-44. Bläser rightly points out that the question raised in Rom. 6:15 and the exhortation of Gal. 5:13 would be meaningless had Paul meant by Christian freedom only a release from the law's ritual demands (*Gesetz,* 228-229).

27. Cf. Mishnah *Aboth* 2.1; 4.2

28. Cf. Deidun, *Morality,* 154, n. 13.

ity. They remain servants of God (cf. Rom. 6:22), bound to do his will.[29] But what is significant here is the way in which that will is defined. Jews "under the law" know the will of God and are able to "approve what is excellent" because they are "instructed in the law" (2:18); the proper course of behavior for them in any situation may be found by consulting the relevant statute in Torah. No such concrete formula, however, is available for Christians. They discern what is the will of God by presenting themselves to God, by refusing to pattern their way of life after that of this age, by being "transformed by the renewal of [their] mind[s]" (12:2). They "approve what is excellent" (the same phrase as in Rom. 2:18 is used of Christians in Phil. 1:9-10) when their love grows in knowledge and judgment. The fact that, whereas the will of God for Jews was found in the statutes of Torah, Christians must discover it for themselves as their mind is "renewed" and they grow in insight shows clearly that the will of God is no longer defined as an obligation to observe the law's statutes.

iv. The Letter and the Spirit

In the programmatic statement of Rom. 7:6, Paul contrasts the service of God enjoined under the old covenant ("so that we serve not under the old written code") with that enjoined by the new ("but in the new life of the Spirit").

The Pauline distinction between *gramma* (literally "letter"; RSV "written code") and *pneuma* ("spirit") has often been taken to refer to different ways of reading the Old Testament. 2 Corinthians 3 in particular seems to lend itself to such an interpretation:[30] in the latter part of the chapter Paul speaks specifically of the reading of the old covenant and of a "veil" which is present when it is read by Jews (vv. 14-15). Some commentators see in the "veil" a reference to the inadequacies of Jewish hermeneutics: its failure to see Christian truth in the Old Testament, its failure to read the scriptures "spiritually," and the like.[31] Such inadequate exegesis is thought to be indicated by the "letter" of verse 6 and is contrasted with the true, "spiritual" understanding.[32]

---

29. Deidun, *Morality,* 24, 51; Bläser, *Gesetz,* 235. For what follows, see Gerhardsson, *Ethos,* 81.

30. Cf. Prat, *Theology,* II, 435-441; see Allo, *Corinthiens,* 103-111.

31. Cf. Prat, *Theology,* II, 440: the veil is present for "unbelieving Jews, who read the *letter* of the Law without grasping its *spirit.*"

32. Cf. also Kamlah, "Buchstabe," 276-282: *gramma* is said to express

The occurrence of the spirit-letter antithesis in Rom. 7:6 has been similarly understood. Particularly those who believe that the law of Moses, correctly understood, is still binding on the Christian are inclined to interpret the "oldness" of the "letter" as indicating the obsolescence, not of the law itself, but of a certain inadequate understanding of the law. We may cite C. E. B. Cranfield as an example:

> [Paul] does not use "letter" as a simple equivalent of "the law." "Letter" is rather what the legalist is left with as a result of his misunderstanding and misuse of the law. It is the letter of the law in separation from the Spirit. But, since "the law is spiritual" (v. 14), the letter of the law in isolation from the Spirit is not the law in its true character, but the law as it were denatured. It is this which is opposed to the Spirit whose presence is the true establishment of the law.[33]

But does Paul mean by the "letter" a perversion of the law of God? Is the "Spirit" with which the "letter" is contrasted introduced as the guide to a right understanding of scripture? A close look at the passages in which Paul refers to the "letter" shows that it refers rather to the law itself as that which imposed obligations during one period of salvation history which for Christians are no longer binding; the Spirit is introduced as the mark of Christian ethics.

1. According to Rom. 2:27, "those who are physically uncircumcised but keep the law will condemn you who have the written code (literally, the "letter") and circumcision but break the law *(ton dia grammatos kai peritomēs parabatēn nomou)*." In the context, Paul is concerned, not with the legalist's misuse of the law to establish personal righteousness, but with the failure of Jews to measure up to the law's specific demands: You yourself are guilty of the blatant sins you condemn in others (vv. 1, 3); you steal, commit adultery, and rob temples (vv. 21-22); you cause the name of God to be blasphemed among the heathen (v. 24)—not, of course, because Gentiles realize that your perfect fulfillment of the law's demands has blinded you to your dependence on God's grace, but simply because your manifest

---

Paul's reproach against the Jews that they interpret the Old Testament from the perspective of the old world order; this is contrasted with the full understanding of scripture, which is possible only when it is interpreted in the light of the cross of Christ.

For a discussion of Käsemann's understanding of the lettter-spirit antithesis, see my "Letter," 230-233.

33. Cranfield, *Romans,* 339-340; cf. also Michel, *Römer,* 222.

transgressions of the law (v. 23; cf. vv. 25, 27) bring dishonor to the God whose elect you claim to be.

This context is crucial for our understanding of *dia grammatos* in verse 27. Here *gramma* ("letter") cannot refer to the misunderstanding of the law shown by those who observe its statutes perfectly in order to establish their own righteousness. Paul has denounced here the open failure to observe what the law by any reading demands; and the Jewish transgressor of the law *dia grammatos kai peritomēs* is contrasted, not with the person who *understands* the true nature of the law or circumcision, but with the Gentile who *observes* the righteous demands of the law without possessing either the books of the law (cf. v. 14) or circumcision (vv. 26-27).

Hence, in this verse at least, "letter" is an abbreviated way of referring, not to a perverted understanding of the commands of God, but simply to their possession in written form: a possession which, however, in Paul's view carries with it the obligation of observance and sanctions to be imposed if the commandments are transgressed. The genitive with *dia* must indicate attendant circumstance, not instrument:[34] the uncircumcised keeper of the law will condemn those who, *though they have the "letter" and circumcision,* are transgressors of the law. Neither the "letter" nor circumcision is here considered a liability. If there is a negative ring to the words *dia grammatos kai peritomēs,* it is due to the fact that it is only the possession of the *scrolls* of the law and only *physical* circumcision which Jewish transgressors can claim in their favor. We may compare Paul's words in verse 20: "having in the law the embodiment (*morphōsin,* literally "form") of knowledge and truth." The choice of the word, "letter," like that of "form" in verse 20, does indeed stress that it is only the written scrolls, the external form, which such Jews possess, while they lack the righteous observance to which possession of the "letter" obligates them; but the fault lies in what they lack, not in what they possess.[35]

2. In Rom. 7:6, both "not under the old written code (literally "letter")" and "in the new life of the Spirit" qualify the infinitive *douleuein,* "to serve." Clearly, then, "letter" and "Spirit" here mark different ways of rendering service which characterize the old and the

---

34. Cf. Bauer, Arndt, Gingrich, Danker, *Lexicon,* 179.

35. The circumcision *(en) grammati* of Rom. 2:29 is simply physical circumcision, a benefit which the Jew possesses (2:25; 3:1-2), but which entails the obligation to obey the commands of the law.

new dispensations respectively. Nothing in the context suggests that the "old way" of the "letter" refers to a legalistic misuse of the law.

In Romans 6, far from speaking of a misguided zeal to observe the law as being characteristic of life "under the law," Paul describes a time when the "members" of his readers were "instruments of wickedness" (v. 13) and in bondage to "impurity" and "iniquity" (v. 19), when they did things of which they now are ashamed (v. 21). The "sin" which is not to master them *because they are not under the law* (v. 14; the phrase of course implies that such sin normally accompanies life "under the law") is certainly, as the sequel shows, not a desire to establish their own righteousness by observing statutes, but lawless and shameful activities which a freedom from the obligation to observe statutes might seem to encourage.

The same note continues into Romans 7, as verse 5, with its reference to "our sinful passions, aroused by the law," indicates. And in 7:7-13, the commandment leads to death, not because the law has been observed in an attempt to establish one's own righteousness, but because the law has been transgressed.

Romans 7:6, then, can hardly be speaking of the misunderstanding of the legalist. Rather serving God by the "letter" must refer to the *obligation* of those subject to the old covenant to carry out the concrete commands of the law of God—a situation which led to obvious sin and death.

3. In 2 Cor. 3:6, as in Rom. 7:6, the antithesis between "letter" and "Spirit" refers to two different ways of rendering service. The ministers *(diakonoi)* of the new covenant are contrasted with those of the old: those who served under the old covenant are called ministers of the "letter"; Paul claims to be a minister of the Spirit. In the verses which follow, he develops the contrast between the two ministries, the "ministry *(diakonia,* RSV "dispensation")* of death" and that "of the Spirit," noting in particular the greater glory attached to that of the Spirit, its permanence, and the boldness *(parrhēsia)* which characterizes his ministry, but not that of Moses (vv. 7-12). Here, as in Romans 7, then, "letter" and "Spirit" express, not two ways of reading scripture,[36] but the essence of service under the two covenants.

36. This remains true in spite of the references to the reading of the old covenant and the "veil" which is said to be present when Jews read it (vv. 14-15). The point of the passage is not that Jews fail to perceive the deeper significance of the scriptures, nor that they pervert them into a demand for good works, but that they fail to perceive that the period of the old covenant has passed (note espe-

Indeed, the view that the "letter" refers to a "perversion," a "misunderstanding" of the Old Testament law, seems incompatible with the language Paul uses. It is true that its ministry was one of death (v. 7) and condemnation (v. 9), but this accords well with what we have seen in Romans about the situation which resulted when men and women were under obligation to fulfill the demands of Torah. On the other hand, the reference to the ministry of death "carved in letters on stone" (v. 7) would seem more naturally to refer to the concrete demands of the law, which were so inscribed, than to a perversion of them. The very references to a ministry *(diakonia)* and a covenant *(diathēkē)* of which Moses was a representative would seem to preclude the possibility that a perversion of that covenant is meant. And Paul repeatedly notes that the old ministry was accompanied by a display of divine glory. To be sure, that glory passed away, indicating the transitory nature of the old covenant; but Paul would scarcely have spoken in these terms had he meant that the ministry of the letter was itself a misunderstanding. On the contrary, the only misunderstanding referred to here is the failure to realize that the period of the old covenant and its ministry has passed, giving way to that of the Spirit (vv. 11-14).

Common to these three passages (Rom. 2:27; 7:6; 2 Cor. 3:6) is the divinely given but limited role assigned to the "letter." Paul means seriously that those who lived under the law were obligated to fulfill the "letter"; indeed, the purpose of the law could only be achieved if those who were under its yoke were bound to observe its terms. This is certainly supported by his references to the (now obsolete) obedience to the "letter," and it is confirmed by such texts as Gal. 3:10, 12; and 5:3. Now, however, the way of the "letter" (i.e., obedience to the law) has become, for believers, a thing of the past; service is now rendered "in the new life of the Spirit" (Rom. 7:6).

4. That the Spirit of God had been poured out on the early Church was the common interpretation of charismatic signs in their midst. Paul, however, may well have been the first to see the indwelling Spirit as the abiding guide and enabler of Christian moral behavior (Gal.

---

cially the frequent forms of *katargein,* vv. 7, 11, 13, 14). The purpose of the "veil" according to v. 13 was to keep the Israelites from looking *eis to telos tou katargoumenou;* presumably we are to see here a reference to the passing of the old dispensation itself (cf. Barrett, *Second Corinthians,* 119). "That same veil," i.e., that which conceals the transitory nature of the old covenant, is present when Jews read the scriptures even today, so that they do not see "that in Christ it is being abolished" (so we may read v. 14). See further Bläser, *Gesetz,* 207-213.

5:16-25; Phil. 3:3; Rom. 8:4-14, etc.; cf. already Ezek. 36:27),[37] and it was almost certainly Paul who introduced the notion that "walking in the Spirit" is an ethical norm *replacing* the law: "If you are led by the Spirit you are not under the law" (Gal. 5:18; cf. Rom. 7:6; 2 Cor. 3:6-17).[38] A full discussion of Paul's understanding of the Spirit would take us far afield; several comments are nonetheless in order.

a. The ethic determined by God's Holy Spirit cannot, for Paul, be capricious. Paul points out areas of possible human behavior which are incompatible with the leading of the Holy Spirit of God (1 Cor. 12:3; Gal. 5:16-21; 1 Thess. 4:7-8) and other moral characteristics which the Spirit inevitably produces (Gal. 5:22-23). In fact, of course, Paul's understanding of the moral behavior which the Spirit induces corresponds nicely with the moral demands of the Mosaic law.[39] But this, as we have seen, does not mean that Paul derives Christian duty from the law. The ethical instruction of the epistles would have looked very different had Paul continued to find the will of God in the way he did as a Pharisee, by interpreting and applying the relevant statutes from Torah.[40]

b. Paul clearly does not conclude that, since all believers possess the Spirit, ethical instruction and encouragement are no longer necessary.[41] As long as believers remain "in the flesh," the risk of succumbing to temptation remains. Furthermore, Paul recognizes that some believers are "babes" (1 Cor. 3:1), some "weak" (Rom. 14:1), and that the encouragement and guidance of those stronger and more mature is needed. Authority to provide such help, to "build up" the faith of his converts (2 Cor. 10:8; 13:10), had been entrusted to the apostle.[42]

c. Certainly there are times when Paul speaks as though his own authority or (still more clearly) that of the Lord ought by itself to de-

37. Cf. Bultmann, *Theology,* I, 337.

38. Cf. Lyonnet, "Freedom," 156-161. Note that the replacement of the (Mosaic) law is the Spirit, not another law. Paul does, to be sure, use the phrase "law of Christ" elsewhere (Gal. 6:2; cf. 1 Cor. 9:21), but the phrase is used loosely, by analogy with the Mosaic code, for the way of life fitting for a Christian. No specific collection of commands is in view. Cf. Räisänen, *Law,* 77-82. Nor is the language Pauline when Stuhlmacher speaks of the Mosaic Torah as *itself* "freed from the power of sin" and "eschatologically transformed and put in force as a way of life" (*Reconciliation,* 126; cf. "Understanding," 99).

39. Cf. Feine, *Evangelium,* 215; Deidun, *Morality,* 169-171, 187.

40. Cf. Gundry, "Grace," 6-8; Deidun, Review, 50.

41. Cf. Lyonnet, "Freedom," 161-174; Gerhardsson, *Ethos,* 82.

42. Cf. Longenecker, *Paul,* 196-202.

cide an issue; the degree of sympathy with which a democratic age reads the apostle depends in no small measure on the emphasis placed upon such passages. But another side to Paul should at least not be lost to view: one which reckoned seriously with each believer's possession of the Spirit and responsibility to follow the Spirit's guidance. On a number of occasions, Paul took great care not to give the impression that he was a dictator over others' faith (2 Cor. 1:24; 8:8; 1 Thess. 2:7; Phlm. 8-9; and note Rom. 1:11-12).[43] He also carefully pointed out that the basis of his instruction was his possession of the Spirit of God (1 Cor. 7:40);[44] he asked his readers, since they themselves had received the Spirit, to acknowledge that his directives came from the Lord (1 Cor. 14:37; cf. Rom. 15:14; Phil. 3:15), to participate in the reasoning which led to his conclusions,[45] or even to judge them for themselves (1 Cor. 10:15; 11:13); he insisted that he was merely reminding them of what they already knew (cf. Rom. 15:15; 1 Cor. 4:17);[46] and so on.

d. Räisänen asks why Paul does not attribute to his own apostolic instructions the negative results he assigns the law.[47] The question may fairly be put, but it should be obvious what Paul's answer would be: the Spirit has now been given.

Humanity outside of Christ has only the "flesh" to live by, a "flesh" which, according to Paul, cannot please God (Rom. 8:5-8). Nor are the manifestations of the "flesh" restricted to the grievous sins listed in Gal. 5:19-21. Even attempts to conform to God's law remain, in Paul's thinking, the endeavors of the flesh (Phil. 3:3-6; Gal. 3:2-3; cf. Rom. 8:3). But those who belong to God's new creation are "indwelt" and "led" by his Spirit (Rom. 8:9, 14; Gal. 5:18); and though the Spirit's power is expressed in human activity, the results remain the Spirit's "fruit" (Gal. 5:22). Paul's terminology, to be sure, is neither

43. Cf. Holmberg, *Paul,* 82-83.

44. Similarly, those responsible for exhortation in the local church do so, according to Paul, on the basis of a *charisma* of the Spirit (1 Cor. 12:7-8, 11; 14:3; cf. Rom. 12:6-8). The contrast with Pharisaism, where trained experts in the law provide guidance as to the proper course of behavior, also witnesses to the change from letter-service to Spirit-service.

45. Cf. von Campenhausen, *Begründung,* 20; Holmberg, *Paul,* 186.

46. Cf. Dahl, *Jesus,* 15.

47. Räisänen, *Law,* 148-149; but see Bläser, *Gesetz,* 240-241. In fact, Jewish eschatological expectation itself assumed that the behavior of God's people in the new age would mark a vast improvement over their conduct in the old. Paul differed here only in his conviction that the new age had come.

technical nor consistent; he is quite prepared, in some contexts, to speak of a Christian's own "work" (1 Cor. 3:13; 15:58; 16:10, etc.). Still his conviction that the effective power within the believer is divine finds constant expression: "it is no longer I who live, but Christ who lives in me" (Gal. 2:20).[48] Since such divine power comes as a gift to the Christian, Paul can insist that divine grace, not the individual's own energy, is the active force (cf. 1 Cor. 15:10; 2 Cor. 1:12). Hence, though Paul's own terminology is not consistent, deeds done in obedience to the old covenant are the doer's *own* works in a sense which does not apply to those performed under the new; and the latter are themselves an expression of divine grace and power in a sense impossible when the Spirit was not yet given.[49]

v. The Origin of Paul's View

Paul defends his positions on the law with every tool at his disposal; nowhere, however, does he explain how he himself arrived at his views. Two suggestions deserve consideration here.[50]

1. Räisänen proposes that Paul at first merely adopted the liberal attitude of the Hellenistic Jewish Christians toward the ritual Torah. A Gentile mission free of circumcision had already been undertaken, though it arose in a "haphazard" way without a theological justification ready to hand. It was when the practice of free admission for Gentiles was challenged by Palestinian Jewish Christians that Paul first attempted to devise a rationale for his position. The tensions and contradictions which mark his argumentation are best explained by supposing that Paul was suddenly confronted in a polemical setting with the need to defend procedures he had long taken for granted.[51]

Much of Räisänen's hypothesis is plausible enough. That, prior to his conversion, Paul persecuted Hellenistic Jewish Christians because of their laxity toward the ritual demands of Torah is very likely. Naturally, his conversion to the cause of those he persecuted would lead him to adopt their practices and views.[52] Moreover, the hypothesis is compatible on the one hand with the evidence of Galatians 1 and

48. See also the passages cited above, Chapter 8, section iii.
49. Cf. van Dülmen, *Theologie,* 172-173; Deidun, *Morality,* 51-84.
50. Räisänen discusses, adequately and at length, a number of other proposals that have been made (*Law,* 229-251).
51. Räisänen, *Law,* 252-263.
52. Cf. Dibelius-Kümmel, *Paul,* 51-53.

2 that Paul proclaimed salvation without circumcision from the very beginning of his Christian ministry and, on the other hand, with the inherent likelihood that the complex views of the law expressed in Galatians and Romans developed over a number of years. However dramatic Paul's Damascus transformation may have been, its implications would be the subject for years of reflection.

The question remains, however, whether Paul would have waited for the criticism of others before attempting to justify abandoning Torah. I think it unlikely, given his erstwhile devotion to its laws and his well-documented bent for placing practical issues of the most trivial sort in a theological framework. The case that Paul long took laxity for granted seems very weak. (a) Some of the tensions which Räisänen finds in Paul seem soluble; others concern complex problems that have vexed theologians for centuries. Neither category requires us to believe that the questions had recently occurred to the apostle. (b) While it is true that Barnabas and Paul worked long together, then parted ways, it is not certain that a shift in Paul's thinking was the cause. Paul himself would have us believe that Barnabas and Cephas succumbed to pressures from Jerusalem and abandoned practices which they previously embraced (Gal. 2:11-14). His account may be one-sided, but we have no evidence with which to confute it. (c) From the silence of 1 Thessalonians on matter of the law we may infer, not Pauline indifference, but only that the law was not an issue in the Thessalonian community. For my own part, I find it hard to believe that the practice of Hellenistic Jewish Christians could have dictated Paul's conduct without—from the very beginning—stirring his thoughts.

2. The second hypothesis is that of Sanders, and it is beautiful in its simplicity. If salvation comes through faith in Christ, then it cannot come through Torah. Paul's exclusivist soteriology compelled him to reject the law.[53]

Such an explanation is certainly true, whether or not other factors (such as the practice of the Hellenists) played a contributing role. Paul perceived that the claims of the gospel to provide salvation competed with those of Torah, whose commands are accompanied by sanctions of life and death. If, then, Christ and not the law brings life, then Torah can only bring death, its demands must have been transgressed, and its subjects must need deliverance. Furthermore, since the law's demands cannot be detached from its sanctions, deliverance from the

---

53. Cf. Sanders, *Law,* 17-64; also Pfleiderer, *Paulinism,* I, 74.

law's curse inevitably means freedom from its commands as well. Paul could not conceive of Torah as a mere guide for moral behavior. Once he had rejected the law as the means of salvation, then ethical conduct required different norms.

Again, these implications would no doubt have become apparent to Paul in the course of considerable reflection; and, again, there is no reason to believe that Paul's reflections were first sparked by the attacks of Palestinian Jewish Christians. Preoccupied with Torah, Paul the Pharisee set out to persecute Christians in Damascus. A heavenly vision changed his commission completely, but only in part his preoccupation.

Chapter Eleven

Paul's Contribution

May we not, after all, speak of a *contribution* by the apostle Paul?

Scarcely, according to Räisänen, on the intellectual level. Credit is given to the Pauline *intuition* which led him to insights concerning Christian freedom; but the tensions, contradictions, false paths, and unsolved problems in Paul's writings show that it is a "fundamental mistake" to portray Paul as the "'prince of thinkers' and the Christian 'theologian par excellence.'"[1]

Räisänen's case is serious, his erudition immense, his argumentation rigorous and sensitive to nuances. And when we list the merits of his study we should not omit the possibility that he may be right as well. Doubtless to some extent he is. Clearly the genre in which Paul wrote, the polemical situations which he addressed, and the nature of his own personality combined to produce arguments in which the terminology is neither strictly defined nor consistently used and in which the propositions made are not examined with the careful order, logic, or detachment required of the makers of systems. However worthy of note the righteous Gentiles of Romans 2 may have been, Paul's argument would have been clearer had he reserved their praise for a different context. However common the lot of Jews and pagans may have appeared, a more systematic thinker would have confined the phrase "under the law" to the former or justified its extension to the latter. Misunderstandings would have been avoided had Paul refrained from speaking of a Christian's "work," or declined the one-upmanship of claiming that Christian morality "fulfills" the law.

1. Räisänen, *Law*, 266-267.

We could of course continue in this vein, applying our shovels to the mountain of Paul's thought, pausing only to wipe our ever so high brows and to admire the pile of soil we have managed to remove. The mountain remains, however; and exegetes too, if only on vacation, should relax from their spadework and acknowledge its grandeur.

Crucial to an appreciation of Paul's understanding of the law is the realization that he normally means by *nomos* the divine commandments imparted to Israel on Mount Sinai with their accompanying sanctions. The "works of the law" are the concrete deeds which this legislation manifestly requires. The "law" promises "life" to those who comply with these commands, but threatens transgressors with "death" (Chapter Seven above). Naturally, those convinced of the adequacy and eternity of the Sinaitic covenant harbor no suspicion that Israel has proved incapable of showing the measure of obedience God requires to maintain relations with his people.

A second crucial factor in understanding Paul is the recognition that his rethinking of the law takes as its starting-point faith in a crucified Messiah. The evidence of the epistles does not support the view that Paul, before his encounter with the risen Christ, was tormented by an inability to keep the law (Chapter Four). Moreover, the claim of a number of recent scholars has here been affirmed, that Jews of Paul's day attributed Israel's enjoyment of divine favor to God's gracious election of his people. They did not believe they "earned" his approval by the "works" they did in compliance with the law (Chapter Three). When Paul distinguishes the path of the divine law and human works from that of human faith and divine grace, the two paths must be seen as reflecting, not the self-understanding of first-century Jewish and Christian communities respectively, but rather Paul's own attempt to grapple with theological problems posed by faith in a crucified Christ.

The questions with which Paul struggled appear in many cases to have been first posed by himself. The second-century writer to Diognetus could accept the message of Christ and dismiss the demands of Moses without hesitating at the thought that the same God commissioned both. Others, while affirming both revelations, betrayed no suspicion that the presence of the new might imply the inadequacy of the old. It was clearly Paul's estimation, however, that the offer of salvation made in the Christian gospel competed with the promises of Torah. Acceptance of the gospel as God's remedy for the human dilemma meant accepting as divine the assessment of the human predicament implicit in the redemptive death of God's Son. It meant that the Sinaitic covenant, with its laws, sanctions, and means of atonement, did not convey the life it promised—for otherwise Christ died to no purpose. Paul was thus forced to account for Torah's *failure* (see the discussion in Chapters Five and Eight above).

His answer was both anticipated in the prophetic charge that Israel, by breaking its covenantal obligations, had rendered the Sinaitic covenant obsolete, and given in the Christian creed that "Christ died for our sins." The covenant of Sinai had not conveyed life because the demands of its way had not been met: the cross of Christ imposed on Paul a more pessimistic view of human capacities than one normally encounters in Judaism. And though a Jew convinced of the efficacy of Torah would never distinguish its works from divine grace, Paul, convinced that the way of Torah had failed because men and women had transgressed its demands, naturally contrasted the works required under the old covenant with the redeeming grace offered in the new. To Paul, then, we owe the thesis of justification by grace, through faith (Chapter Eight). The doctrine must not be perceived as merely polemical (see Chapter Two above), though there is no doubt that we owe its articulation to a crisis in the life of the early Church. Utter dependence on divine grace is a constant and characteristic feature of Pauline theology *wherever* we meet it.

"Why then the law?" Again, the question posed marks a problem percieved. Paul's answer here is striking indeed, though the convictions at its base are traditional. If the law led to sin, then God must have so designed it. If the law precedes the gospel, then the sequence serves a purpose. God consigned all to sin, with the law serving both to demonstrate human guilt and to vindicate divine justice; but God's ultimate design was to show mercy to all (Chapter Nine).

Finally, it was Paul who realized that when the sanctions of the law have been removed, its demands have no force. The old covenant, of which the Mosaic law was an essential component, had now been replaced by a new covenant. And while others, with or without reflection, continued with the old observances, Paul set about the task of formulating the ethics of the new covenant. The gift of God's Spirit, recognized by the Christian community in the charismatic signs in its midst, became for Paul the basis for a new kind of service: discharged from the law, Christians serve God by the Spirit (Chapter Ten).

To this point we have considered Paul's contribution in terms of theological abstractions; nothing has been said of the integration of

Jew and Gentile into one Church through the exclusion of circumcision as a requirement. The emphasis on theology is needed, for though
the first century social reality was long overlooked and theology alone
considered, the pendulum has perhaps swung the other way. *Of course*
Paul's discussions were occasioned by disputes with his contemporaries; *of course* his practical goal was the promotion of the Gentile mission. But Paul could raise no practical issue without resolving its place
in a theological framework. His contribution to first-century Christianity was that of a pioneer missionary, coping with concrete problems as they arose in his assemblies. On the other hand, the Church of
the centuries is indebted to his persistence in relating ephemeral issues
to the themes of eternity. What influence Paul's discussions of the Gentile problem had in Galatia or Rome in the first century remains a mystery; their later effects in Hippo, Wittenberg, and Aldersgate are better known. Nor need the giants of the latter sites have perverted the
apostle's larger meaning because they show little understanding for
the halachic disputes of Paul's day or the perspective of his opponents.
Impervious to the problems which preoccupy the moderns, they had
eyes for the mountain.

Bibliography

Allo, E.-B. *Seconde Epître aux Corinthiens*. Etudes Bibliques; Paris: Gabalda, 1956.

Bacher, W., *Die exegetische Terminologie der jüdischen Traditionsliteratur*. Two vols. in one; Hildesheim: G. Olms, 1965 (= 1899, 1905).

Badenas, R. *Christ the End of the Law*. Sheffield: JSOT, 1985.

Barr, J. *The Semantics of Biblical Language*. Oxford: Oxford University, 1961.

Barrett, C. K. *The Second Epistle to the Corinthians*. Harper's New Testament Commentaries; New York: Harper and Row, 1973.

Barth, K. "Gospel and Law," *Scottish Journal of Theology Occasional Papers* 8 (1959), 3-27.

Bauer, W., W. F. Arndt, and F. W. Gingrich. *A Greek-English Lexicon of the New Testament and Other Early Christian Literature*, revised by F. W. Gingrich and F. W. Danker. Chicago: University of Chicago, 1979.

Beker, J. C. *Paul the Apostle: The Triumph of God in Life and Thought*. Philadelphia: Fortress, 1980.

Betz, H. D. *Galatians*. Hermeneia; Philadelphia: Fortress, 1979.

Bläser, P. *Das Gesetz bei Paulus*. Münster: Aschendorff, 1941.

Bornkamm, G. *Early Christian Experience*. New York: Harper & Row, 1969.

Bruce, F. F. *The Epistle to the Galatians*. New International Greek Testament Commentary; Grand Rapids: Eerdmans, 1982.

Bultmann, R. "Christ the End of the Law," in *Essays, Philosophical and Theological*. London: SCM, 1955, 36-66.

———. "Jesus and Paul," in *Existence and Faith. Shorter Writings of Rudolf Bultmann*. Cleveland: World, 1960, 183-201.

———. *Jesus Christ and Mythology*. New York: Charles Scribner's Sons, 1958.

———. "New Testament and Mythology," in *Kerygma and Myth*, ed. H. W. Bartsch. London: SPCK, 1953, 1-44.

———. "Paul," in *Existence and Faith*, 111-146.

————. *Primitive Christianity in its Contemporary Setting*. New York: New American Library, 1974.

————. "Das Problem der Ethik bei Paulus," in *Exegetika. Aufsätze zur Erforschung des Neuen Testaments*. Tübingen: J. C. B. Mohr, 1967, 36-54.

————. "Romans 7 and the Anthropology of Paul," in *Existence and Faith*, 147-157.

————. *Theology of the New Testament*. I. New York: Charles Scribner's Sons, 1951.

Burton, E. D. *A Critical and Exegetical Commentary on the Epistle to the Galatians*. International Critical Commentary; Edinburgh: T. & T. Clark, 1921.

Byrne, B. *'Sons of God'—'Seed of Abraham.'* Rome: Biblical Institute, 1979.

Callan, T. "Pauline Midrash: The Exegetical Background of Gal 3:19b," *Journal of Biblical Literature* 99 (1980), 549-567.

von Campenhausen, H. F. *Die Begründung kirchlicher Entscheidungen beim Apostel Paulus*. Sitzungsberichte der Heidelberger Akademie der Wissenschaften, Philosophisch-historische Klasse, 1957, 2.

Clements, R. E. *Old Testament Theology*. Atlanta: John Knox, 1978.

Cranfield, C. E. B. *A Critical and Exegetical Commentary on the Epistle to the Romans*. 1-2. International Critical Commentary; Edinburgh: T. & T. Clark, 1975-1979.

————. "St. Paul and the Law," *Scottish Journal of Theology* 17 (1964), 43-68.

Dahl, N. A. *Jesus in the Memory of the Early Church*. Minneapolis: Augsburg, 1976.

————. Review of E. P. Sanders, *Paul and Palestinian Judaism*, *Religious Studies Review* 4 (1978), 153-158.

————. *Studies in Paul*. Minneapolis: Augsburg, 1977.

Davies, W. D. *Jewish and Pauline Studies*. Philadelphia: Fortress, 1984.

Deidun, T. J. "'Having His Cake and Eating It': Paul on the Law" (Review of E. P. Sanders's *Paul, the Law, and the Jewish People*), *Heythrop Journal* 27 (1986), 43-52.

————. *New Covenant Morality in Paul*. Rome: Biblical Institute, 1981.

Dibelius, M. and W. G. Kümmel. *Paul*. Philadelphia: Westminster, 1953.

Dodd, C. H. *The Bible and the Greeks*. London: Hodder & Stoughton, 1935.

Donaldson, T. L. "The 'Curse of the Law' and the Inclusion of the Gentiles: Galatians 3, 13-14," *New Testament Studies* 32 (1986), 94-112.

Drane, J. W. *Paul: Libertine or Legalist?* London: SPCK, 1975.

van Dülmen, A. *Die Theologie des Gesetzes bei Paulus*. Stuttgart: Katholisches Bibelwerk, 1968.

Dunn, J. D. G. "The New Perspective on Paul," *Bulletin of the John Rylands Library* 65 (1983), 95-122.

————. "Works of the Law and the Curse of the Law (Galatians 3.10-14)," *New Testament Studies* 31 (1985), 523-542.

Ebeling, G. *Word and Faith.* Philadelphia: Fortress, 1963.

Espy, J. M. "Paul's 'Robust Conscience' Re-examined," *New Testament Studies* 31 (1985), 161-188.

Feine, P. *Das gesetzesfreie Evangelium des Paulus nach seinem Werdegang dargestellt.* Leipzig: J. C. Hinrichs, 1899.

Friedrich, G. "Das Gesetz des Glaubens Röm. 3, 27," *Theologische Zeitschrift* 10 (1954), 401-417.

Fuller, D. P. *Gospel and Law: Contrast or Continuum?* Grand Rapids: Eerdmans, 1980.

————. "Paul and 'The Works of the Law,'" *Westminster Theological Journal* 38 (1975-1976), 28-42.

Gaston, L. "Works of Law as a Subjective Genitive," *Studies in Religion/ Sciences Religieuses* 13 (1984), 39-46.

Gerhardsson, B. *The Ethos of the Bible.* Philadelphia: Fortress, 1981.

Grafe, E. *Die paulinische Lehre vom Gesetz nach den vier Hauptbriefen.* Freiburg und Tübingen: Akademische Verlagsbuchhandlung von J. C. B. Mohr, 1884.

Gundry, R. H. "Grace, Works, and Staying Saved in Paul," in *Biblica* 66 (1985), 1-38.

Gutbrod, W. and H. Kleinknecht, *"nomos,"* etc., *Theological Dictionary of the New Testament,* ed. G. Kittel. Vol. 4. Grand Rapids: Eerdmans, 1967, 1022-1091.

Hahn, F. "Das Gesetzesverständnis im Römer- und Galaterbrief," *Zeitschrift für die Neutestamentliche Wissenschaft* 67 (1976), 29-63.

Hawthorne, N. *The Marble Faun.* The Centenary Edition of the Works of Nathaniel Hawthorne, IV; Ohio State University, 1968.

Hays, R. B. *The Faith of Jesus Christ: An Investigation of the Narrative Substructure of Galatians 3:1–4:11.* Society of Biblical Literature Dissertation Series; Chico: Scholars, 1983.

Herford, R. T. *Judaism in the New Testament Period.* London: Lindsey, 1928.

Holmberg, B. *Paul and Power.* Philadelphia: Fortress, 1980 (1978).

Hooker, M. D. *Pauline Pieces.* London: Epworth, 1979.

Howard, G. E. "Christ the End of the Law: The Meaning of Romans 10.4ff.," *Journal of Biblical Literature* 88 (1969), 331-337.

————. "On the 'Faith of Christ,'" *Harvard Theological Review* 60 (1967), 459-465.

————. *Paul: Crisis in Galatia.* Cambridge: Cambridge University, 1979.

Hübner, H. *Law in Paul's Thought.* Edinburgh: T. & T. Clark, 1984.

————. "Pauli Theologiae Proprium," *New Testament Studies* 26 (1980), 445-473.

Hultgren, A. J. "The *Pistis Christou* Formulation in Paul," *Novum Testamentum* 22 (1980), 248-263.

Jackson, B. S. "Legalism," *Journal of Jewish Studies* 30 (1979), 1-22.

Kamlah, E. "Buchstabe und Geist. Die Bedeutung dieser Antithese für die alttestamentliche Exegese des Apostels Paulus," *Evangelische Theologie* 14 (1954), 276-282.

Käsemann, E. *Commentary on Romans*. Grand Rapids: Eerdmans, 1980.

―――. *Perspectives on Paul*. Philadelphia: Fortress, 1971.

Kim, S. *The Origin of Paul's Gospel*. Tübingen: J. C. B. Mohr, 1984[2].

Kümmel, W. G. *Römer 7 und das Bild des Menschen im Neuen Testament*. Munich: Christian Kaiser, 1974.

Kuss, O. "Nomos bei Paulus," *Münchener theologische Zeitschrift* 17 (1966), 173-227.

Lapide, P. and P. Stuhlmacher. *Paul: Rabbi and Apostle*. Minneapolis: Augsburg, 1984.

Lindars, B. "Torah in Deuteronomy," in *Words and Meanings: Essays Presented to David Winton Thomas,* ed. P. R. Ackroyd and B. Lindars. Cambridge: Cambridge University, 1968, 117-136.

Lohse, E. "*ho nomos tou pneumatos tēs zōēs*. Exegetische Anmerkungen zu Röm 8, 2," in *Neues Testament und christliche Existenz*. Festschrift H. Braun. Tübingen: J. C. B. Mohr, 1973, 279-287.

Longenecker, R. N. *Paul, Apostle of Liberty*. Grand Rapids: Baker, 1976 (1964).

Luther, M. *Luther's Works*. Vols. 26 and 27, ed. J. Pelikan. Saint Louis: Concordia, 1963-1964.

Luz, U. "Die Erfüllung des Gesetzes bei Matthäus (Mt 5, 17-20)," *Zeitschrift für Theologie und Kirche* 75 (1978), 398-435.

Lyonnet, S. "Christian Freedom and the Law of the Spirit according to St. Paul," in *The Christian Lives by the Spirit*. Staten Island, New York: Alba House, 1971, 145-174.

―――. "Gratuité de la justification et gratuité du salut," in *Studiorum Paulinorum Congressus Internationalis Catholicus 1961*. Vol. I. Rome: Biblical Institute, 1963, 95-110.

―――. "Le sens de *eph' hō* en Rom 5, 12 et l'exégèse des pères grecs," *Biblica* 36 (1955), 436-456.

Marshall, I. H. *The Epistles of John*. New International Commentary; Grand Rapids: Eerdmans, 1978.

Maurer, C. *Die Gesetzeslehre des Paulus*. Zurich: Evangelischer Verlag A. G. Zollikon, 1941.

Meyer, B. F. *The Early Christians. Their World Mission and Self-Discovery*. Wilmington: Michael Glazier, 1986.

Michel, O. *Der Brief an die Römer*. Göttingen: Vandenhoeck & Ruprecht, 1978[14].

Montefiore, C. G. *Judaism and St. Paul*. London: Max Goschen, 1914.

Moo, D. J. "Israel and Paul in Romans 7.7-12," *New Testament Studies* 32 (1986), 122-135.

———. "'Law,' 'Works of the Law,' and Legalism in Paul," *Westminster Theological Journal* 45 (1983), 73-100.

Moore, G. F. "Christian Writers on Judaism," *Harvard Theological Review* 14 (1921), 197-254.

Moule, C. F. D. "Obligation in the Ethic of Paul," in *Christian History and Interpretation: Studies Presented to John Knox*, ed. W. R. Farmer, C. F. D. Moule, and R. R. Niebuhr. Cambridge: Cambridge University, 1967, 389-406.

Parkes, J. *The Conflict of the Church and the Synagogue*. New York: Atheneum, 1969 (1934).

———. *The Foundations of Judaism and Christianity*. Chicago: Quadrangle, 1960.

Pfleiderer, O. *Paulinism*. I. London: Williams and Norgate, 1877.

Prat, E. *The Theology of Saint Paul*. II. London: Burns, Oates and Washbourne, 1957.

von Rad, G. *Old Testament Theology*. II. New York: Harper & Row, 1965.

Räisänen, H. "Galatians 2.16 and Paul's Break with Judaism," *New Testament Studies* 31 (1985), 543-553.

———. "Das 'Gesetz des Glaubens' (Röm. 3.27) und das 'Gesetz des Geistes' (Röm. 8.2)," *New Testament Studies* 26 (1979-1980), 101-117.

———. "Legalism and Salvation by the Law," in *Die paulinische Literatur und Theologie*, ed. S. Pedersen. Aarhus: Aros, 1980, 63-83.

———. *Paul and the Law*. Philadelphia: Fortress, 1986 (1983).

———. "Sprachliches zum Spiel des Paulus mit *Nomos*," in *Glaube und Gerechtigkeit. In memoriam R. Gyllenberg*, ed. J. Kilunen, V. Riekkinen, and H. Räisänen. Helsinki: Exchange Centre for Scientific Literature, 1983, 131-154.

Rhyne, C. T. *Faith Establishes the Law*. Society of Biblical Literature Dissertation Series; Chico: Scholars, 1981.

Ridderbos, H. *Paul: An Outline of His Theology*. Grand Rapids: Eerdmans, 1975.

Sanday, W. and A. C. Headlam. *A Critical and Exegetical Commentary on the Epistle to the Romans*. International Critical Commentary; Edinburgh: T. & T. Clark, 1902[5].

Sanders, E. P. "The Covenant as a Soteriological Category and the Nature of Salvation in Palestinian and Hellenistic Judaism," in *Jews, Greeks, and Christians: Studies in Honor of W. D. Davies*, ed. R. Hamerton-Kelly and R. Scroggs. Leiden: E. J. Brill, 1976, 11-44.

———. *Paul and Palestinian Judaism*. Philadelphia: Fortress, 1977.

———. *Paul, the Law, and the Jewish People*. Philadelphia: Fortress, 1983.

Schechter, S. *Aspects of Rabbinic Theology.* New York: Schocken, 1961 (1909).

Schnabel, E. J. *Law and Wisdom from Ben Sira to Paul.* Tübingen: J. C. B. Mohr, 1985.

Schoeps, H. J. *Paul: The Theology of the Apostle in the Light of Jewish Religious History.* Philadelphia: Westminster, 1961.

Schweitzer, A. *The Mysticism of Paul the Apostle.* New York: Seabury, 1931.

——. *Paul and His Interpreters.* London: Adam & Charles Black, 1950 (1912).

——. *The Quest of the Historical Jesus.* New York: Macmillan, 1968.

Stendahl, K. *Paul among Jews and Gentiles.* Philadelphia: Fortress, 1976.

Stowers, S. K. *The Diatribe and Paul's Letter to the Romans.* Society of Biblical Literature Dissertation Series; Chico: Scholars, 1981.

Stuhlmacher, P. "Paul's Understanding of the Law in the Letter to the Romans," *Svensk exegetisk årsbok* 50 (1985), 87-104.

——. *Reconciliation, Law, and Righteousness: Essays in Biblical Theology.* Philadelphia: Fortress, 1986.

Tov, E. *The Text-Critical Use of the Septuagint in Biblical Research.* Jerusalem: Simor, 1981.

Trilling, W. *Das wahre Israel.* Munich: Kösel, 1964[3].

Tyson, J. B. "'Works of Law' in Galatians," *Journal of Biblical Literature* 92 (1973), 423-431.

Vanhoye, A. "Un médiateur des anges en Ga 3, 19-20," *Biblica* 59 (1978), 403-411.

von Wahlde, U. C. "Faith and Works in Jn VI 28-29," *Novum Testamentum* 22 (1980), 304-315.

Watson, N. M. "Justified by Faith, Judged by Works—an Antinomy?" *New Testament Studies* 29 (1983), 209-221.

Wendland, H. D. *Ethik des Neuen Testaments.* Göttingen: Vandenhoeck & Ruprecht, 1978[3].

Westerholm, S. "Letter and Spirit: The Foundation of Pauline Ethics," *New Testament Studies* 30 (1984), 229-248.

——. "On Fulfilling the Whole Law (Gal. 5:14)," *Svensk exegetisk årsbok* 51-52 (1986-1987), 229-237.

——. Review of H. Hübner, *Das Gesetz bei Paulus, Svensk exegetisk årsbok* 44 (1979), 194-199.

——. "*Torah, nomos,* and Law: A Question of 'Meaning,'" *Studies in Religion/Sciences Religieuses* 15 (1986), 327-336.

Wilckens, U. "Die Bekehrung des Paulus als religionsgeschichtliches Problem," in *Rechtfertigung als Freiheit.* Neukirchen-Vluyn: Neukirchener, 1974, 11-32.

——. *Der Brief an die Römer.* 1-3. Evangelisch-katholischer Kommentar; Cologne: Benziger; Neukirchen-Vluyn: Neukirchener, 1978-1982.

——. "Christologie und Anthropologie im Zusammenhang der paulinischen Rechtfertigungslehre," *Zeitschrift für die Neutestamentliche Wissenschaft* 67 (1976), 64-82.

——. *Resurrection.* Atlanta: John Knox, 1978.

——. "Was heisst bei Paulus: 'Aus Werken des Gesetzes wird kein Mensch gerecht'?" in *Rechtfertigung als Freiheit,* 77-109.

——. "Zum Römerbriefkommentar von Heinrich Schlier," in *Theologische Literaturzeitung* 103 (1978), 849-856.

——. "Zur Entwicklung des paulinischen Gesetzesverständnisses," *New Testament Studies* 28 (1982), 154-190.

Wilson, S. G. "Paul and Religion," in *Paul and Paulinism. Essays in honour of C. K. Barrett,* ed. M. D. Hooker and S. G. Wilson. London: SPCK, 1982, 339-354.

Wrede, W. *Paul.* Lexington: American Library Association Committee on Reprinting, 1962 (1908).

Wright, N. T. "The Paul of History and the Apostle of Faith," *Tyndale Bulletin* 29 (1978), 61-88.

Zeller, D. *Juden und Heiden in der Mission des Paulus.* Stuttgart: Katholisches Bibelwerk, 1976[2].

Zimmerli, W. *The Law and the Prophets.* Oxford: Blackwell, 1965.

Index of Authors

Index of Scripture Passages